ALSO BY RICHARD LAVOIE

It's So Much Work to Be Your Friend: Helping the Child with Learning Disabilities Find Social Success

THE MOTIVATION BREAKTHROUGH

6 Secrets to Turning On the Tuned-Out Child

RICHARD LAVOIE

A TOUCHSTONE BOOK
Published by Simon & Schuster

NEW YORK LONDON TORONTO SYDNEY

Touchstone
A Division of Simon & Schuster, Inc.
1230 Avenue of the Americas
New York, NY 10020

First Touchstone hardcover edition October 2007

Designed by Ruth Lee-Mui

Manufactured in the United States of America

10 9 8 7 6 5 4 3 2 1

Library of Congress Cataloging-in-Publication Data is available.

ISBN-13: 978-0-7432-8960-3
ISBN-10: 0-7432-8960-9

To: Tom and Barbara Hunt . . .
their daughters and son . . .
Thanks for letting me in

To: Jennifer Reichert
and Jennifer Carnig . . .
Thanks for loving our boys

To my Meggi . . . "When I first saw
you, I said, 'Oh, my . . . Oh, my . . .
that's my dream . . .'"

And, as always . . .
to Janet . . .
more today than yesterday,
less than tomorrow

"In those whom I like, I can find no common
denominator. In those whom I love,
I can: They all make me laugh."

—W. H. AUDEN

ACKNOWLEDGMENTS

I EXTEND MY DEEPEST GRATITUDE AND APPRECIATION to the extraordinary team at Touchstone/Fireside for their ongoing faith in this project.

Editor in chief Trish Todd has been unwavering in her support and has provided me with a seemingly limitless supply of encouragement, inspiration, and wisdom. She approached this project with the mind of an editor and the heart of a mom . . . an unbeatable combination.

Kimberly Brissenden, Jessica Napp, Jamie McDonald, and Kelly Bowen have been of invaluable assistance over the past two years. Walking a rookie author through the maze of media interviews and book signings is no easy trick. Kimberly, Jessica, Jamie, and Kelly accomplished this task masterfully.

My literary agent, Liza Dawson, envisioned me as an author long before I did. Her faith, persistence, encouragement, persistence, loyalty, persistence, diligence, and persistence made all the difference.

When I was a young professional, I had very strong feelings and beliefs about the education that struggling children should receive. I had passion, fervor, spirit, commitment, and a compelling message. In fact, I had everything that a successful speaker needs . . . except an audience.

One man changed all that. Bill Halloran had faith in me and my message and added me to his national Teacher Revival Tour in the early 1980s. He helped me to hone my speaking skills and was a kind and gentle mentor. His confidence and belief in me made all the difference. My wish for every young educational professional is that a "Bill Halloran" enters your life.

The Motivation Breakthrough: 6 Secrets to Turning On the Tuned-Out Child was not the product of extensive research, surveys, computer searches, or interviews. Its content is based upon my thirty years of experience teaching, coaching, and observing children who struggle in school. During my career I have worked with or observed countless teachers and coaches who have been extraordinarily effective at motivating children. I have learned from each of them. I am in their debt.

On a recent long plane trip, I made a list of the names and character traits of the twenty-five best teachers whom I have seen over the past thirty years. One of the most common traits listed was "humility." Most truly great teachers simply don't know how great they are and constantly strive to improve.

So, if you have worked with me in the past and you think that your name is on the list—it probably isn't. And if you think that you didn't make the list—you probably did. Congratulations.

—RDL

"We must not, in trying to think about how we can make a big difference, ignore the small daily differences we can make which, over time, add up to big differences that we often cannot foresee."

—MARIAN WRIGHT EDELMAN

CONTENTS

PREFACE

"I was successful because you believed in me."

—ULYSSES S. GRANT IN A LETTER
TO ABRAHAM LINCOLN

I HAVE BEEN INFORMED AND INSPIRED by innumerable colleagues and students over the past thirty years. There are two people who have been greatly on my mind as I've written this book. One is a teacher. The other is a student.

Our daughter, Meghan, confronted significant struggles with language in her elementary school career. Spelling and reading were a particular challenge for her and she had great difficulty breaking the code. Schoolwork was a daily struggle, but her ebullient personality and her irresistible charm carried her through the first three years of school. She had friends who embraced her, a family that adored her, and a personality that earned her admirers wherever she went. She was a winner. We knew it . . . and so did she.

Her world began to unravel when she reached fourth grade. She had an overly stern, inflexible teacher who did not find Megg's shenanigans particularly endearing. She was a stickler for spelling accuracy and was renowned for her fifty-word Friday spelling tests. Megg began to fail. She failed often and publicly. The sparkle began to leave her eyes. "Monday morning tummy-aches" became commonplace. She had trouble sleeping. She lost confidence. She became sad and introverted and no longer carried tales of school to the dinner table to entertain her parents and her adoring brothers.

Kids go to school for a living. It's their job—their workplace. And she was failing daily at her job.

We tried to intervene, but with minimal success. The teacher had her policies and procedures and saw no compelling reason to modify these to meet our daughter's needs. She was intransigent, and Megg went through each school day with the fear of impending failure and the wrenching knowledge that the adult in her classroom simply did not like her. Megg's attempts to please her teacher were fruitless. Praise or encouragement was simply not part of the teacher's repertoire.

We tried to "ramp up" the praise and reinforcement that we provided Megg at home in order to offset her daily rejection and failure at school, but we were fighting a losing battle. Our joyful little girl was becoming sad. My wife, Janet, and I had five education degrees between us and were professional teachers, but our daily doses of success, praise, and encouragement were offset by the rejecting and critical comments that Megg received at school every day.

One Friday, Megg disembarked the school bus and slowly opened the door to the kitchen. She had invested several hours in studying for that day's fifty-word spelling test, and her teacher had returned the test to the students that same day. Megg's efforts had paid off. She'd gotten forty-nine words correct!

But the only written comment on the paper, in bright red ink, read, "one wrong—write misspelled word ten times."

It has been said that "A mother is only as happy as her unhappiest child." The teacher's insensitive response to Megg's effort propelled Janet to action. Megg had previously begged us not to intervene in her school situation because she feared that the teacher would retaliate against her, but Janet could no longer contain her maternal instincts.

Janet met with the teacher, and as a result, the situation improved a bit. Megg received no support or praise at school, but she was no longer publicly embarrassed or chastised in front of her classmates. Small steps.

Megg completed fourth grade. The joyful little girl who loved school was lost to us. Our only hope was that her sadness and melancholy were temporary.

In early September of her fifth-grade year, she began to dread and obsess about her first day of school. She was worried . . . and so were we. I was unsure that she could handle another difficult school year. She was a rough-and-ready kid in many ways and I would never have described her as "fragile." But as she walked toward the bus on her first day of fifth grade, that adjective fit her perfectly.

We waited anxiously for her to return home that day. We watched her get off the school bus. There was a bit of a bounce in her step—a bounce that we had not seen for a while. We asked her the inevitable "first day of school" question: *How was your teacher?*

"Pretty nice. Her name is Miss Nunes. She smiles a lot . . . and she smiled at me. She said that she liked my shoes and told us about her pets. Yeah . . . pretty nice."

Each day that week, Megg shared tales of Miss Nunes. Megg was beginning to enjoy school again. She smiled at supper. She laughed when getting ready for school. She ran to the school bus. We were cautiously optimistic.

On that Sunday evening, Megg went to her room to do her homework. Within five minutes, she returned to the kitchen. She was beaming.

"Look, Dad," she said. "Look at what Miss Nunes sneaked into my math book."

Megg had a weekend math assignment on page 16 of her computation notebook. Unbeknownst to her, Miss Nunes had secreted a twenty-eight-word note between page 15 and page 16, so it fell into Megg's lap when she opened the book. It read:

> You had a great first week, Megg. I think that this will be a good year for all of us.
> See you Monday,
>
> Miss Nunes
>
> P.S. Love those shoes!!

Now, perhaps Miss Nunes did that for every one of her students. I don't know. And I don't care. She did it for *my* kid and it brought a smile to Megg's face that we hadn't seen in months. Through similar random acts of kindness during the year, Sue Nunes made Megg happy again. Megg was back!

Sue taught Megg's dad something that year as well. She taught me the Power of One. She showed me that one skilled and compassionate teacher can make a difference. Just like in the fairy tales, one caring adult can change and save the life of a child.

I acknowledge Sue Nunes. Teacher. Motivator. Dream maker.

The second person who has taught me much about motivation is our nephew, Daniel.

When I was introduced at a speaking engagement several years ago, the master of ceremonies referred to me as a "hero." Although the use of that noun was well intentioned, I found it to be inappropriate and a bit embarrassing. I am not a hero. I am very good at what I do. I am well trained and equipped to serve as a school administrator, consultant, and speaker. I love addressing ballrooms filled with people. It does not take courage or heroics for me to do that. I'm no hero . . . and I'm not particularly courageous.

Lou Gehrig taught a generation of Americans about courage when he said, "Courage does not mean the absence of fear. Courage means being afraid and doing it anyway."

"Courage" and "fearlessness" are antonyms. Courage can exist only in the presence of fear. If you are not afraid to do something, it does not take courage to do it. Conversely, if the act *does* make you afraid, you cannot attempt it without courage.

Are you looking for a hero? Look no further than Daniel.

Daniel is a high school student who has struggled mightily throughout his school career. He has attentional problems and marked difficulty with the writing process. He is exceptionally bright and his inability to communicate his dynamic and innovative ideas in writing is a source of great frustration for him. His limited writing skills have, of course, impacted greatly on his performance in classes that require essays, compositions, and extensive reports.

Daniel's motivation in school might be described as "whimsical." At times, he applies himself fully and works diligently on assignments. At other times his effort is, at best, shaky or, at worst, imperceptible. Perhaps this is because even his best and most focused efforts seldom result in meaningful success or progress. He has learned the bitter lesson of learning disorders: The amount of effort that he invests in a task seldom translates to the amount of success that he has in accomplishing the task.

Basically, what he puts into it has little to do with what he gets out of it. The chronic and repeated failure that he faces during the school day has served to all but obliterate his intrinsic motivation and his drive to succeed.

I have attended several meetings with Daniel's teachers, at his mom's request. I have invariably been impressed with their devotion and sincerity. They like Daniel and want him to succeed. But their reports and discussions are peppered with the phrases that adults use to describe a child who is unresponsive to the adults' strategies, techniques, and approaches:

> "If he would only apply himself . . ."
> "He can do it when he puts his mind to it . . ."
> "He's so inconsistent . . ."
> " . . . doesn't seem to care . . ."
> " . . . just not trying . . ."

But young Daniel has other parts of his life besides the classroom. He is an extraordinary sailor who has won numerous awards as a skipper and a crew member. His nautical skills are legendary. He can troubleshoot a computer expertly, and his knowledge of popular music and politics is unsurpassed.

All little boys are fascinated with flight, but Daniel's interest in planes and flying always seemed unusually intense. As a toddler, his aunt Janet would often take him to the local regional airport, where he delighted in watching the planes arrive and depart. Two years ago, Daniel was searching for a summer job. His dad suggested that he apply at a small light-plane airport with a grass runway that was a mile or so from their home.

Daniel was told that they had no paid positions available, but the airstrip's owner instantly liked Daniel and offered to have him do some basic yard work and painting on the property . . . in exchange for flying lessons. All of the adults in Daniel's life were skeptical. But our doubts paled in comparison to Daniel's enthusiasm and delight at the prospect of flying.

As I write this, Daniel has had a relationship with the airstrip staff for two years. They love him. He loves them. He is never happier than when he is at the strip. He has painted several buildings, mowed and re-mowed countless runways, cleaned airport restrooms, washed endless windows. . . . And he flew a Cessna solo two weeks after his sixteenth birthday.

When Daniel's teachers discuss him, they commonly use words such as "unmotivated," "lazy," "inconsistent," "resistant," "passive," and "inattentive."

When you talk to his flight instructor, his sailing coach, or the airstrip's owner, their conversations are peppered with words such as "enthusiastic," "go-getter," "dependable," "valued," "industrious," "indispensable," "initiative," "devoted," and "focused."

Why the difference?

Many education professionals would read the preceding paragraphs and ask, "Why won't Daniel apply the same consistent effort in class that he seems willing to invest in flying and sailing?"

I believe that this question misses the point.

In this book, I attempt to pose a very different question: "What are the flight instructor and sailing coach doing with Daniel that lights his motivational spark, that his teachers are *not* doing?"

If you were to ask Daniel that question, he would respond that the airstrip gives him approval, support, acceptance, toleration for errors, belonging, encouragement, camaraderie, understanding, praise, reassurance . . . and success.

Daniel has earned the love, respect, and admiration of all who know him for his efforts and expertise on the seas and in the air. The joy he finds on a sailboat or in a Cessna is diametric to his frustration in the classroom. If only the year consisted of an endless succession of Julys and Augusts. Then HE would be writing a book, and I would find myself unhappily imprisoned in beginning sailing class. Quite simply, Daniel is a summer kid.

As teachers, let us commit to learning why "unmotivated" kids are able to find their drive and inspiration on playing fields, on skateboard courses, in poolrooms, in video arcades, on mall concourses . . . or at nine thousand feet. What do these settings provide that we do not provide in the classroom?

We constantly search for ways that we can "change the child." Perhaps the first significant change should come from us. Perhaps we should first analyze and change *our* policies, procedures, and practices when dealing with hard-to-reach kids.

I acknowledge Daniel. Sailor. Pilot. Summer kid.

—RDL

Part I

UNDERSTANDING AND FOSTERING STUDENT MOTIVATION

1

Student Motivation: What It Is and What It Is Not

"If there is anything that we wish to change in a child, we should first examine it and see whether it is not something that could be better changed in ourselves."

—CARL JUNG

SEVERAL YEARS AGO, I designed and delivered a workshop entitled "I Can't" Versus "He Won't": Motivational Issues in Special Education. This awkwardly titled seminar was designed to acquaint teachers and parents with basic information about motivation, the impact of learning problems on motivation, and strategies to improve a student's efforts in the classroom and at home.

I was delivering the seminar to the faculty of a small Midwestern high school during a staff development day. Among the audience members was a stern-looking middle-aged gentleman who—I later learned—taught United States history and civics. He sat tight-lipped with his arms crossed firmly throughout the seminar. Although we never spoke to each other during the workshop, his body language clearly communicated that he was not buying what I was selling. He rolled his eyes and sighed audibly several times during my presentation. He shifted impatiently in his seat and glanced at his watch repeatedly. His behavior demonstrated that he had not begged his supervisor to allow him to attend a motivation workshop that day.

At the conclusion of the seminar, I opened the floor to questions. I was disheartened—but not surprised—to see this gentleman's hand shoot up. I acknowledged him and he stood and stared icily at me. "Your workshop had a lot of suggestions and plenty of reasons why kids aren't motivated to learn, but I am in total disagreement with your premise."

"And what is the source of our disagreement?" I asked, tentatively.

"Quite simply, *it's not my job to motivate these kids*. If they come to my class and they want to sit quietly and learn history, I will gladly give them the facts, information, and concepts that they need. If they are not motivated to learn, they can sit in the back of the class and sleep if they wish. It's their choice. It's their loss. I communicate information . . . and I do that very well. But if a kid doesn't care to learn it, that is not my problem. It's *his* problem. I'm a teacher, not a cheerleader."

We discussed . . . and argued . . . and debated . . . and dickered . . . and quarreled.

Because we disagreed so fundamentally on this issue, the discussion became quite heated. Finally, I said in some frustration, "But there are many legitimate reasons why a student can lack motivation: fear of failure, lack of understanding, learning disorders, frustration. Every learning theorist from Piaget to Gardner has stated that the learning process begins with motivation. Without motivation, there is no learning. Attempting to teach a child who is unmotivated is as futile as hammering on cold steel."

"But it's not my job!" he countered.

"It *is* your job, sir. Quite simply, kids don't come *with batteries included*. You've got to provide the batteries if you want them to function."

I don't believe that I was successful in changing the gentleman's mind, but our exchange *did* give me a better title for the seminar. I renamed the workshop "Batteries Not Included: Motivating the

Struggling Learner," and have delivered programs throughout North America, Australia, Hong Kong, and New Zealand.

Most teachers and parents recognize that motivation is the key to learning. Reflect for a moment on your favorite teacher in high school. The chances are that he was an effective motivator. He inspired you. He was not merely a teacher, he was also a leader.

He did not necessarily make learning fun, but he made learning attainable and purposeful. Whether you serve children as a teacher, parent, coach, or instructor, you will multiply your effectiveness immeasurably if you learn how to motivate your charges and maintain that motivation throughout the learning process.

I began my study of student motivation in the twentieth year of my education career. I interviewed dozens of teachers about student motivation and was surprised and disheartened to find how little my colleagues knew about this important topic. The more I learned about this subject, the more I came to realize that I, also, did not have an effective repertoire of motivational techniques. I tended to use a "one size fits all" approach with my students wherein I expected all of the children to be motivated by the same star chart, checklist, or reward system. This broad approach left many children unmotivated and uninspired. I was able to motivate many of my students. I analyzed the approaches and strategies that were successful with these children. My successes, I came to recognize, were almost accidental—nearly serendipitous. I made no conscious attempt to match the child to the motivational technique. I merely had the good fortune to use a motivational strategy that, by happenstance, seemed to inspire a particular child.

After observing one of my classes a generous superior once commented that I was "a natural motivator." I wasn't, and now that I have a better understanding of the intricacies of this complex process we call "motivation," I realize a truly "natural motivator" is a rare, rare person indeed. In order to establish and maintain the motivation of a fellow human being, or a classroom filled with fellow human beings, one must understand the complexities inherent in this elaborate motivation process.

It is important that adults learn what motivation is! But it is equally important that they *unlearn* what motivation is not! I have yet to find an undergraduate- or graduate-level curriculum that effectively addresses this fundamental concept. Teachers' lack of training and exposure to the basic tenets of childhood motivation results in a corps of American teachers who are unable to understand or implement effective motivational techniques.

The media bombards us incessantly with the bad news emanating from America's classrooms. Test scores are down, dropout rates are up, and school violence is on the rise while school attendance declines. Students' high-risk behaviors (drug use, sexual activity, delinquency) increase while SAT scores plummet in some communities. There are innumerable reasons for these statistics, many of which are beyond the control of parents and school personnel. But student motivation is clearly a factor in these upsetting educational trends. This fact should serve as a clarion call to America's parents and professionals to focus time, energy, and other resources on the study and exploration of motivation.

This book is designed to explore and, to a degree, demystify the complex process of motivating school-aged children. First, we will explore and explode some of the most common myths and misconceptions that impact our understanding of motivation. Following this *unlearning*, the processes of *learning* and *relearning* can begin. Second, we will discuss and demonstrate the significant impact that learning disorders can have upon a student's ability to maintain his motivation in the classroom, at home, and on the playing field.

The final, and perhaps primary, focus of the book will be a collection of field-tested strategies designed to create, foster, and maintain the motivation of children in a variety of settings.

It is not overstating the case to say that our nation's future depends greatly on our ability to motivate our children today. This fact should inspire all adults to become more effective motivators. In the sage words of Charles Kettering, "My interest is in the future because I am going to spend the rest of my life there."

MYTHS AND MISCONCEPTIONS ABOUT STUDENT MOTIVATION

> "Do something. If it works, do more of it. If it doesn't . . . do something else."
>
> —FRANKLIN DELANO ROOSEVELT

Today's teachers and parents should heed FDR's sage advice. Often, we continue to repeatedly use traditional "motivational techniques" despite the obvious fact that these strategies are not working effectively. I recall a simmering teacher bringing an errant and unmotivated student into my office and complaining, "I have kept Josh in for recess *fifteen days in a row* and he *still* isn't doing his math homework."

Well, let's circle the slow learner in this picture. The strategy is not working. Try something else!

Because we are unable to inspire our students by igniting their intrinsic (internal) motivation, we try to motivate them extrinsically by establishing a complex tapestry of tests, quizzes, evaluations, and grades. In effect, we *force* them to be motivated to master the targeted curriculum. ("I know that you will never need to use these algebra equations in real life, Tucker, but you *must* learn them because they will be on Friday's test.") This unrelenting coercion seems to be a rather unfair use of our power over children. We can do better.

I have come to recognize that most teachers and parents adhere to a false and shaky set of beliefs related to motivation. These misconceptions must be shelved before we can embrace a more enlightened motivational approach.

Motivation Myth #1

"That Danny . . . NOTHING motivates that kid."

Any teacher or parent who makes this statement is displaying a sad lack of knowledge about the true nature of student motivation.

We must come to understand the most basic tenet of human motivation. This concept is the keystone upon which the remaining pages of this book rest. The simple but profound concept is the following: *All human behavior is motivated*!

EVERY behavior that we manifest on any given day is motivated. If a reader decides to stop reading this book at this point, I cannot state that the person is "not motivated." She was motivated to *stop reading*. If a friend of mine stops calling me on a weekly basis, I cannot say, "He is unmotivated to maintain the friendship." Rather, he is *motivated to end the relationship*.

Let's consider that student who sits in the rear of the classroom in your fifth-period math class. He rests his head on the desk, never volunteers an answer, and fails to participate in class discussions and demonstrations. The temptation is to say "This kid is unmotivated." You would be wrong. Rather, he *is motivated to rest his head on the desk, keep silent, and not participate!* In point of fact, he *is* motivated and may indeed be among the most motivated students in your class. But his motivation is not to learn math. His motivation focuses on avoiding failure, preventing frustration, or even angering the teacher.

It is incorrect to say "This kid is not motivated." Rather, the correct assessment of the situation is that *he is not motivated to do that which you wish him to do*.

At the conclusion of a speaking engagement in a major northwestern American city, a young man approached me from the audience and asked if he could share a story with me. He was visibly upset, as evidenced by his shaky hands and mournful voice. We sat backstage in the auditorium as he related his experience.

"My dad left my life when I was in the third grade. I came downstairs one morning and he was gone. He simply packed up his belongings and left my mother, my two older brothers, and me.

"That was seventeen years ago and I have not seen him since. I do not know where he is. I do not know if he is alive or dead and—God help me—I don't care. I have come to realize that the day he left was, on reflection, the greatest day of my life.

"He was a terrible person. Probably the most evil person I have ever known. I was the youngest of three brothers. I was the smallest and the weakest. As a result, my dad used to beat me. Regularly and severely. He beat me for the simple reason that he ENJOYED beating me. He didn't need a reason. He would reach across the dinner table and slap me without provocation. He was a bully and I hated him for that.

"But generally when he beat me, he had been drinking and he would hit me in the living room or the kitchen. I was faster than he was, and I could easily escape by running outside, waiting until he fell asleep, and then sneaking back into the house.

"But on the occasion when I made a mistake or did something wrong, I got what my brothers and I called a 'bathroom beating.' My father would drag me into the bathroom, close and lock the door behind us, and simply beat me until he got tired of beating me. In a 'bathroom beating' you couldn't escape. If you ran into the shower, he was there. If you hid behind the toilet, he was there. If you sought shelter in the linen closet, he was there. A bathroom beating was reserved for situations in which I had broken a rule or made a mistake.

"In the first grade I couldn't read. I struggled and struggled to break the code, but I was simply unable to do so. They had a unique way of teaching reading in my school district at that time. On the first Thursday of each month—shortly after morning recess—Mrs. Donovan, the reading specialist, would arrive at our classroom. She would require all the poor readers to come to the front of the class and read aloud to the other children. This ritual was extremely embarrassing for me. But I devised a strategy to avoid the humiliation.

"On the day that Mrs. Donovan was scheduled to visit our class, I would go into the boys' room during recess. I would take my reading glasses and crack one of the lenses on the sink or simply twist the glasses until they broke in half.

"I would approach Mrs. Donovan as soon as she arrived and explain to her that I couldn't read that day because my glasses were broken.

"I did that every first Thursday for five months—with the full knowledge that when I showed my parents the broken glasses that evening, I was going to receive a bathroom beating."

A sad and troubling story, indeed. But the most disturbing aspect of the tale is this: I am certain that, if you were to review this young man's first-grade assessments, Mrs. Donovan doubtless labeled him "unmotivated." After all, nobody recuses himself from remedial reading five sessions in a row with the same excuse unless he is purposely trying to avoid it.

I would submit that this child was *extremely* motivated. In fact, he was probably one of the most highly motivated children that Mrs. Donovan would meet in her career. HIS MOTIVATION WAS TO AVOID EMBARRASSMENT, and he was willing to receive a beating from a grown man once each month in order to achieve his goal. Imagine the magic that would have occurred if Mrs. Donovan had been able to transfer that boy's motivation to *learning to read* and away from *avoiding reading*.

The boy's problem was not a lack of motivation. Rather, it was misdirected motivation.

Motivation Myth #2

"That kid! One day he is motivated, the next day he is not!"

This oft-stated complaint is generally untrue. The field of psychology recognizes motivation as a *relative constant*. That is, if a child is motivated to learn math, he is motivated to learn math all the time. If he is not motivated to learn math, he is not motivated to learn math—all the time.

The child's performance, productivity, and progress may vary from day to day, but this generally does not reflect inconsistent motivation. This behavior more likely reflects the child's inconsistent and often unpredictable learning style, which will be detailed later in this chapter.

An analogy may be helpful. Let's substitute "love" for "motivation." You love your husband. That love is a constant in your life and his. Now, as in any marriage, some days are better than others. On any given day you may be angry or upset with him as the result of an argument or disagreement, but despite these temporary feelings, *you still love him*. If he were to become ill unexpectedly, you would assist and care for him because of this love. Annoyance is temporary; love is permanent. Poor school performance and productivity are temporary; motivation is permanent.

It is important to understand and embrace this concept because it provides insight into the frustration that children often feel when they have difficulty mastering information and skills despite their motivation to learn.

Motivation Myth #3

"Give him something; that will motivate him."

Many—perhaps *most*—parents and teachers attempt to motivate children by giving them rewards as incentives. Dad may promise Shannon five dollars for every A that she receives on her report card. Her teacher awards her stickers based on her homework performance. Her soccer coach buys the team pizzas after a particularly good practice. Although these responses are well intentioned and may even have a temporary impact on Shannon's *behavior*, they will do little to improve or enhance her *motivation*.

Providing rewards in an attempt to boost motivation is a corruption of a widely used behavior management technique known as the Premack Principle. This strategy is often referred to as Grandma's Rule: If you eat your vegetables, you will get dessert. If you do X for me, I will give you Y. Although this technique may modify a child's behavior, it will do little to modify his motivation. Shannon may work diligently in school in order to receive an A and be granted the five-dollar reward. But her goal is *not* to progress in school or gain new skills. Her goal is to receive the money.

In order to be an effective motivator, one must understand the significant difference between *intrinsic motivation* and *extrinsic motivation*. Our goal with children is to foster lasting motivation that is inspired by their desire to learn and grow. Reward systems that emphasize tangible incentives can actually serve to decrease motivation in the long run.

Extrinsic motivation consists of systems or policies that encourage the child to earn rewards by behaving in a manner that promotes learning. These systems can serve a useful and constructive purpose by reminding children of classroom or household rules. However, children can become overly reliant on these rewards and may be unable to monitor or evaluate their own performance. They become totally dependent upon the rewards when attempting to evaluate their daily progress. ("I *must* have been good today. Mrs. Scranton gave me two stickers." Or "I must have been bad today—no stickers.") The child is unaware of which behaviors contributed to his plethora or paucity of stickers. He has surrendered the entire self-assessment process to Mrs. Scranton. The primary warning sign of an ineffective or overused reward system is when a student asks a teacher "What will I get if I do this right?"

For most of us, our salaries constitute the extrinsic motivation for daily work. However, our desire to effectively serve our clients, students, patients, customers, or colleagues constitutes our intrinsic motivation. You would undoubtedly leave your job if the extrinsic reward (salary) was discontinued, but it is the intrinsic reward (service) that truly fosters your day-to-day motivation. Personal satisfaction for a job well done is the greatest reward.

Similarly, intrinsic motivation comes from within the child. This internal drive will inspire the child to work to her fullest potential whether or not a reward is promised. Learning becomes its own reward. Intrinsically motivated children believe in themselves and their abilities. They enjoy learning and are self-directed. They do not rely on the approval or approbation of others in order to work toward their potential.

That is not to say that rewards and incentives should not be granted to children. A well-planned and implemented reward program can be helpful in meeting short-term goals, modifying behavior, and ensuring children's cooperation, but we should remain ever mindful that *intrinsic* motivation is our long-term goal.

Encouraging or requiring students to set and establish individual goals for themselves can foster intrinsic motivation. Children with learning disorders often have great difficulty establishing performance goals and often aim too high ("I want to be captain of the soccer team and score three goals per game") or aim too low ("I know that I'll *never* get to play—everyone is better than me"). In order to foster intrinsic motivation, it is useful to assist the child in establishing attainable and appropriate personal goals. ("I will attend and participate in all practices and will score an assist at some time during my first four games.")

Motivation Myth #4

Competition: The Great Motivator

Many educators are greatly concerned about two conflicting and mutually exclusive movements that are currently impacting the field of education. The first is the high-stakes testing movement, which emphasizes and requires intense student-on-student competition in our classrooms. The second is the inclusion movement, which emphasizes placing children with learning problems in classes with nondisabled peers. These movements are akin to oil and water: They simply do not mix.

If special needs children are going to be placed in general education classes, teachers need to downplay and decrease the use of inherently unfair competitive activities. If classrooms are going to feature intense competition, we need to remove special needs students from those environments because they become academic casualties in such a system.

Recent surveys conducted by the University of Massachusetts in suburban American school systems indicate that competitive classroom activities (games, quizzes, test, bees) occupy nearly 80 percent of the on-task time in elementary schools. It is, by far, the most widely used classroom approach. Teachers utilize competition in the belief that it motivates children to do their best. However, research and experience teach us that this belief is untrue and unfounded.

The most important and profound reality regarding the link between motivation and competition is the following: *The only person motivated by competition is the person who believes that he has a chance of winning.*

Therefore, if a fourth-grade teacher decides to use bees, quizzes, and games to teach spelling, who are the students that she is motivating? The good spellers. The students who are already motivated in this skill area. The struggling spellers—the ones who would greatly benefit from increased motivation—are not stimulated or energized by these activities.

There are several common misconceptions regarding the fragile link between motivation and competition:

- *Most people do their best work when involved in head-to-head competition with others.*

This widely held belief is simply untrue. In order to demonstrate this, I often ask audiences to reflect upon one of the premier annual sporting events in the world: the Boston Marathon. Each April, Boston plays host to twenty thousand runners from across the globe who come to run the grueling twenty-six-mile course from the suburbs to historic Copley Square. These runners train intensively and participate in exhausting regimes in order to prepare for the challenging, and at times overwhelming, course. The participants come to Boston at their own expense.

Each marathoner enters the race with the full knowledge that there will be only two prizes awarded at the completion of the event. One prize goes to the man who finishes first, and the second goes to the first woman to complete the course. Twenty thousand runners . . . two prizes.

Reflect for a moment on this question before responding: How many of those runners enter the marathon with the hopes of winning the race? All of them? Most of them? Many of them? Some of them?

I would submit to you that only twenty or thirty world-class runners go to Boston with the expectation and hope that they will win the coveted laurel wreath. But there are twenty thousand people in the race. Who are the other 19,970 runners competing against?

Themselves!

We do our best work when we compete against ourselves—not against others.

Each time I deliver a speech, my goal is not to be superior to other educational speakers such as Mel Levine, Bob Brooks, Ned Hallowell, or Reid Lyon. Rather, my goal is to deliver a better speech than the one I delivered yesterday. My goal for tomorrow's speech is that it will be better than today's. You see, I cannot control the behavior of Mel, Bob, Ned, or Reid. I can control and improve only my own behavior, so that is what I try to do.

I recall a distraught fifteen-year-old boy barging into my office at school several years ago. He was deeply shaken about his performance in that afternoon's cross-country meet. He had finished in fifth place and was greatly disappointed because he'd had a second-place finish two days before.

I attempted to comfort him by reminding him that all athletes have good days and bad days and that he should use this temporary setback to motivate himself to train even more intensely than before. However, as the discussion went further, I learned that his time in that day's race was 29:35. His time in the previous race was 31:05. Although he had a superior performance in the second race, his placement among the finishers was lower. This information changed the entire course of our discussion. I reminded him that there was only *one* runner's performance that he could control—his own. He actually ran a better race when he finished in fifth place than he had run when he'd finished second. His placement was determined by variables that he could not control. By happenstance, we were competing against a superior team in the second race, and some of the boy's teammates ran unusually well that day. But again, these variables were beyond his influence. He improved his own performance and that was cause for delight, not dejection.

As educators and parents, we must downplay competition and emphasize the concept of "personal best." We should encourage students to continually strive to improve their own performance and be less mindful of comparing themselves to others. *Personal Best* should replace the drumbeat of *The Best*.

Unfortunately, most schools emphasize *the* best and reserve their awards, plaques, certificates, and rewards for the most-skilled students. This approach has a negative impact on the children who struggle with learning, because they never have the opportunity to "shine."

When I served as director of education at the Eagle Hill School in Greenwich, Connecticut, I proposed an idea to the faculty. I purchased an oversize bulletin board and mounted it in the school's lobby. Above the board was a large banner saying CLASS OF THE WEEK. I explained to the staff that I would be distributing a schedule, and on a rotating basis each teacher's class would be designated as Class of the Week. On that specific week, the teacher was expected to display representative samples of her students' work on the board, thereby allowing visitors to see the type of work being done at the school. My colleagues were very enamored with my idea.

Within an hour of distributing the schedule, one of the teachers asked to see me. She was quite certain that I had made an error on the schedule because I had designated her fifth-period literature class as Class of the Week later that month. She explained that most of the students in that class were sixteen or seventeen years old, and she felt that they would feel that a bulletin board displaying their work was "baby stuff" and that they would be insulted by this primary-school approach. I did not agree and I asked her to display the students' papers on the assigned week. She dutifully—if reluctantly—complied and on the scheduled Monday, their papers were put on display.

The following day, I arrived at the school's lobby unusually early because I had a meeting with a parent. As I entered, I was surprised to find three of the literature students examining the bulletin board with their parents. I was running late for my meeting so I did not have time to inquire as to why the display had sparked such wide interest.

Later in the day, I met Scotty, who was one of the students I had seen in the lobby earlier that morning. I asked him why he had brought his parents to school to see the display.

This wonderful kid, who had attended a highly competitive school system before enrolling at Eagle Hill, look downward and self-consciously shuffled his feet.

"I'm sixteen years old, Mr. Lavoie," he began. "I've never had a piece of my work put up on a bulletin board before."

Scotty had attended a school that celebrated The Best. Because of his learning problems, he never wrote The Best essay on Abraham Lincoln or The Best composition about his summer vacation. He never did The Best in science, math, geography, or spelling. As a result, he attended school for ten years and never had a piece of his work displayed on a bulletin board. Pediatrician Mel Levine refers to this as "chronic success deprivation."

With all that we currently know about self-esteem, it is inexcusable that such a thing should happen to any student in any classroom. I encourage elementary school teachers to take a different and more enlightened approach. If you have twenty-five students in your class, divide your room's bulletin board into twenty-five sections so that each child is given his own section. Each Friday, allow each student to select the piece of work that he is most proud of and let him post it on his section. In this way, *every* child's performance is celebrated *every* week.

No child should be required to wait until he is sixteen years old to show his mom and dad his paper on a bulletin board. In Scotty's case, the system—not the child—had failed.

- *It's a big, bad world out there and we need to prepare children for the competitive adult world.*

Our nephew attended a very competitive suburban elementary school and had ongoing difficulty performing academically. His parents asked that I meet with his teachers occasionally in an effort to help the teachers meet his needs. His teachers were outstanding, but invariably, each of our meetings became a debate about the intensity of the competition that the child faced daily. Each time I asked about the rationale for this constant competition, I received the same response: "We live in a competitive society and we must prepare children for the dog-eat-dog work environment that they will be joining."

There are a number of flaws in that argument. First, the boy is only nine years old! He will not be entering the "real world" for a dozen years. Isn't it a bit early to begin preparing him for the workplace by turning his fourth-grade classroom into a replica of a Wall Street boardroom?

Second, a 2003 governmental survey indicated that less than 20 percent of America's workforce is paid according to individual performance (paid on commission) and only 1 percent of workers are in situations where their continued employment is exclusively determined by their accomplishments (sales quotas). Most employment situations are *not* competitive in nature. In fact, if the American workplace were as competitive as America's classrooms, the result would, doubtless, be low worker morale. Most employees who lose their jobs are dismissed because of lack of motivation, poor interpersonal skills, incompetence, or cyclical economic forces. The oft-repeated warning to children that "when you grow up, you will lose your job if you can't compete" is simply false.

The keys to success in the workplace are competence, cooperativeness, and motivation—not the ability to compete.

The third flaw in the "real world" argument is that the competition that we use in schools is totally dissimilar to the competition that the student will be facing as an adult. There are two criteria that characterize competition in the adult world. First, *as an adult, you compete only when you choose to compete*! I am not required or coerced to enter a golf tournament, join a tennis ladder, or apply for a new job unless I desire to do so. Second, *when adults compete, they compete against peers* (with similar background, training, experience, and affinities). When a principal evaluates a speech therapist, he compares her to other speech therapists in order to assess her skills. He does not expect her to be as effective a wrestling coach as his school's wrestling coach. Nor does he expect her to know Shakespeare's sonnets as well as the English teacher across the hall. When he evaluates the English teacher, he compares her with other members of the English department.

Does the daily classroom competition that my nephew confronts meet these two criteria? Certainly not! The Monday-Wednesday-Friday spelling bee ritual is not voluntary. His participation is required. Further, the bee may find him competing head-to-head with the most able speller in the class. Unlike adults, children are constantly required to compete with others who have far different skills and abilities from those they might possess.

Many sociologists posit that twenty-first-century America is not a competitive society at all. In point of fact, we may well be the most cooperative society in the history of mankind. We greatly depend upon the cooperation and collaboration of others. The simple act of driving is reflective of the cooperative spirit that characterizes our society. As you drive down the street, you trust that all the other strangers in their cars will stay in their designated lanes and will stop at stop signs and red lights. Further, they have placed the same trust in you. We cooperate with one another in order to survive on this planet.

Some will argue that it is competition that is the driving force in American society and will cite the 1957 launch of the USSR's Sputnik I, which led to the space race and America's triumphant 1969 landing on the moon's surface. I disagree. Although it was the competition with the Soviets that got us involved in the space program, it was the cooperation of thousands of American scientists, researchers, legislators, designers, and industrialists who actually created that miracle. In the "real world," competition generally occurs between companies, teams, and countries, not individuals.

Competition does not ensure success or progress; cooperation does. The 2004 Boston Red Sox ended their eighty-six-year drought by winning the World Series because they collaborated so effectively that year. Successful competition relies entirely upon the cooperation that exists within the organization. The hallmark of every great human endeavor—from the Egyptian pyramids to the NASA space station—is cooperation. Go visit the business section of a major bookstore and you will see countless volumes related to collaboration, cooperation, and team building. Wouldn't our nephew be better served if his teachers fostered cooperation among his classmates rather than intensive and often hurtful competition? The ability to collaborate and cooperate in the workplace is one of the most admirable and valuable skills that an employee can possess. The conventional wisdom in management is that an organization greatly enhances its external competitiveness by minimizing its internal competition. If you wish to be competitive in the marketplace, you must be cooperative in the workplace.

Even if you accept the flawed premise that we live in a highly competitive world, it does not necessarily follow that children should be exposed to "doses" of competition in order to prepare them for adulthood. Following that logic would also require you to expose children to doses of liquor and pornography in order to ease their transition to adulthood.

It is important to remember that competition is a learned behavior. Most preschool children are highly cooperative. However, the competitive culture of the classroom often cancels out their natural desire to work together. I remember the response of our son Dan when I asked him about school after his first week in kindergarten:

> "How's school going, Dan?"
>
> "Pretty good, Dad. I can run faster than Zack and I can jump higher than Justin, but, boy, can Sally ever pass out napkins!"

How sad. After only fifteen hours in the classroom, he had learned that it simply did not matter how well *he* was doing; it only mattered how well he was doing in comparison with his classmates.

My negative attitude toward classroom competition stems from an incident with our firstborn, Christian, when he was in the first grade. I came home from work one day to be greeted by a very excited and exuberant Christian. Our conversation went like this:

> "Hi, Dad! Guess what? I had a great day at school today."
>
> "Why is that, pal?"
>
> "Well, the teacher taught us how to carry numbers in addition today. My best friend, Jason, didn't understand it and he got a fifty on his quiz and had to stay in for recess. I got a ninety on my quiz."

Christian beamed. I was crestfallen. I never taught or expected my son to take delight in the failure of his best friend. I knew Christian to be a fiercely loyal friend and once observed him confronting a sandbox bully because the boy took Jason's toy. Where did my son learn to take delight in his buddy's failure? He learned that in school. In the classroom it was acceptable and anticipated that Christian would celebrate his friend's failure. In effect, his classmates had become obstacles to his own success.

Many teachers will argue that competition is inevitable, unavoidable, and necessary in our classrooms. Actually, every teacher does have options when planning and implementing daily lessons, and it is important that we understand the distinctions among those options.

Every classroom lesson can be placed in one of three types of categories:

Individualized
Cooperative
Competitive

In order to illustrate each, imagine that there are two fourth-grade classmates named John and Sasha. If their teacher wishes to conduct an *individualized* activity, she might ask John to complete a work sheet on the five times table while Sasha simultaneously completes a work sheet on the seven times table. The students work independently at their desks. The dynamic of this activity is that John's success or failure has no impact upon Sasha's success or failure. Neither does Sasha's performance impact upon John's.

Then imagine that the teacher wishes to conduct a *cooperative* activity. She asks John and Sasha to go to the whiteboard and draw a mural of a farm scene to celebrate National Dairy Month. She asks them to work jointly on the project. Sasha begins to draw the farm animals while John draws the farmhouse and silo. He sees that Sasha is having difficulty drawing a cow, so he volunteers his assistance by showing her how to draw the animal based on some drawing tips that his cartoonist grandfather had given him. John is eager and willing to help Sasha because, in a *cooperative* activity, his success is largely determined by her success. If he draws a nice farmhouse and she draws nice animals, they will have a nice mural.

In an *independent* activity, John's success or failure is not impacted by Sasha's performance. In a *cooperative* activity, John's success is largely determined by Sasha's success. In a *competitive* activity, John's success is largely determined by Sasha's failure. Only if she fails can he succeed.

In a *competitive* activity ("John and Sasha, see which one of you can alphabetize these words the fastest!"), each child hopes that the other child—his opponent—will do poorly. In a highly competitive classroom, the teacher creates an environment wherein each child hopes that the children next to him *do poorly*—because it is in his best interests for them to do poorly.

Have you ever worked in an office, a store, a factory, or a school where workers in one department wanted workers in another department to fail? It creates the most stressful and unproductive work environment that one can imagine, and yet that is precisely the work environment that we create in competitive classrooms. We can do better.

As teachers and parents we need to place greater emphasis on *individual* and *cooperative* strategies. The former strategy allows and encourages the child to work toward his own unique tailored goals. Research indicates that failure to meet one's own goals can encourage tenacity, resilience, effort, and self-discipline. However, failure to meet imposed public goals often results in humiliation, timidity, and lowered self-esteem.

Cooperative education strategies are significantly different from the methods used in a typical classroom. In a traditional classroom children work quietly on teacher-directed activities; independence is celebrated and support comes solely from the teacher.

By contrast, a cooperative classroom features active learners working busily in small groups, where they share ideas, initiate discussions, and reinforce one another. *Interdependence* is celebrated. Competition is replaced by collaboration and every student's active participation is assured. Youngsters provide one another with positive feedback, support, praise, and affirmations.

Remember that all "small group work" does not necessarily qualify as cooperative learning. Teacher-directed remedial groupings, for example, do not qualify. Cooperative learning activities meet the following criteria:

- *Interdependence:* Students share ideas, information, skills, and materials. Each student's success and progress is largely dependent upon the performance of his learning partners.
- *Accountability:* Each student has assigned tasks that he must complete in order to ensure the success of the project. These tasks are tailored to each child's strengths, skills, and affinities. This ensures that each child is an active participant in the process.
- *Social component:* Cooperative strategies promote positive social interaction among children. The children talk, plan, discuss, share, and praise.

As will be discussed in chapter 2, cooperative education activities provide students with valuable experience with group work. Students learn tolerance, patience, acceptance, and generosity in addition to the academic content. These skills are fundamental to success in postsecondary programs and in the workplace, where cooperation and teamwork are the order of the day. The communication skills learned in cooperative activities will also be useful for the child when interacting with family and friends. In addition, the success that results from active participation in cooperative activities can do much to enhance the child's confidence and self-esteem.

Cooperative learning activities can be used for myriad purposes and to meet a wide variety of academic goals. A teacher can temporarily stop a lecture or demonstration and ask cooperative groups to assemble in order to summarize, discuss, or debate the topic at hand. These groups can also discuss and solve problems, review previously learned material, prepare for tests, conduct research, or review topics.

If conducted properly, cooperative learning activities can provide the people-oriented person with invaluable opportunities to interact with others. Because *all* students are actively involved in these activities, the entire class benefits.

Motivation Myth #5

"Punishment is an effective motivator."

Many adults attempt to motivate children by punishing them. In most cases, this is an ineffective and short-lived solution to a motivation problem. There are several reasons why punishment simply does not work.

Many kids, particularly those who have a history of academic difficulty, have been punished enough. They are largely immune and desensitized to this approach. By the time the learning disabled child enters your fifth-grade classroom, it would be nearly impossible for you to devise a punishment that has not already been applied to him. He has lost recesses, had privileges revoked, written his transgressions ten thousand times, and stood outside the principal's office for countless hours. All of these punishments have not served to enhance his motivation, so perhaps we ought to investigate alternative approaches.

Punishment does not have a lasting impact upon a child's motivation because punishment is effective only as long as the threat of punishment exists. Suppose you are late for an important engagement and you are barreling down the highway at a speed that greatly exceeds the posted limits. As you come up over the top of a hill, you see a police cruiser parked on the shoulder a few hundred yards ahead. You immediately apply your brakes and assume the speed limit. You do not slow down because a sudden epiphany causes you to recognize your responsibility to follow the highway laws. Rather, you decrease your speed because you don't want to receive a ticket. As soon as you can no longer see the cruiser in your rearview mirror, you resume your excessive speed.

If you are a teacher or a parent who controls or "motivates" children by constantly punishing them, you must understand that they will doubtless begin to misbehave the moment you leave the room or turn your back, because the threat of punishment does not exist. They behave and perform only when you are watching. Such parents and teachers should consider granting combat pay to their babysitters and substitute teachers!

Another reason that punishment is an ineffective motivator is that children tend to associate the punishment with the punisher, not with the offending behavior. ("Mr. Stewart took away my recess today." Versus "I cursed in class today and lost my recess.") Therefore, constant punishment has a negative impact upon your relationship with a child, and a positive teacher-pupil relationship is fundamental to enhancing motivation. Of course there are times and situations when punishment is appropriate and effective. But punishment does little to motivate children toward long-term, lasting effort.

PERFORMANCE INCONSISTENCY: THE LINK BETWEEN LEARNING DISORDERS AND MOTIVATION

I often remind audiences of the simple but profound fact that kids go to school for a living. That's their job. Their entire identity. When you meet an eleven-year-old neighbor on the street, what is your first question? "Hi, Teddy. How's school?"

Children with learning disabilities struggle mightily in the classroom. Their frequent failures and frustrations have an understandable impact upon their motivation. It is difficult to remain motivated and inspired when you are consistently unable to meet adult expectations—through no fault or choice of your own.

One of the least-understood aspects of learning disorders is the concept of performance inconsistency. Teachers' comments on report cards and at parent-faculty meetings often reflect this frustrating aspect of learning disabilities.

> "His performance is very spotty."
>
> "He has good days and bad days."
>
> "He seems to be able to do the work when he wants to."
>
> *And the classic:* "If he only applied himself . . ."

These comments, unwittingly, reflect the challenge of performance inconsistency. Any child with a learning disability has experienced the following scenario innumerable times:

Peggy has a test on the original thirteen colonies on Friday and she wants to do well. She practices several times on Monday evening in lieu of watching her favorite television program.

On Tuesday morning, her dad quizzes her on the colonies over breakfast. Tuesday night she reviews them again. Wednesday morning she studies them on the bus on the way to school. By now, she has mastered the thirteen quite solidly. Massachusetts, New York, New Hampshire, New Jersey . . .

On Wednesday night she forgoes a family trip to the local ice cream stand and remains in her room to review the colonies list once again. She rehearses them with her friend while waiting for the school bus on Thursday morning. That evening she neglects all of her other homework and focuses her complete attention on studying the list.

Her dad drives her to school on Friday, the day of the colonies quiz. She proudly announces to him that she has mastered and memorized the list and demonstrates by rattling off the names of the thirteen states from north to south . . . then from south to north. Peggy's hard work has paid off!

During her first-period class, the teacher is offering instruction on the food pyramid, but Peggy is focused on the second-period American history quiz. She is eager to demonstrate the newfound knowledge!

Second period comes. . . . The teacher distributes the quiz. . . . Suddenly, inexplicably, Peggy's information is gone. Vanished. She desperately searches the deepest recesses of her mind and her memory, but to no avail. The list is gone. Lost in her complex and flawed memory system. Peggy fails the quiz.

That evening, while she is watching television with her sister, the list suddenly reappears in perfect order. Virginia, Massachusetts, New Hampshire, Maryland, Connecticut, Rhode Island, Delaware, North Carolina, South Carolina, New Jersey, New York, Pennsylvania, Georgia.

For kids with learning problems, this scenario occurs over and over. Eventually, they come to accept a profound reality about their idiosyncratic learning style: For them, school is a game of chance. A crapshoot.

As one adolescent confided in me, "Mr. Lavoie, I have good days and bad days that are beyond my control. I have come to realize that. If test day is going to be a good day for me, I'll pass the test whether or not I study. If the test day is going to be a bad day for me, I'll fail the test whether or not I study. Sometimes, I think that it is useless to study at all."

When viewed from the child's perspective, it is easy to see why her motivation would wax and wane. Imagine that you had a relative and, despite your tremendous efforts to please and impress her, she simply did not like you. Eventually, you would recognize that all of your efforts were for naught, and you would simply stop trying to win her over.

This spotty motivation on the part of students with learning problems is caused by performance inconsistency. Basically, this neurologically based problem causes the child to have good days and bad days that are largely beyond her control.

An analogy: It is as if the child has three clocks in her brain. Each clock is set at a different time and moves at a different speed. As a result, the child is constantly confused and out of sync with her environment. However, the law of averages dictates that eventually, and inexorably, the clocks will tell the same time for a period. Then they will again go out of sync.

So it is with the child with learning problems. Inexplicably she will have bursts of forward movement wherein she makes observable, measurable progress for a period of time. Basically, her "clocks" are telling the same time. But then the clock hands move and she once again is out of sync.

This inconsistent progress and motivation is a source of great frustration for parents and teachers. Reflect for a moment on how frustrating it is for the student. In a study conducted by Jonathan Cohen at Columbia University, eight hundred adolescents with learning problems were asked to identify the most troubling and frustrating aspect of their learning disability. The majority of the students cited performance inconsistency. As one respondent stated, "The problem seems to come and go. I never know from one day to the next how I will perform in school." Frustrating, indeed.

This frustration is heightened by the fact that adults view this as a motivational problem rather than a neurological problem. Teachers and parents will often cite this inconsistency as a lack of focused effort. This leads to the mistaken but oft-heard belief that "He can do the work when he puts his mind to it." In the wise words of Dr. Mel Levine in his book *All Kinds of Minds*, "It will be a great day in education when we recognize performance inconsistency as part of the child's profile . . . rather than as evidence for the prosecution."

These accusations can create great anxiety and confusion for the child. She is constantly told that her learning capabilities are within her control, but in large part, this is simply untrue. She may become anxious or even depressed regarding her erratic and unpredictable performance. She begins to view herself as a failure or a slacker, and her motivation to succeed wanes even further.

It is useful to teach the child about her inborn inconsistencies.

She should not be allowed to use this irregularity as an excuse. Rather, she should learn to embrace and maximize those periods of time when her "clocks" are all telling the same time!

Decades ago, I heard Dr. Levine speak about performance inconsistency and I began to utilize the concept in my classroom. I explained to my students that—through no fault or choice of their own—their day-to-day performance would vary widely. In light of this, I explained that we would want to take full advantage of those occasional "good days." I purchased twenty hot-pink file folders and labeled each with a student's name. Inside each folder was a work sheet related to a skill or concept that was particularly difficult for that specific student. Tiffany's folder might contain a sheet on multiplication tables; Victoria's might focus on a specific spelling rule; Charlie's folder might contain some map work. I placed the folders on my desk, and when a student appeared to be having a good day, I would dispense with the planned lesson and give him his hot-pink folder. Maybe that day would be the day when he would learn that "*i* comes before *e*, except after *c*!"

My students began to embrace this concept and it was not unusual for a child to enter my classroom and say, "I'm feeling hot today, Mr. Lavoie. Gimme my good-day folder!" This demonstrated that they were beginning to understand and embrace—and compensate for—an important aspect of their learning style.

OVERCOMING LEARNED HELPLESSNESS

> "Tell a man that he is brave, and you help him to become so."
>
> —THOMAS CARLYLE

It is nearly impossible to understand or empathize with struggling children unless and until you have gained an appreciation for the complex concept of learned helplessness. Children who experience this phenomenon are often mislabeled as simply "lazy" and "unmotivated." The misdiagnosis occurs because educational professionals are often unskilled and untrained in the area of differential diagnosis.

Physicians receive intensive training in differential diagnosis and utilize the concept on a daily basis. Differential diagnosis recognizes the fact that two patients can have identical symptoms and yet their diagnoses and treatments may be significantly different. For example, Josh and Henry may go to their doctor suffering from excruciating headaches. After thorough examination, the physician determines that Josh's headaches are caused by seasonal allergies; Henry's headaches are caused by a growing cerebral tumor. Although the men's outward symptoms are identical, the treatment regimes that will be used will be drastically different. Josh gets antihistamine; Henry gets radiation.

As educators, we tend to view all children with similar symptoms (or behaviors) as having the same problem or diagnosis. If three boys in your third-period English class often sit passively with their heads lying on their desks, you make the assumption that all three are "lazy." In reality, one, two, or possibly all three of the boys may be experiencing learned helplessness.

Research into this intriguing phenomenon began in the 1960s. Researchers demonstrated that animals could be "taught" that they were helpless, and once they accepted the fact that they could not help themselves, they became very passive and nonassertive. For example, dogs were placed in a double-chambered cage with a low wall that allowed them to move easily from one chamber to another. While in one chamber, they were given low-voltage shocks, and they would invariably move to the other chamber to avoid these shocks. However, some dogs were placed in inescapable hammocks and were forced to endure shocks. When those dogs were then placed in the chambered cage and shocked, they made no attempt to escape. They merely accepted the shock passively. In effect, they had learned that they were helpless and so they simply stopped trying to escape.

These experiments demonstrated that when any member of the animal kingdom (and I remind you that human beings are part of the animal kingdom) feels that it is helpless, it stops trying.

Another notable example of this phenomenon can be viewed daily on the remarkable nature programs that are currently featured on television. These shows often feature footage of a big cat (leopard, cheetah, etc.) as it chases a gazelle across an open plain. The gazelle uses all of its speed and cunning to outrun the cat, but invariably the cat tackles his prey and begins to kill and devour it. Initially, the gazelle struggles madly to escape, but eventually it ceases struggling and passively accepts its fate. Scientists strongly feel that the gazelle has plenty of fight left in him and is not dead; it simply and instinctively recognizes that it is being held in a death grip from which there is no escape, and so it surrenders.

We all have areas of learned helplessness in our lives. For example, I am extraordinarily incompetent—and therefore extraordinarily helpless—when it comes to automotive maintenance or repair. I simply do not understand the complexities of the internal combustion engine. Suppose I were to go out to my car tomorrow morning, turn the ignition key, and the engine failed to start; I would turn the key again, and a third time. If the car failed to start after the third attempt, I would doubtless call the garage and request that they dispatch a mechanic to assist. It would not occur to me to lift the hood and attempt to troubleshoot the engine problem.

Now, if a neighbor were to observe this scene, he might make the judgment that I am "lazy" because I requested help without first trying to solve the problem on my own. I would submit to you that my behavior would be due to learned helplessness, not laziness. However, if my nephew, an auto mechanic, were to behave in an identical manner, he could be rightfully described as "lazy." Same behavior. Different diagnosis.

Unfortunately for children with academic deficiencies, their areas of learned helplessness include math, science, reading, and writing. As adults, we can generally avoid confronting our areas of learned helplessness. Struggling children cannot ignore theirs. Their chronic failure and frustration related to accomplishing critical language tasks can easily result in feelings of helplessness and hopelessness, withdrawal, and marked reluctance to attempt new or challenging tasks.

They assume that failure at these tasks is inevitable and unavoidable. They begin to develop passive and maladaptive behaviors in response to this anticipated failure.

I recall working with a math class several years ago. I announced, "We are going to try something new today." Immediately, Craig's hand shot up. "I can't do this. I'll need help!" Craig had decided that he would need my assistance before he even knew the nature of the task. That's not laziness. That's learned helplessness. Craig's long history of failure in math led him to believe that this task, too, would result in failure, defeat, and frustration. His effort would be futile. This was not a moral choice. Rather, it was a decision based on past experiences. Learned helplessness becomes a conditioned response to academic challenges and expectations. But conditioned responses are learned behaviors—and all learned behaviors can be unlearned. If attempts are not made to "unlearn" learned helplessness, it can easily become a permanent and continuous response to any unfamiliar or challenging task.

In order to fully understand the concept of learned helplessness, one must also be familiar with the theory of locus of control. This theory holds that human beings will attribute their success or failure to internal or external forces depending upon the degree of control that they have over the events in their lives.

Having an external locus of control would mean that a person's performance is determined by outside forces beyond the person's influence (luck, fate, intelligence, inborn qualities). Having an internal locus of control would mean that a person's actions are controlled by his own effort and energy.

Most of us assume an external locus of control when we fail and an internal locus of control when we succeed. For example, a golfer who has a poor day on the links is likely to cite the weather, his caddy, or his clubs as the source of his failure. Conversely, when he has a superior round, he will say that his continual dedicated practice is responsible for his success. As humans, this is how we remain happy and well adjusted.

However, some children who struggle with learning take an opposite view from the one adopted by our golfer. The child may well credit external forces when he succeeds ("I did well on the test because it was easy" or "I hit the home run because the pitcher stunk") and blame internal forces when he fails ("I failed the test because I'm dumb" or "I struck out twice because I skipped three practices last week").

It is important to realize that internal forces are factors that are within the child's sphere of influence. However, external factors cannot be controlled or predicted. It is easy to see how a child can feel helpless if he believes that he is at the mercy of these external forces.

Parents and teachers need to assist the child in gaining a more realistic and appropriate view of the factors that contribute to his performance.

In order to assist the child who is experiencing learned helplessness and to modify this unproductive thought process, the adults in the child's life must take three definitive but interrelated steps.

First, you must come to fully understand and embrace the nature of learned helplessness. To assist in this understanding, consider the elephant in the zoo. Each day, his handlers escort this huge powerful beast from his cage into his open-air pen. A thin chain is then looped around the elephant's ankle. The other end of the chain is attached to a metal stake that is driven a mere six inches into the ground. Although the elephant could with one tug of his mighty leg easily free himself from his bondage, he never tugs. He merely walks around the stake in the same circular pattern, day after day, week after week, month after month.

Why? Animal behaviorists use learned helplessness to train elephants. When he was a young, feeble elephant, his handlers attached that chain to his ankle and then attached it to the stake. The frustrated animal continually tugged on the chain, but was unable to free himself. After a while, he merely stopped trying and whenever the chain was looped around his ankle, he assumed he was imprisoned—helpless—and he simply circled the stake from that time forward. The elephant's feelings of helplessness were very real to him; just as a child's feelings of helplessness are real after repeated and chronic failure.

You must come to view learned helplessness as a credible and treatable condition and not label this behavior as laziness or a lack of motivation.

The second step in the elimination of learned helplessness involves changing the child's thought process and adjusting his belief that failure is inevitable. You must replace his expectation of failure with a more positive and effective thought process. However, encouraging him to repeat confident, self-affirming statements to himself will not provide significant relief. You must consider not only the failure itself but the child's perception of the reasons for the failure.

The child's assigning of causes for his lack of success is known as "attribution." This concept explains and illuminates the child's perception of what and who are responsible for his failure. The degree to which he is optimistic or pessimistic about his academic abilities is largely determined by his belief either that he has significant control over his skills ("I flunked the test because I didn't study enough" "I got an A because I did my homework every night") or that his performance is beyond his influence ("I failed because I'm dumb" "I got a D because the teacher doesn't like me"). This belief system is fairly well established by third grade and is greatly influenced by interactions with parents, teachers, and peers. Adults need to continually foster the idea that the child can control his progress and performance to a degree and that intensive and consistent effort will, eventually, result in academic progress.

Absent supportive adult intervention, the child can develop a permanent, fixated attitude about the inevitability of failure. His perception of the future and the present is dictated by the past. Further, he begins to generalize his failure in specific tasks (e.g., reading) to unrelated tasks (e.g., swimming, soccer). His feelings of helplessness and failure begin to take on a life of their own. The child begins to view himself as incompetent and assumes that this pattern of school failure will spread to his activities at home and in the community. His negative feelings about himself begin to extend to all aspects of his life. His initial feelings that he is "lousy at reading" expand into the belief that he is "a loser."

Once these feelings of learned helplessness become widespread and intense, learning becomes nearly impossible and the child's daily performance is significantly impacted. The resultant lack of progress serves to confirm his feelings of hopelessness, and a vicious cycle begins. In order to break this cycle, the child's teachers and parents must work closely together to provide the student with consistent reassurance and support. This is a lengthy, complex, and protracted process. Your encouragement must be at least as strong as the child's self-discouragement.

The adults in this child's life must make the child aware of these automatic, negative thoughts. Because this pattern of thinking has become so routinized and constant, the child may be unaware that he has developed such negative and ineffective thoughts. He must learn to recognize and derail these negative thoughts as soon as they occur and replace them with more positive, self-affirming thoughts ("I can do this" "I've gotten through difficult assignments before"). Once the student becomes aware of the nature and the frequency of these negative thoughts, he will be better able to defeat them. Dr. Thomas Tokarz, a Massachusetts-based expert in this area reminds us: "You don't have bad thoughts because you feel bad. Rather, you feel bad because you have bad thoughts. By improving the thoughts, you improve the feelings."

We must provide the child with concrete, observable, measurable evidence that contradicts and refutes his negative thoughts. (For example, "I don't agree that you don't have any friends, Jamal. Remember when Joseph asked you to be on his team in the geography bee?" "Sandra, I think that you will be able to design a good project for the science fair. The book cover that you made for *The Call of the Wild* was beautifully and creatively done.") The child must learn that these particular—negative—thought patterns are invalid and inaccurate.

Once the child has become aware of the negative thought patterns that he has developed and, further, recognizes that the thought patterns are unproductive, untrue, and harmful to his progress, the adults can begin the next step in the remediation process.

The third step involves asking the child what he would do if he were falsely accused of something or if someone called him a thief or a liar. He will likely respond that he would defend himself by assertively disputing the charges and that he would provide contradictory evidence to the accuser. ("I couldn't have stolen your stapler because I was in soccer practice all afternoon.")

Tell the child that his consistent negative thought patterns are, in effect, accusing him falsely and that he should provide himself with contradictory evidence just as he would with a teacher or peer who made an untrue accusation. It may be useful to role-play such a discussion with him.

Martin Seligman, who pioneered much of the research into learned helplessness, suggests in his book *The Optimistic Child* that the child use the following strategies to conduct this self-argument:

- *Gather contradictory evidence.* The child should serve as his own defense attorney and should collect data that refutes his belief that he will automatically fail at the task before him. ("Maybe Patti won't laugh at me if I ask her to work on our homework together. Last week when I asked to sit next to her on the bus, she said okay.")
- *Analyze alternatives.* Teach the child to generate possible outcomes that contradict his automatic negative thought. ("I think that I will be unable to understand the new unit in algebra, but maybe I will be able to get the initial part of the lesson and then my teacher or my dad can help me with the rest . . . or maybe the teacher will have us work in teams and Dawan will be able to help me a bit.")
- *Consider the implications of failure.* In the words of Franklin Roosevelt, "The only thing we have to fear is fear itself." Often the child's anxiety about a negative outcome magnifies the situation beyond reality. Enable him to understand this. ("Max, suppose you submitted a poem to the poetry contest and it didn't get selected for the class anthology. . . . So what? What damage would be done?")

The child with learned helplessness needs a learning environment that is supportive and nonthreatening. Mistakes must be viewed as inevitable—and useful—steps in the learning process. I often told students that I couldn't actually begin teaching them until they made some mistakes. The errors were the invaluable signal of the student's needs. ("If you keep getting every answer correct, I won't know where to start my instruction.")

In order to reduce the child's fear of mistakes, utilize correction techniques that recognize how a student's response is partially accurate, then coach him to the accurate answer.

TEACHER: *Kyle, who was the founder of Rhode Island?*

KYLE: *William Penn.*

TEACHER: *Good answer because William Penn did found one of the colonies. William Penn founded Pennsylvania. In fact, that is how the state got its name. We talked about the fact that the founder of Rhode Island has a college named after him in Providence. Does that help?*

KYLE: *Oh, yeah! Roger Williams.*

TEACHER: *Excellent.*

As much as possible, try to eliminate the word "wrong" from your classroom vocabulary, particularly when working with the child who has learned helplessness. Refer to his responses as "good," "better," and "best." ("Is there a better answer than that?" Or "That's much better, but let's try to find the *best* answer.") Encourage the child to use this vocabulary as well.

Measurable success and progress must be an integral part of the child's learning environment. He should be taught how to establish and work toward realistic goals, to monitor his performance, and to accept responsibility and credit for his progress.

Another instructional strategy that is effective with children with learned helplessness is the learning-teaching cycle. This four-step process can be used to teach nearly any academic, social, recreational, or household skill. I have used this process to teach children the times tables, how to fry an egg, spelling rules, how to mow a lawn, and how to wash the family dog.

This simple, sequential strategy must be followed closely with appropriate emphasis on and practice with each of the four steps. The strategy will not be effective if steps are skipped or abbreviated. Although the process can be time consuming, it should be viewed as an effective investment in the child's growth, progress, and attitude. Again, it is a particularly valuable approach to use with a learned-helpless child.

In order to illustrate the method, I will use the example of teaching Tyler to make a bed. Tyler is twelve years old and is unable to make his own bed, although his younger siblings are required to complete this daily chore. He has strong feelings of learned helplessness regarding this task and is convinced that he is simply incapable of making his bed properly.

Step One: Do It for Him

Make his bed while Tyler observes the process closely. As you complete each step, explain what you are doing. Encourage him to ask questions. As the process proceeds—over a period of several days—require him to verbally guide you through the procedure.

MOM: *What do I do next, Tyler?*

TYLER: *Now you spread out the quilt and line up the pillows.*

Do not require him to physically participate or assist during step one.

Step Two: Do It with Him

Gradually include Tyler in the process.

MOM: *Okay, Tyler, let's have you put on the top sheet.*

At the outset of step two, Tyler will be assisting you. As step two proceeds and an increasing number of the subtasks are assigned to

Tyler, you are in effect assisting him. By the conclusion of step two, he is completing the task virtually on his own.

Step Three: Watch Him Do It

This step is often forgotten, and its omission from the sequence can render this technique ineffective. Once Tyler has mastered the bed-making task, ask him to call you into his room whenever he makes his bed. Observe him and offer suggestions, praise, and reinforcement. Once you are convinced that he has gained mastery of the task, move on to step four.

Step Four: Have Him Do It

Parents and teachers commonly invest tremendous amounts of time in teaching a child a skill, only to fall into old patterns and begin doing the task for the child even though he is now capable of doing it independently. For several years, I served as curriculum director for a special education day school in Connecticut. I recall entering a local family restaurant and seeing one of my students seated in a booth with his dad. The father was dutifully reading the menu to the twelve-year-old, as he had countless times over the years. I approached them, took the menu from the dad, and handed it to the boy. I gently reminded the father, "You have invested a great deal of money and we have invested a great deal of time in teaching this child how to read. He can read now. . . . Let him read!"

Well-meaning parents unintentionally feed the learned helplessness by continually doing things for the child that she may be capable of doing independently. I often advise parents to conduct a monthly review—just as they pay their monthly bills—of tasks that they complete daily for their child that she should be completing by herself. For example, Mom has been selecting and laying out Bethany's wardrobe every evening since Bethany was six years old. Now, ten years later, Mom continues this nightly ritual even though Bethany is doubtless completely capable of doing this task independently and would probably greatly enjoy it. Mom should initiate the previously outlined process and encourage Bethany to select her own clothing. Parents need to continue to break this ongoing dependency cycle, lest the child's learned helplessness becomes more deeply ingrained.

Parenting expert Chick Moorman in his book with Thomas Haller, *The 10 Commitments: Parenting with Purpose*, advises parents and teachers to avoid using ritualistic language or phrases that may enhance the child's feelings of learned helplessness. Review his list of common phrases to determine if perhaps you are unintentionally exacerbating the problem by communicating a lack of faith in the child's abilities and potential.

Phrases that increase feelings of learned helplessness:

- Let me do that for you.
- I'll handle it.
- I'll talk to your mother (teacher) to see if I can get her to change her mind.
- I'll send the teacher a note.
- That's too difficult for you.
- I'll call the store and see if they have any left.
- Let me pour (get, fix, bring, carry, etc.) that. You might drop (spill, break, forget) it.

Phrases that enhance independence and decrease learned helplessness:

- I'll get the job started and you can finish it.
- Take a chance. See if you can do it.
- I know you can . . .
- Sounds like you have a problem. What solutions have you thought about?
- Let me teach you how to do this yourself.

Which phrases do *you* use most commonly?

We must remain mindful of the fact that learned helplessness is a real and potentially destructive psychological construct. The presumption of failure can cause significant damage to a child's self-esteem and worldview. He can become consumed and obsessed by a dark pessimism that will prevent him from taking risks in any setting.

MOTIVATING THE CHILD WITH ATTENTION DEFICIT DISORDER

"Sometimes I just get all scribbly."

—NINE-YEAR-OLD BOY WITH ADD, AS QUOTED BY MAUREEN NEUVILLE

One of the factors that can have a substantial impact on a child's academic performance and his degree of motivation is attention deficit disorder (ADD). This debilitating disorder affects the child's ability to focus and control his behavior. These are the two factors that contribute most significantly to a child's daily progress and performance in the classroom. School is quite literally a stacked deck for the child with ADD.

I often use an analogy to help people better understand the needs of ADD children. Recall if you will your junior high school science class. You probably were required to spend countless hours peering into microscopes in order to observe the single-celled amoebas and paramecia as they gyrated endlessly on the glass slides. You were taught that these creatures never slept, rested, or stopped. They were involved in a constant, vigilant search for food and nutrition.

So it is with the child with ADD. However, this child is not searching for nutrition; he is searching for stimulation. The ADD child needs stimulation to the same degree that you require oxygen. He simply cannot function without it.

In fact, if the child is not provided with stimulation, he will create stimulation by acting out or disrupting his environment in some way. Again, this is not being done for any negative reason. He is creating excitement because he needs it.

When viewed from this perspective, it is easy to see the impact that ADD would have on a child's academic progress and his motivation to succeed. Because the skills that he lacks are precisely the skills he needs in order to progress in school, he begins to develop negative associations regarding the learning process. He may be continually blamed, reprimanded, and censured for behavior that is beyond his control. He begins to feel angry, resentful, and frustrated. This frustration is exacerbated by the fact that ADD children are often exceedingly bright, and they are well aware of the discrepancy between their potential and their performance.

Current research by the Council for Exceptional Children indicates that nearly 10 percent of school-aged children struggle with ADD. The majority of these students also have some sort of academic learning disability, so their inability to sit still in class is complicated by their difficulty in mastering the content of the curriculum. These children tend to fail at a rate 250 percent higher than their peers without ADD, and nearly half of them will be required to repeat a grade in elementary or middle school.

When these factors are considered, the link between ADD and motivational problems is easily understood.

Our knowledge of ADD has expanded significantly in recent years. In the 1980s, the disorder was associated with three basic symptoms: hyperactivity, distractibility, and impulsivity. Current research demonstrates clearly that these three symptoms represent the literal tip of the iceberg and that there are numerous concomitant symptoms and traits that impact greatly upon the child's academic and social performance.

Success in school requires children to pay attention to assigned tasks and expectations. Children with ADD have significant difficulty sustaining attention, particularly during rote, repetitious, or prolonged tasks that are not particularly novel, entertaining, or stimulating.

Success in social situations requires children to complete three basic tasks consistently: listen, follow direction, and wait their turn. If a child is able to accomplish these simple procedures, he will likely enjoy social success. However, for the child with ADD, these "simple" skills are greatly compromised. For the ADD child, "simple" is not always "easy."

The key to motivating the child with attentional problems is to modify and adjust the learning environment. Often, teachers will invest significant time and effort in attempting to change the child. Their time might be better spent trying to change the policies, practices, and procedures that they are using with the child.

If you consider the skills and abilities that a child requires in order to succeed in the classroom, and then consider the deficits and weaknesses inherent in ADD, you will recognize that a significant mismatch exists. The expectations of the classroom are in direct conflict with the limitations of the child. Consider the following:

Classroom Expectations	**ADD Symptoms That Interfere**
"Wait until you are called on."	Impulsivity
"Don't interrupt."	Impulsivity
"Keep your hands to yourself."	Impulsivity
"Stay in line."	Impulsivity
"Take your time."	Impulsivity
"Read the directions carefully."	Impulsivity
"Sit still."	Hyperactivity
"No pencil tapping."	Hyperactivity
"Stay in your seat."	Hyperactivity
"Play/talk/work quietly."	Hyperactivity
"Stop fidgeting."	Hyperactivity
"Keep your desk/book bag orderly."	Organizational problems
"File your homework."	Organizational problems
"Where's your pen/pencil/ ruler/glasses?"	Organizational problems
"Drill, drill, drill!"	Low frustration level
"If at first you don't succeed . . ."	Low frustration level
"Be patient."	Low frustration level

"How many times have I told you . . ."	Inability to learn from experience
"Don't you remember what happened last time?"	Inability to learn from experience
"Follow the rules!"	Inability to learn from experience
"Arrive on time."	Impaired sense of time
"Adhere carefully to due dates."	Impaired sense of time
"Estimate how long it will take you to . . ."	Impaired sense of time
"Figure it out yourself."	Difficulty with sequencing, prioritizing, analyzing, synthesizing
"How would you solve this problem?"	Difficulty with sequencing, prioritizing, analyzing, synthesizing
"What's your solution?"	Difficulty with sequencing, prioritizing, analyzing, synthesizing
"Don't forget to . . ."	Memory deficits
"Always remember to . . ."	Memory deficits
"Memorize this."	Memory deficits
"The due date was . . ."	Memory deficits
"Come prepared."	Memory deficits
"Watch those careless mistakes."	Inattention
"Listen closely."	Inattention
"Pay attention."	Inattention
"Follow the main idea."	Inattention
"You should have finished that by now."	Inability to sustain effort
"You seem to be able to do it when you want to."	Inability to sustain effort
"Great start, but then you fell apart."	Inability to sustain effort
"Unacceptable handwriting."	Inability to sustain effort

When all of the above is considered, it becomes clear that the ADD child and the traditional classroom basically represent a mismatch. In order for the child with ADD to be successful—and, therefore, motivated—the teacher must make significant adjustments in her policies, procedures, and expectations. Basically, if the child cannot learn in the way we teach, we must teach in the way he learns.

For the child with ADD, his performance and his motivation are influenced by three major factors: his degree of interest in the activity, the difficulty of the activity, and the duration of the task. He will have significant difficulty with tasks that require organization, planning, inhibition, self-monitoring, and sustained effort.

The implications of this are readily apparent and it is easy to see that many traditional classroom activities will be inappropriate for this student. Included among these are: heavy emphasis on work sheets, independent work, long-term assignments, extended silent reading, and multistep tasks. Conversely, active, collaborative, spirited activities are very likely to motivate and inspire the child.

As much as possible, the curriculum should be stimulating and relevant to the child's life experiences. Research has shown that a curriculum that is irrelevant to the student's social and economic interests generally results in disruptive behavior, poor academic performance, limited progress, and dropping out. It is extraordinarily difficult for a child with ADD to remain engaged in a curriculum that is not interesting or challenging. These children live very much in the present. Therefore, long-term goals and rewards (e.g., grades and report cards) are often ineffective motivators.

Dr. Edward Hallowell, a Boston-based psychologist and author of *Driven to Distraction,* crystallized how important the present is to children with ADD. He explains that in the world of ADD children, there are basically two time frames—now and not now.

Friday Afternoon

TEACHER: *Be sure to read chapter 4 for Tuesday's quiz.*

ADD CHILD: *Tuesday? That's Not Now.*

Tuesday

TEACHER: *This is the quiz on chapter 4.*

ADD CHILD: *Uh-oh. That's Now.*

This Now/Not Now worldview causes great frustration for the child, his teachers, and his parents, and must be seriously considered when designing activities and approaches for motivating the child with ADD.

The child with ADD will respond more positively to a curriculum that allows him choices and options. He will also be more likely to participate actively in tasks when there is a degree of creativity and novelty (e.g., presenting a history review using a *Jeopardy!* game). In order to maintain the motivation of this child, the teacher must simultaneously consider *what* is being taught and *how* it is being taught. The content alone is unlikely to hold the child's attention or motivation for an extended period. The content should be stimulating and relevant; the presentation should be creative, colorful, multimodal, and enjoyable.

Among the specific teaching strategies that may foster the child's motivation are:

TEACHING STRATEGIES TO MOTIVATE THE STUDENT WITH ADD

- Provide a structured, predictable environment.
- Give simple single-step instructions.
- Simultaneously provide verbal and visual input (e.g., dictate instructions as you write them on the board).
- Provide modified testing and assessment procedures.
- Offer the child positive reinforcement, praise, and encouragement.
- Teach note taking, outlining, and other useful study skills.
- Assign the child a seat within close proximity of the teacher but away from high-traffic areas.
- Clearly outline rules, limits, and expectations. Post them.
- Avoid overloading the child with information, data, or instructions that he is unable to process.

- Allow for occasional breaks to let the child relax and reenergize.
- Institute a "study buddy" or "good neighbor" system wherein a classmate may assist the child with organization and preparation.
- Utilize a cue or a private signal that you can send to the child if her behavior or attention is beginning to deteriorate.
- Divide large, complex tasks into smaller, manageable segments. For example, if the child is assigned twenty math problems, give them to him five at a time. As he completes one set, give him the next five. This will be less intimidating and overwhelming. Gradually, increase the length of the segments.
- "Legitimize" the child's need for movement and activity by designing classroom activities that allow and encourage movement.
- Require that the child maintain an assignment notebook, and assist her with this task.
- Assist the child in getting started on a task and then encourage him to complete it independently.
- Give the child as much notice as possible if a major change or transition is coming.
- Establish a daily checklist communication system to ensure ongoing contact between home and school.
- Provide the child with a basic course syllabus to assist her in organization and planning.
- Provide him with two sets of textbooks. One set remains at home to facilitate homework, while the second set stays in school. This strategy ensures that he has the necessary materials in both settings.
- Make organization of books, desk, locker, and book bag a regular routinized part of her day. She should be assigned to spend a few minutes organizing at the beginning, middle, and end of the school day. Be aware that she may need assistance with this. Merely telling her to "straighten out your book bag" will not be effective.
- Be sure that you have the child's attention before giving him a direction or instruction. This can be done by calling his name or using a hand signal. After the instruction has been given, ask him

to repeat it back to you prior to carrying it out. Many ADD children are adept at appearing to understand when, in fact, they do not.

- Remain mindful of the three levels of instructional material:
Independent Level: Child can read the material at 97 percent accuracy and comprehend at 90 percent accuracy.
Instructional Level: Child can read the material at 90 to 96 percent accuracy and comprehend at 75 percent accuracy.
Frustration Level: 90 percent or below in reading accuracy and below 75 percent accuracy in comprehension. Reading is halting, slow, and laborious.

    Independent Level work should be assigned for homework and seat work. Material at a child's *Instructional Level* should be teacher-directed or monitored. Material at the *Frustration Level* should not be assigned.
- Never take good behavior for granted. Praise and reinforce the child for not interrupting, for working patiently, remaining in his seat, staying on task, cooperating.
- Remember that hyperactive behaviors during seat work (e.g., drumming fingers, pencil tapping, squirming in seat, fidgeting) are actually a release for the child's hyperactivity. Unless the movements are distracting or disruptive for others, ignore them. If it doesn't make a difference, what difference does it make?
- Do not emphasize quality and quantity simultaneously. Lengthy, complex assignments are exceedingly difficult for the child with attentional problems. It is better to assign five math problems and emphasize/expect accuracy than to assign twenty problems that will overwhelm the child and result in twenty inaccurate responses.
- Provide the child with a study carrel or a quiet section of the classroom where she can go when she needs a distraction-free area to study or memorize. Allow other students to have access to this area so it is not viewed as punitive or negative by the class.
- Remember that the child with ADD can become easily frustrated and this frustration greatly impacts his motivation. Stress, pressure, and fatigue can initiate and increase these feelings of

frustration. Be aware of the child's tendency to become frustrated, and take proactive steps to avoid or diminish anxiety-producing situations.

- Provide this child with several (e.g., ten to fifteen) seconds to respond to verbal questions. It may well take him that long to process and comprehend the question. Whenever possible, supplement verbal questions with visual input.
- Try alternative methods of assessment, such as oral testing or demonstration testing. Written tests and assessments will present particular difficulty for children with attentional problems because of the children's language and organizational weaknesses.
- Be certain that the child has the materials she needs before she begins a task.
- Carefully observe the child in order to determine when the child is particularly focused and attentive (e.g., early in the day, after recess, before lunch). Schedule his most difficult and challenging assignments and activities at these times.
- Follow difficult activities with more interesting or rewarding activities. ("Joseph, when you finish the math work sheet, you can feed the gerbil.")
- Avoid attributing moral or judgmental reasons for the child's inconsistency and impulsivity. Remember that these behaviors occur through no fault or choice of the child's. Accusatory feedback is counterproductive. Don't blame the victim.
- Provide the ADD child with ample opportunities to show divergent, creative, and imaginative thinking and to receive recognition for originality.
- Allow the child to doodle or squeeze a soft ball. Some children with ADD are better able to focus and attend when they are doing something with their hands during quiet activities (lectures, discussions, story time, videos).
- When giving instructions, be sure that you have the child's focused attention and ask her to paraphrase the instruction before beginning the task. Many children with ADD may also have difficulty with auditory processing. This disorder makes it

exceedingly difficult to understand and follow oral directions. These students will also have difficulty taking notes from lectures, so it may be useful to provide her with class notes.

- Encourage the child to focus his attention on the task at hand, and reinforce appropriate behavior when it occurs. These students have significant difficulty working independently and have a tendency to procrastinate and dawdle. These behaviors can be disruptive for the class and frustrating for the teacher.

Teachers and parents should view attention deficit disorder as a pervasive and complex disorder that impacts nearly all of the child's activities and interactions. The child's impulsivity ("Ready, fire, aim!") can present serious safety concerns; his distractibility makes it extraordinarily difficult for him to understand and follow instructions; his memory difficulties make even rote learning troublesome; his executive processing problems (ability to plan and prioritize) present great challenges when he attempts to plan simple daily activities; his organizational deficiencies cause him tremendous problems with homework, household tasks, and long-term projects.

The neurological causes and the medical treatment of ADD continue to be sources of research, experimentation, and debate. However, educators have developed methods and strategies that have proven successful with these children. Teachers and parents should remember the two most important words when dealing with these special children: "support" and "challenge." The adult should continually challenge the child by presenting him with activities designed to improve his behavior and his learning, while *simultaneously* providing him with the support that he requires to meet these goals. Support without challenge is meaningless. Challenge without support is equally ineffective.

2

The Motivating Classroom

"If you want to build a ship, don't recruit the men to gather the wood, divide the work and give orders. Instead, teach them to yearn for the vast and endless sea."

—ANTOINE DE SAINT-EXUPÉRY

EDUCATORS OFTEN BELIEVE THAT most of the factors that impact negatively on motivation (home life, parental attitudes, peer influence) are beyond the teacher's control. I speak to many teachers who feel that they are powerless to motivate and inspire children. This widely held belief runs contrary to current research in the field. Teachers can use strategies and techniques that can have a marked impact on student motivation and engagement. Basically, students expect to learn only if the teacher expects them to learn.

As we will explore in chapter 3, teachers and parents must come to recognize that there is no "one size fits all" solution to low student motivation. Just as each student *learns* in her own way, each child is *motivated* in a manner that is unique. The key to developing long-term effective motivational strategies is to analyze each child's motivational needs and design curricula and management techniques that are responsive to those needs.

However, there are general methods and approaches that tend to motivate and inspire most children regardless of their learning style, personality, or affinities. Teachers, coaches, instructors, and parents should be mindful of these global strategies and should attempt to make them fundamental ingredients in any learning situation.

These strategies do not focus on changing or modifying the *child* in any way. Rather, they are designed to make adjustments in the learning environment, whether it is a classroom, a playing field, a club meeting, or a household. These techniques are nothing more or less than sound field-tested procedures and policies that will provide the student with the drive and impetus to learn. Absent these approaches, the child will have little desire—or reason—to apply himself.

According to university research by Thomas L. Good and Jere E. Brophy, and presented in their book *Looking in Classrooms,* teachers seem to—perhaps unintentionally—treat low-achieving students differently than they treat students who are more academically competent. The researchers' study indicated that teachers provide low-achieving students with less praise and less feedback than they offer their classmates. Further, teachers interrupt these children more often, seat them in distant locales in the classroom, call on them less often, and give them less time to respond to questions. These students are given fewer compliments and far more criticism. These teacher behaviors are in response to the child's lack of progress but may indeed *contribute* to his chronic failure and underachievement.

This pattern can be reversed and the student's motivation can be greatly enhanced if the teacher remains mindful of the six C's of a motivating classroom:

Creativity
Community
Clarity
Coaching
Conferencing
Control

CREATIVITY

"The creative mind plays with the objects that it loves."

—CARL JUNG

A wise educational mentor of mine once counseled, "There are two ways that you can get twenty years' teaching experience. One is to get twenty years' teaching experience. The other is to get one year's experience twenty times." Astute observation.

We have all known teachers who present the same curriculum, activities, assignments, and bulletin boards year after year after year. My mother and I had the same teachers from the first grade to the fifth grade in our Massachusetts hometown. She had the teachers at the outset of their careers, and I had them in the twilight of their teaching. At every holiday she could tell me, with precise detail, what each teacher's bulletin board and holiday assembly poem would be! They made no significant changes in their curricula in the thirty years between the time when she was in their classes and I was assigned there. I well remember Easter of 1959, when Miss Counihan erected an Easter bulletin board featuring a bunny holding a sign urging the students to buy war bonds.

In order to foster motivation, teachers must inject variety and creativity into their lesson planning. This not only ensures increased motivation from the students, but also stimulates and energizes the teacher.

Today's teachers must recognize that our students exist in a highly visual world. The flood of videos, computer games, television images, and movies that children are currently exposed to have strengthened the link between memory and visual input. Teachers should capitalize on this by the extensive use of drawings, pictures, charts, graphs, and so forth, in the classroom. We are teaching in a different time, for a different time.

In order to provide a creative curriculum it is not necessary to spend tremendous amounts of money on the latest software or teaching equipment. In fact, some of the most creative curriculum approaches that I have seen have been conducted in rural and urban schools where resources are limited and scarce. Necessity is, indeed, the mother of invention.

I was once supervising a group of teacher interns at a hospital school in the Bronx. On their first day, they placed a harried phone call to me saying they were having an emergency and requesting that I come to the site as soon as possible. Anticipating a disaster, I left for the school immediately after receiving their SOS.

When I arrived at the teachers' lounge, my three interns were waiting for me and two of them were in tears. They explained that they were assigned to teach the ten-year-old students in the program, but the school had only one language arts series available in the curriculum library, and it was not the series that the interns had used in their Introduction to Language Skills classes. "How can we teach these kids any language skills if we don't have our language arts books?" they asked.

Admittedly, I was already a bit miffed at having been called in for a pseudo-emergency. But I was also genuinely troubled that these teachers had become so dependent on commercial materials. They failed to understand that they could modify the available materials or even design material themselves. I reached up to a shelf and grabbed a box of breakfast cereal that happened to be there. I said, "I will bet that we can construct ten language skills assignments from this box. I'll do the first three: List the vitamins and ingredients in alphabetical order. Divide your paper into three columns and list all of the one-, two-, and three-syllable words that you find on the back of the box. How many words can you make using the letters in the words General Mills? Now you try."

Within a minute or two the teachers began developing solid, effective activities to teach composition, grammar, alphabetizing, spelling, and handwriting. They got it.

Of course, it is important to adhere to the curriculum guidelines of your school district, but you will greatly enhance your students' motivation if you give yourself permission to "think outside the box" on occasion.

COMMUNITY

"What is learned in school depends far less on what is taught than on what one actually experiences there."

—EDGAR FRIEDENBERG

Physicians, nurses, social workers, and counselors are trained to adhere to a simple but profound concept when dealing with patients and clients: *Before clients care how much you know, they must know how much you care.*

Teachers would be well advised to apply this concept to their classrooms, and most effective teachers do. If a child is to be consistently and effectively motivated, she must feel that she is part of an accepting and caring "community of learners." She must feel safe, welcome, and a deep sense of belonging. Such an environment is the soil in which motivation can grow and flourish.

A classroom is a community with its own culture, values, and standards of behavior. Each classroom develops and fosters the ways in which students will receive recognition and achieve success. The classroom culture may be comforting or cruel, accepting or exclusionary, hospitable or hostile, welcoming or wary. The culture can provide a child with reinforcement or ridicule, compassion or criticism, inspiration or isolation.

Who determines the cultural climate of the classroom? I share the belief of legendary child care expert Haim Ginott, who reminds us in his book *Between Teacher and Child:*

> *I have come to the frightening conclusion that I am the decisive element in my classroom. It is my personal approach that creates the climate. It is my daily mood that makes the weather. As a teacher, I possess tremendous power to make a child's life miserable or joyous. I can be a tool of torture or an instrument of inspiration. I can humiliate or honor, hurt or heal. In all situations, it is my response that decides whether a crisis will be escalated or de-escalated and a child humanized or de-humanized.*

So how does a teacher convert a roomful of disparate and self-focused children into a sharing and caring community? First, we must recognize exactly what a community is. *Merriam-Webster's Collegiate Dictionary* defines "community" thus: *"a body of persons having a common history or common social, economic, and political interests."*

Unfortunately, that sterile definition is not particularly helpful for the teacher who is trying to create a community of learners in her classroom. A more useful definition can be found in *The Road Less Traveled* by renowned author M. Scott Peck. He outlines the four basic characteristics of a functioning and effective community. The community, according to Peck, must be:

Inclusive—each member is recognized, accepted, and embraced
Responsive—the community meets individual needs
Contemplative—the group continually examines and monitors progress
Safe—each member feels secure and protected

Upon consideration, you will recognize that every successful community you have been involved with—whether it was a sports team, a family, a workplace, or a committee—has had and practiced those four characteristics.

If you are to have an effective and motivating classroom, you should think of it as a working community with its own culture, values, and standards. You should establish the common goals of creating, fostering, and recognizing the success and progress of the members of that community. Further, you should establish community rules that are recognized by all members. The classroom rules, in and of themselves, do not create a constructive classroom structure; rather, the rules are merely reflections of and vehicles for the values of the community.

Your goal in creating a community within the classroom is to develop each student's sense of belonging and identification with the group. Each child must feel valued, accepted, included, and safe.

Once the children's emotional needs are met, they are far more likely to abide by the established norms of the community, and further, the children are more likely to support and validate other members of the community when *they* abide by the standards. For example, if bullying is contradictory to the cultural values of the classroom, children will be far less likely to bully others and will have little tolerance for a classmate who bullies.

As Peck reminds us, the community must be *inclusive*. New members should be welcomed and accepted warmly. Any hierarchical structures, cliques, or groups should be avoided and all children should be valued and recognized.

I once served as director of a residential school for students with special needs on Cape Cod. The extraordinary staff created a school culture that was caring, compassionate, and inclusive. The students, faculty, and staff shared wonderful relationships, and "random acts of kindness"' abounded throughout the campus. We all really cared about one another, and each member of the community enjoyed unconditional support and acceptance.

I recall watching a twelve-year-old prospective student who was spending a two-day visit at the school as part of the admissions process. He was sitting with a group of boys and was obviously attempting to ingratiate himself to them.

A very heavy young girl walked by their table. The visitor leaned into the group and whispered, "Look at that cow. Does she need two beds in her dorm room?" I will never forget the looks on the faces of the students. They looked at the newcomer as if he were speaking a foreign language. *Why would he say that? Why be so mean?* they thought.

The new boy unwittingly violated the inclusive culture of the school. His comment—which would have received hearty laughter in many schools—simply ran contrary to the culture of acceptance and generosity that we had created. The students were not entertained by his comments. They were puzzled and troubled by them.

By the way, the boy *did* eventually understand and embrace our culture. During the exit interview at the conclusion of his visit, he told the admissions director, "I really like this place. It's not like my other school. Here you don't have to be mean to be popular."

Creating an inclusive community is a significant challenge for a teacher, particularly in a middle school or high school classroom. Students at that age have a natural tendency to isolate and reject fellow students, often for reasons that seem petty and arbitrary. When I conduct seminars for parents and teachers of adolescents, the attendees often describe teenagers as mean, vicious, or cruel. Actually, these labels are inaccurate and misleading.

The cruelty that is commonplace among teens and preteens is somewhat understandable when we consider the "spotlight principle." I often use this analogy when discussing adolescence with parents and professionals. The primary fear of any adolescent is to be embarrassed in front of his peers. Teens spend nearly every waking hour in an ongoing mission to not be humiliated. A teen's great fear is that the dreaded spotlight will shine on her—that something she says, wears, or does will be singled out by her peers as decidedly "uncool" and the spotlight of embarrassment will mercilessly shine on her.

Teenagers soon realize that the best offense is a good defense. That is, the most effective way to keep the spotlight off me is to focus the group's spotlight on a peer. Four classmates—Sasha, Linda, Becky, and Lisa—are seated at a cafeteria table. Each girl harbors the same secret fear: that she will say or do something that is viewed as uncool by her tablemates. Suddenly, Linda makes a positive comment about a song she heard on the radio that morning. Becky sees this as her opening, her chance to deflect the spotlight by locking its beam on Linda. "You like that song?" Becky scoffs. "That group is *so* gross! I can't believe that you like *them*."

Of course, Lisa and Sasha gladly "pile on" in order to avoid the spotlight, and suddenly hapless Linda finds herself bombarded with criticisms and taunts from all sides. Such is the world of adolescence.

Empathy requires a child to understand and assume the roles and feelings of another person. This represents a tall order for the adolescent or preadolescent, who by his very nature is egocentric and self-absorbed. One effective strategy that adults can use to promote empathy is I messages. This makes the child more aware of the feelings or needs of others. Rather than saying "Stop being a pain and quiet down," you say "I can't help this group with their math when the other group is talking so loudly." By consistently emphasizing the impact that the child's behavior has on you, you will make him better understand the needs and feelings of others in his social environment.

The classroom culture should also be tolerant of differences and, in fact, should embrace differences as a fundamental aspect of the human condition. Tolerance is an integral part of a respectful classroom community, and students should be encouraged to be accepting of differences and difficulties among classmates. They should also be accepting of their own idiosyncrasies, quirks, and eccentricities. Children must come to recognize that "different" is not synonymous with "bad" and that prejudice or intolerance of any type is inappropriate and unacceptable. The maturing child not only must practice tolerance in his own life, but also must promote and foster it in others.

The teacher can demonstrate acceptance for her students in several ways. Many of these strategies are quite simple and require minimal time or resources. However, by using these techniques consistently and by making them an integral part of your daily routine, you will be showing your students that you genuinely care about them, their feelings, and their progress.

- Greet the students at the door of your classroom as you would a guest in your home. Smile and make eye contact. Call them by their preferred nickname (but don't assume that every William is "Bill" and every Robert is "Bob").
- Use attentive, active listening when talking to students, even during informal conversations.
- Attend school plays, games, and other activities that your students may be involved in.

- Criticize in private; praise in public.
- Circulate around the room in a natural nonthreatening manner; walk and talk.
- Acknowledge student progress, accomplishments, efforts . . . and birthdays.
- Inquire about their health after an absence.
- Always avoid humiliation, ridicule, impatience, anger, or disappointment when dealing with students.
- Use their names when writing comments on assignments. ("Great improvement, Jenn.")

The second trait of Peck's community is *responsiveness*. The members of a community must recognize and respond to the needs of the other members. This requires the teacher to modify and adjust expectations in response to the individual needs of a child. She must be aware that some children will require more of her time and energy than others will. She must come to practice and embrace the concept that "fair" is not always synonymous with "equal."

Students must also recognize their duty to be responsive to the needs of classmates and the adults in the community. I recall teaching a literature class early in my career. The students were an extraordinary group and, together, we created a remarkable community. Meeting with this class was invariably a high point of my day. One morning, I was not feeling well. I had a nagging headache and was quite congested. I entered my literature class and saw that my students were exceptionally "wired" and aroused. They were anticipating that afternoon's soccer game and the annual sports award dinner that evening. They were loud, boisterous, and noisy, jostling one another and eagerly getting an early start on the afternoon's festivities.

As I entered the room, the students did not go to their seats and settle down as they customarily had. They continued their noisy conversations and most ignored my request that they return to their seats and begin the class. Finally, I got their attention and plaintively said, "Guys, please, not today. I feel lousy."

They immediately took their seats, retrieved their literature notebooks, and looked up at me anticipating my next instructions. I was duly impressed by their responsiveness and empathy. Their sensitivity to my temporary needs reflected the responsive community that we had created. Absent this community feeling, the students would have doubtless taken advantage of my vulnerability and would have ramped up their disruptions and celebrations.

In a responsive community, the teacher must be willing and prepared to modify her instruction in order to meet the unique needs and limitations of her students. This requires her to provide remediation when necessary and possible, and to assist the child by making accommodations and modifications in the curriculum. This is particularly important when dealing with children who have special educational needs. As learning disabilities pioneer and lecturer Laurence Lieberman reminds us: In regular education, the *system* dictates the curriculum. In special education, the *child's needs* dictate the curriculum.

The third requirement for a successful community is Peck's concept of *contemplation*. The community must continually strive to improve itself and must constantly monitor, analyze, and evaluate its progress toward its goal and mission. Without this ceaseless striving toward betterment, the community can become stale, flat, and ineffective.

In the 1950s many American business leaders were greatly impressed by the manner in which Japanese industries were recovering from the devastation and destruction they had experienced during the Second World War. Teams of Western executives went to Japan to study the processes and procedures that their Japanese counterparts were using to produce such high-quality products in such an efficient and timely manner. While observing these Japanese business communities, the Western executives were introduced to the concept of *Kaizen*.

Kaizen (*Kai* = change; *zen* = good) is a widely used Asian business technique that expects and requires every member of an organization to make continual and ongoing improvement in all aspects of the program. Improvement should be gradual and continuous, even in areas and aspects of the organization that are going well and running smoothly. This approach runs contrary to the traditional philosophy of "if it ain't broke, don't fix it." Kaizen is based on the belief that every aspect of an organization can and should be continually improved and enhanced.

Your classroom community will be far more responsive and effective if you adopt the Kaizen philosophy and consistently monitor and adjust your curriculum, policies, and procedures. For example, your homework program may be going quite well, but Kaizen would dictate that you still examine your home study system to see if improvements are possible. The Kaizen philosophy states that every action taken by the leader should be aimed at improving the program and, further, that a day should not pass without making some sort of modification or improvement in some aspect of the organization. All adjustments are directed at one solitary goal—improving the services that are being delivered to the clients and the customers.

As educators, we are unaccustomed to viewing our daily duties from a business perspective, but we would do well to adopt this outlook. There are three basic ingredients that constitute a business environment: customers, clients, and competition. Upon reflection, you will come to realize that schools have all three of these criteria. Our *clients* are the students. Our *customers* are the parents. And with the advent of charter schools, vouchers, and private schools, the concept of *competition* has become a reality in public schools. If teachers are not able to effectively motivate and educate their *clients* (students), the *customers* (parents) will seek out *competitors* (educational options) that can. When twenty-first-century American education is viewed from this perspective, it makes sense to investigate and adopt proven business practices such as Kaizen.

In order for Kaizen to be effective, all members of the organization must embrace the concept and develop ideas and suggestions to improve the services. Teachers should solicit and respond to suggestions and recommendations made by students, aides, colleagues, and parents. Generally, these recommendations do not call for major or significant changes. Rather, they suggest minor adjustments that serve to make the organization more effective and responsive. For example, a student might suggest that Friday's vocabulary quiz be moved to Monday to allow the weekend for study; the janitor may recommend that you move your computers away from the windows to prevent sun damage; a parent might propose that homework assignments be posted on a website to assist children who have difficulty remembering instructions. All of these recommendations are positive and will contribute to the common purpose of the classroom.

Again, teachers should solicit, consider, and—when appropriate—implement these suggestions made by others. Problem solving should be viewed as a collaborative community activity. These small, incremental changes all contribute to the overall effectiveness of the class. Kaizen reduces waste, increases quality, improves communication, and enhances morale. Instead of focusing on large, significant projects, Kaizen places attention on small, creative investments and modifications. The practice emphasizes teamwork, cooperation, and responsiveness.

Peck urges continual, ongoing evaluation and contemplation in order to improve the community. The concept of Kaizen provides a useful and effective vehicle to accomplish this.

The final criterion in Peck's formula for an effective community involves the *safety* of all members of the community. Nearly a half century ago, pioneering psychologist Abraham Maslow posited that a person could not learn, function, or reach his fullest potential unless and until his need for safety was assured. If a person feels insecure, endangered, or threatened, he will simply be unmotivated to learn. Rather, his entire being becomes focused upon his personal well-being.

I was once speaking with an administrator of a very troubled and violent urban high school. He asked me, "How can you expect these kids to focus on high-stakes testing? They are worried that they might not survive lunch break or the walk down the hallway between classes."

In order for a child to feel safe in the classroom, he must believe that he is insulated and protected from bullying, embarrassment, assault, rejection, indignity, shame, and humiliation. Most of us work in schools where physical safety is relatively assured, but student motivation is also greatly impacted by the insecurity related to psychological humiliation and rejection. Will a child be motivated to participate in a classroom discussion if he knows that an incorrect or inappropriate response will result in merciless taunting by his classmates or an insensitive public criticism from his teacher? I think not.

Teachers should create a classroom environment in which students feel secure and accepted. In order to learn and progress, a student must occasionally take risks. He must be willing to volunteer his opinions during class discussions, respond to a teacher's question even though he is not totally sure of the accuracy of his answer, submit a proposal for the science fair, and ask the cute redhead in the third row if she would like to sit with him at lunch. All of these daily school rituals require confidence and self-esteem. These two traits will develop only in an environment where the child is willing and able to take risks without fear of embarrassment or humiliation.

This, of course, is particularly important for the student in middle school or high school. At those stages of human development, the child has minimal interest in or concern for the opinions of his parents or teachers. Rather, the adolescent's self-concept and self-worth are determined nearly exclusively by his peers. Pediatrician and author Mel Levine reminds us that adolescence is a five-year seven-days-a-week twenty-four-hours-a-day battle to *not be embarrassed.* If the student does not feel safe and protected from daily humiliation, he will doubtless be reluctant to participate in academic or social activities.

It is widely held that September 11, 2001, was a momentous day in America's history, that it changed the course of our society. However, I feel that America's schools were impacted to a greater degree by the horrific incident at Columbine High School on April 20, 1999. The wonton and brutal attack by two troubled students changed the American school forever. Twelve students and a teacher went to school one morning in a bucolic American suburb and never returned home. On that dark day, teachers, parents, and students were forced to recognize that our schools were no longer the sanctuary that we had believed them to be. As a result, a cottage industry of books, curricula, consultants, and websites related to school safety was born.

Of course, we all want our children—and the adults who teach them—to be safe and secure from physical violence. But—we must also be concerned about the verbal assaults, rumors, bullying, humiliation, and rejection that occur in our schools daily. These factors also impact upon the safety needs of children.

If your "classroom community" is to be a safe harbor for your students, you must be aware of, and have little tolerance for, any sort of abuse or rejection that may occur in your classroom.

The caring teacher must first examine her own interactions with students. Do you act in a way that is perceived as threatening or intimidating? Do you respond to student errors in a supportive way? Are you warm and accepting of the children in your charge? Are you approachable and welcoming? Basically, do your students feel safe with you?

I have a long-standing bias against teachers and coaches who are chronic yellers. They use their voices to intimidate children. I view this as a significant abuse of their positions and authority because they clearly would not tolerate a child yelling at them and would respond strongly and punitively to this behavior.

I recall consulting with an elementary school in a small Midwestern town. Their sixth-grade teacher, Mrs. Da Point, was widely known as a hollerer, and her voice would reverberate through the hallways several times each day. Students feared her. Parents dreaded her. The principal was puzzled by her.

"She's actually a very effective teacher and a good person," the principal told me. "I have worked with her for years and have come to respect her knowledge and skills. She can also be very sensitive to kids and has been known to provide extraordinary support to some of our most troubled kids. If only I could break her of the yelling. Would you give it a try?"

I met with her and discussed several curriculum issues. I found her to be quite astute and knowledgeable. Her concern for her students was obvious and she seemed eager to modify her strategies to better meet their needs.

I tentatively and gingerly brought up the reports of her chronic yelling at students. Her demeanor changed immediately and she became stern and defensive.

"I know that I yell at kids. But I get so frustrated after I have told them the same thing twenty times. Yelling *really* gets their attention. They are just going to have to learn to live with it!"

She squared her shoulders and glared at me.

I once saw a bumper sticker that read, AS LONG AS YOU ARE ON THIN ICE, YOU MIGHT AS WELL DANCE. . . . So I decided to dance with her a bit.

"I want you to think about something, Grace. Please recall for me the last time that someone yelled at *you*."

"Oh, this is silly," she responded.

"No, please. Adults seldom yell at other adults. Maybe it was years ago. Think."

She became intrigued. "Well, it was several years ago at Christmastime. I was backing my car out of a parking spot at the mall. The backseat was filled with gifts and they blocked my view as I was backing. Suddenly, I heard a young lady yell, 'Hey, look out!' She was in my blind spot and I nearly struck her. I rolled down my window to apologize, but she approached the car and began yelling loudly at me. She just stood there and hollered. It was terrible. I'll never forget it." She shuddered as she spoke.

"How did you feel at that moment?" I asked.

"Terrible! I was embarrassed, humiliated, and frightened. Even though we were in a public place and I was securely in my car, I felt . . . unsafe."

She suddenly stopped, and in a moment of insight, she murmured, "That must be the way my kids feel . . ." Her voice trailed off.

Yes, Grace, that is *precisely* how they feel. Embarrassed. Humiliated. Frightened. Unsafe.

The teacher can do a great deal to ensure that students feel safe in the classroom. A child's feeling of safety springs from the knowledge that powerful adults care for him and are willing and able to help. When a teacher intimidates a child or fails to intervene when the child feels unsafe, the student comes to feel very vulnerable and fearful. It is important to remember that there is a clear link between the child's sense of safety and his ability to learn, concentrate, and be motivated.

Insecurity, of course, is common among children in all settings. I once asked my mentor why children were so insecure. He responded, with tongue firmly in cheek, "Well, if you were smaller than everyone else and didn't have any money, you'd be insecure, too." However, for some youngsters, this feeling of powerlessness can become pervasive and damaging. This powerlessness can lead to feelings of hopelessness that impact significantly on the child's motivation.

The sole antidote to this hopelessness is empowerment. The child must come to feel that he can influence his environment, feel safe there, and seek assistance when he feels threatened or insecure.

Meeting Physical Needs

As we have outlined, it is crucial that a child feel safe and secure in the classroom if he is expected to be motivated to learn. Expanding the definition of "security" a bit, we must also consider whether a child's basic physical needs are being met. Research has shown that when a basic, primary physical need is unmet, it is extraordinarily difficult for the child to be motivated.

For example, if a child is hungry or thirsty, the related sensations will impact upon his motivation. This phenomenon also commonly occurs with adults. When I address a large audience of teachers at a morning seminar, I can easily determine which audience members had breakfast before coming to the workshop. Those attendees who are hungry begin to stir a bit as lunch approaches. They find it difficult to focus or even to sit still. Their basic need (hunger) overcomes their motivation and their ability to attend. If hunger has this impact upon adult learners, we can assume that a child's unmet basic needs affect the child in the classroom as well.

As we all know, many students in our classroom come to school hungry for a variety of reasons. By late morning, they may become anxious, irritable, and unfocused. I offer a novel solution to this common problem: *Give them something to eat!*

One of the most valuable weekly purchases you make may be a simple box of crackers. When a child begins to "fade" because of hunger, simply give him a handful of crackers and instruct him to get back to work. Some teachers may be reluctant to use this strategy, but consider the alternative: You can either provide him with the nutrition to satisfy his primary need . . . or deal with his daily meltdown from eleven A.M. until noon! To me, the choice seems simple.

Another primary physical need that can impact on classroom performance and motivation is thirst. When I give a seminar to a ballroom filled with teachers, I often ask them to note that nearly every person in the audience has brought something to drink with them. The tables are filled with bottled waters, cans of soda, and Styrofoam coffee cups. In addition, the sponsoring organization also provides unlimited liquid refreshments at each table or in a common location in the ballroom. Even when a seminar is held in an auditorium where signs announce that food and drinks are not permitted, the majority of attendees manage to smuggle a bottle, can, or thermos in their bags or briefcases.

Yet these are the same folks who forbid students to bring drinks into their classrooms, and may go apoplectic when a child requests permission to leave the classroom for a moment to get a mouthful of water from the hallway bubbler.

Just as it would be difficult for a teacher to attend a lengthy lecture without something to slake her inevitable thirst, it is very difficult for a young child to sit through his morning classes without a drink. This is particularly noteworthy for teachers whose students may be on prescribed psychotropic medications, of which thirst and dry mouth are common side effects. Perhaps that boy in your fourth-period English class who constantly asks to leave the room to get a sip of water is not plotting to avoid schoolwork or have a clandestine meeting with his friends. Perhaps he is simply *thirsty.*

For over a decade, I was director of a school for adolescents with learning disorders. We allowed students to bring small water bottles to class with the caveat that any child who misused his bottle would forfeit the bottle and the privilege of using it. In seven years, *one* student had his water bottle confiscated. There is something a bit troubling and ironic about watching a teacher refuse a child's request to get a drink from the water fountain during class . . . while she takes another sip of the Big Gulp that sits on her desk!

Human beings also have a physical need for air and space. The working conditions in a typical classroom are extraordinarily close and tight. What if you were expected to function for six hours each day in a workplace where you could reach out your arms and easily touch five or six coworkers? You would doubtless find these conditions intolerable. However, that is the precise environment in which we expect students to function every day. Because this environment is so cramped and close, students are deprived of the space that they need to feel comfortable. They need an occasional break from this stifling environment.

Remember the wise old teacher in your brick elementary school who would occasionally have her students "stand up and shake" after a particularly tedious or challenging activity? She knew instinctively that the youngsters needed some air, space, and activity before they could tackle the next task.

If the child feels cramped and closed in, it will be very difficult for her to maintain her motivation. It is for this reason that recess has become a centuries-old staple in America's schools. This break time at midmorning is not a luxury but a necessity for most students. A troubling trend in schools is the elimination of recess periods in order to allow additional preparation for high-stakes testing. Denying a child recess not only deprives him of the air and rest he physically requires, but also eliminates an invaluable social laboratory where children learn the three basic skills of childhood social success: sharing, following directions, and waiting their turn.

I once consulted with a nine-year-old named Beth. She was a sweet and generally compliant youngster with significant attentional and hyperactivity difficulties. She was particularly needy in regards to air and space, and it was extraordinarily difficult for her to sit quietly in her seat for hours. She could maintain herself—with great investment of effort and energy—for the initial two hours of school, but she needed the daily activities and rituals of recess in order to maintain her attention for the final two hours of the morning.

A few minutes before the ten-thirty recess bell would ring, Beth would often become anxious and overly active in anticipation of running and frolicking on the playground. This anxiety would frequently result in minor misbehaviors—speaking loudly, leaving her seat, looking out the window—and her teacher would respond by *taking away her recess*! In effect, the teacher was eliminating the *solution* to her misbehavior.

I conferred with the teacher and explained that for Beth recess was a *right*, not a privilege, and I asked that recess no longer be used as a punishment for her. The teacher was quite intransigent and refused to modify her approach. At the next assessment meeting with school personnel, I had the following phrase added to the addendum page of the Individual Education Plan document: "At no time and under no condition (save medical constraints) is Beth to be denied participation in recess."

From that point forward, anyone depriving Beth of her recess was in violation of federal law.

Elimination of Waste

The final physical need that we must consider is the elimination of waste. When a person needs to urinate or void, his bodily systems send him innumerable uncomfortable messages. These sensations can easily and understandably overshadow the person's desire to learn or participate. I have long been puzzled by the inflexibility with which teachers approach this issue.

Teachers view "the bathroom issue" as a major problem in today's classrooms and generate a fascinating array of "solutions." Below is a list of the most interesting ones that I have seen or heard over the years. As you will see, they range from dubious to draconian.

- A middle-school teacher allows two "potty passes" per semester. Each pass allows the student a two-minute bathroom break. Any time beyond the two minutes requires the child to make up the time after school.
- A fifth-grade teacher requires her students to write their names on the blackboard when they use the bathroom and that child automatically misses five minutes of recess that day.
- An elementary-school teacher gives every student five laminated tickets at the beginning of each month. When a child uses the bathroom, he must turn in a ticket . . . two tickets are required if he uses the bathroom within a half hour of recess.
- A fourth-grade teacher requires children to spend their recess picking up litter from the playground if they use the bathroom during the morning.
- In one third-grade class, all students are required to have a "silent lunch" if three or more students request to use the bathroom on the same morning.
- A fourth-grade teacher requires students to stand against the wall for five minutes at recess if they use the bathroom during the class day. If a child spends more than three minutes in the bathroom, she loses bathroom "privileges" for a week.
- One teacher reports that she grants no bathroom privileges without a doctor's note.

Why does the bathroom issue continue to be such a hot-button topic for teachers? Surely a child's departure from the class can be a disruption, and *some* children will attempt to use bathroom breaks to avoid work, but—quite simply—"if you gotta go, you gotta go!" You may want to deal with the "frequent flyer" who asks for a pass daily, but in the majority of cases, children will ask for permission to use the bathroom only when they truly need it.

If you work with special needs children, you might walk in the student's shoes for a moment in regard to the bathroom issue. I once worked with an eleven-year-old boy named Alec. He had significant learning and social problems and was isolated and rejected by his classmates and peers. His teacher was greatly frustrated by his daily request to go to the bathroom immediately after recess and lunch, despite several reminders to use the facilities during recess and lunch . . . like the other kids do.

One day, Alec asked to use the bathroom shortly after the students returned from lunch. The teacher posed her oft-asked question, "Why didn't you use the bathroom at lunch?"

In response to this, a frustrated Alec unloaded his pent-up frustrations and fears. "You want to know *why*?" he began. "I'll tell you why! Because you people don't protect us in there. Every time I go into the boys' room at recess, the kids in the bathroom splash me with water and call me SpEd Head. One time, they pushed me into the urinal and flushed it. I was soaked. The last place that you will ever find *me* is in the boys' room at lunchtime!"

The teacher had a momentary glimpse at Alec's world. From then on, she willingly approved his occasional requests to use the bathroom during class time, and recommended that the principal occasionally patrol the boys' rooms during lunch and recess.

In summary, teachers: *Let my people go!*

CLARITY

> "When children enter school, they should discover that each classroom is a working, problem-solving unit and that each student has individual and group responsibilities."
>
> —WILLIAM GLASSER

Clarity is another crucial trait of Peck's community. It is important that all members understand the rules and expectations of the community. If these requirements are not generally understood, it is doubtful that compliance will occur.

Nearly every effective and functioning classroom that I have ever observed features a large tag board sign that outlines the classroom rules. This has become a staple in America's classrooms. Although the publishing of the class rules will not ensure a neat, orderly, effective class, it *is* an important step in creating clarity in the room.

As you design the class rules, you should be mindful of the differences among philosophies, policies, and procedures. The classroom should have a *philosophy:* a basic belief system that reflects the class values and goals. You also need *policies*: the regulations that allow the community members to carry out that philosophy. Lastly, you should have *procedures*: the specific practices and activities that support the philosophy and allow the policies to work.

For example:

Philosophy: Homework is an important aspect of the curriculum because it provides valuable reinforcement of academic material and develops independent functioning and academic skills.

Policies: Homework assignments should be:

Relevant: Homework material will be related to units and topics currently covered in class.
Review: New, unfamiliar material should not be introduced through homework.
Realistic: Because homework is completed in a relatively

unstructured environment at home, it is anticipated that the child will be only 30 percent as productive as he will be in the structured classroom.

Procedures: Homework is assigned, corrected, and returned on a daily basis.

Care must be taken to ensure that policies and procedures support and reflect the philosophy. Any procedure that is not in keeping with the philosophy is counterproductive. For example, if the teacher fails to include homework in her lesson plans for a substitute teacher or if she occasionally gives a "No Homework Day" for students, she is using *procedures* that violate the *philosophy*.

The philosophy and policy aspects of the community are largely designed and dictated by the teacher. However, the procedures consist of rules and regulations to be followed by the teacher and the student. For example, in the homework guidelines listed above, the teacher's role is to prepare and distribute homework; the child's role is to carefully complete homework and place it in the homework folder upon entering the class each morning.

The most common mistake made by teachers when designing their classroom rule charts is that they utilize philosophies, not procedures. For example, I have seen teachers include statements such as "Be nice to each other" or "Work hard." These are ineffective because they describe behaviors that cannot be readily observed or measured. These statements identify philosophies, not procedures.

Keep the following guidelines in mind when designing class rules:

EFFECTIVE CLASSROOM RULES

1. Although the teacher designs the majority of the rules, you may want to seek and implement student input on occasion. They are more likely to follow rules that include their input.
2. Each rule should begin with an action verb and should be clear and concise. Your posted rules should describe the behavior that you

want (e.g., "Walk in the hallways"), not the behavior to be avoided ("No running in the hallways"). By stating the rule positively, you have enhanced the rule's clarity; only *walking* is permitted. The "no running" rule does not eliminate skipping, galloping, sprinting, dashing, scampering, scurrying, hopping, or cantering.

3. All rules should be measurable and observable. An effective rule should be reasonable, positive, succinct, enforceable, and enforced.
4. Rules should reflect effective work habits and safety. When explaining a rule to the class, present scenarios that demonstrate the safety implications. All rules should reinforce the basic belief that students are in school to study and learn.
5. Rules should be somewhat flexible. Add or eliminate rules as the school year proceeds. Try to create rules that can be generalized to other settings outside of the classroom (e.g., media center, field trips, cafeteria). Of course, class rules should be adapted to reflect the age, abilities, and dynamics of the students.
6. Limit the number of rules to seven or less and list them in a sequence that follows the order of a typical school day. Post the rules prominently in the classroom so they can be referred to often. ("Kaylee, remember rule number four.") You may want to distribute them to parents as well.
7. When establishing rules at the beginning of the school year, have a discussion with the class that outlines the reasons behind the rules, and the specific regulations that are subsumed under the general rules.

Again, it is important to remember that merely posting the rules will not ensure compliance. The teacher *and* the students must play a role in promoting and following the rules. For example, consider the rule "Enter the classroom quietly." The students are expected to speak softly, take their assigned seats, and stow backpacks and supplies. The teacher is expected to stand at the door and greet the arriving students, create a permanent seating plan, praise and reinforce appropriate behavior, and establish areas to put coats and submit assignments.

Don't refer to the rules only when a regulation is broken. Also acknowledge the rules when they are followed. ("That discussion went very well. That's because you all followed rule three and raised your hands and listened politely.")

Students are far more likely to be motivated if the behavioral, academic, and social expectations are clearly outlined.

The second aspect of clarity as it relates to motivation involves giving clear and concise directions and instructions. Children with learning and language problems often have significant difficulty understanding and following instructions due to their processing, sequencing, and memory deficits. Because they fail to comprehend part or all of the instruction, they become frustrated, anxious, or noncompliant.

Teachers and parents must see to it that children are able to understand and remember the directions that they are given in academic, social, and recreational situations.

Below are some suggestions designed to help adults give realistic and effective instructions that will enhance the child's comprehension and, ultimately, her motivation.

GIVING EFFECTIVE INSTRUCTIONS

- Provide individual cues (e.g., a wink) or group cues (e.g., flashing lights or pointing to the blackboard) to the students prior to giving an important instruction. This signal tells the children that they need to attend closely. Also use key phrases to let the students know that they should be focusing their attention on the upcoming instruction. ("It's important that you follow these directions exactly or the experiment won't work. Ready?")
- Ask the child to repeat or paraphrase the instruction before he carries out the activity. A child with language problems often becomes quite adept at feigning comprehension and sending body language signals (e.g., nodding) that imply that he understands the instruction although he actually does not, so supportively require him to repeat the instruction. ("Rachel, please go ask Grandma if she has seen the watering can. Now, what are you going to ask her?")

- For multistep processes (cleaning the bedroom, getting ready for bed) you will want to post a checklist of the various steps that the child can refer to when completing the task.
- Encourage the child to ask for clarification if she does not understand an instruction. She should be specific and mannerly when requesting clarification. ("Mrs. McNamara, I didn't understand where I should write my answers on the sheet." Not, *"I don't get this."*)
- Avoid ambiguous terms when giving instructions. ("All right, settle down!" Versus "Please go to your own seats and take out your science notebooks.")
- When possible, present instructions in numbered lists. ("I want you to take three things from your backpack and put them on your desk. Your map skills book, your ruler, and a red pencil.")
- When possible, demonstrate the instruction while you are giving it. ("Now fold your paper in half the long way . . . like I am doing.")
- Activate prior knowledge when giving an instruction by referring to a previous activity. ("I want you to put the date in the upper right-hand corner, the way we did on our science quiz this morning.")
- Provide examples of the correct and incorrect action, to assist the child in comprehending the instruction. ("I want you to put these stickers on the back cover of your vocabulary notebook—not on the front as we did with your grammar notebook.")
- Stop frequently to evaluate their comprehension of the material thus far.

Another aspect of clarity involves the manner in which the students spend their time in the classroom. The teacher must have clear and definitive plans that ensure that the students are spending the maximum amount of time learning the subject material and related concepts.

COACHING

"A good coach will make his players see what they can be rather than what they are."

—ARA PARASHEGININ

Several years ago, I was consulting with the faculty and staff of a middle school in a West Coast town. The teachers were genuinely interested in improving the skills of their students, but they were having great difficulty with children with special needs.

One math teacher became the self-appointed spokesperson for the group. "They are just totally unmotivated," she began. "I've tried everything but they simply don't care. They are good kids, but they don't seem to care if they learn or not."

The physical education teacher interrupted, saying, "You know, I don't know what you guys are talking about. The kids you mentioned are great on the soccer team and in basketball. Motivated. Responsive. Hardworking. You couldn't ask for more. They're just great."

"Well." The English teacher shrugged. "That's easy to understand. They don't have to deal with language when they are on the playing field and they can run around to their hearts' content during practices. No wonder they are motivated with *you*. It's different in the classroom!"

I respectfully disagreed with the English teacher. It is not uncommon to see that children who struggle in the classroom are responsive and motivated on the playing field. But I do not think that this phenomenon is due to the reasons that the English teacher cited.

Rather, I believe that youngsters with learning problems respond more positively to *coaching* techniques than they do to *teaching* techniques. I often suggest that new teachers spend some time observing a good coach. Much can be learned about motivation. If fact, many professional and college coaches—Lou Holtz, Vince Lombardi, Red Auerbach, Tom Landry, Joe Paterno—are internationally revered for their ability to motivate their players. Obviously, coaches do something right, and teachers should try to adopt coaching strategies and techniques into their classroom instruction.

Consider for a moment the characteristics and practices of a good coach. Any and all of these traits would benefit students in a classroom as well as the players on a team.

A good coach wants all of his players to win. In order for a team to be victorious, all members of the team—offense and defense—must do well. Therefore, an effective coach is constantly encouraging and assisting *all* members of the squad. The coach cannot focus all of his attention on the members who play certain positions and allow the remaining players to cope for themselves. Recognizing that the chain is only as strong as the weakest link, the coach works with all players and wants each and every player to succeed and progress.

As a teacher, can you honestly state that there are no "forgotten" students in your class? Are there students whom you have given up on? Are there students who feel that they are not "part of the team" and, further, that you are not invested in their progress?

A good coach knows all his players. When a coach is asked about the profile and potential of his players, he is generally able to outline each player's strengths, weaknesses, personality, and potential. ("Eric has difficulty hitting curveballs from right-handed pitchers, but he has a great batting eye and knows when to back off a bad pitch. He had some elbow problems last year so I moved him from shortstop to second base so he has fewer cross-field throws. He moves well to his left, but often crosses his feet when moving to his right. We'll work on that. He is pretty active in practice and works hard . . . except on Wednesdays. His dad owns a clothing store and Eric works there on Tuesday evenings stocking the shelves and racks. He's usually pretty tired on Wednesdays, so I try to give him a bit of a break on those days.")

If I were to select a child at random from your class, could you provide me with detailed information on his learning style, academic needs, and factors that might impact on his progress and performance? Do you closely observe your students to gain diagnostic insights into their skills? Have you reviewed each child's file? Do you confer with your students regularly to gather this information?

A good coach designs individual goals and group goals. At any point in the season, an effective coach can give you his considered and informed opinion related to the outcome of the team's placement by the end of the season. ("Our goal is to make it to the play-offs and to the third tier once the play-offs begin. Based on the talent of my players and the strengths of the opposing teams, I feel that these are realistic goals.") He also has individual goals for each member of his team. ("Right now I have Aaron playing defensive end, but he has great speed and is a good blocker so I am grooming him to play in the backfield. By his junior year, I think he will be my starting halfback.")

As a teacher, do you have long-term goals for your class? Do you try to make projections or predictions related to the yearly progress of your class, or do you simply work day to day? Do you have goals and objectives for each child? Are goals an integral part of your daily instruction?

A good coach uses the players' strengths. After evaluating and assessing each player's strengths and affinities, the coach puts the players in positions that maximize their individual skill sets. The dependable, consistent hitter with minimal power will be assigned to the beginning of the batting order; the long ball hitter will bat in the cleanup position; the second baseman who sparkles on defense, but does not hit well, will be placed near the bottom of the batting order. In this way, all of the players' strengths are effectively used.

> *Do you identify each student's strengths? Do you use those strengths consistently in order to develop these skills further and boost the child's self-esteem? Is each child in your class an "expert" or "specialist" in some area and recognized as such by you and her classmates?*

A good coach consistently works on each player's weaknesses. Just as a coach recognizes each player's strengths and positions the players in a manner that maximizes these skills, she also identifies areas of weakness and designs a program to assist the player in improving her skills in this area. The coach does not simply ignore the area of deficiency. ("Jessica is an excellent rebounder because of her strength and her jumping ability. Because she is so aggressive, she is often fouled. Unfortunately, she has difficulty making foul shots and we have lost a few games by a point or two. I work with her daily after practice to improve her foul shooting. I also encourage her to do daily wind sprints because her speed and endurance are inconsistent.")

> *As a teacher, do you work directly and intensely on the student's weaknesses? Is remediation a key ingredient in your instruction? If a child struggles with reading, do you try to remediate his reading skills or do you ignore his weaknesses by simply putting the reading material on tape? Do you convene special needs groupings in your class, where you work intensely with small groups of students who are having difficulty with a specific skill?*

A good coach knows the opponent. Coaches regularly send members of their staff to "scout" an opposing team before a big game. The scout carefully observes and records the strengths and weaknesses of the opposition, the plays that they consistently use, and the strategies they apply on offense and defense. These data are then used by the coach to devise a game plan.

Do you know the "opponents" that your students struggle with daily? Those opponents may be ADD, distractibility, disinhibition, sequencing deficits, and so on. The effective teacher gathers current information about these disorders so that she can assist the students. She also takes these disorders into consideration when planning and implementing lessons.

A good coach considers the existing conditions. The effective coach always views his practices and games in a wider context by considering any and all conditions that may impact upon the team's success. On a rainy day, the football coach is going to use fewer pass plays and emphasize his ground game. When the temperature reaches 90 degrees, the wise coach will postpone the wind sprints that he planned for that day's practice. The track coach will doubtless move his scheduled nine A.M. practice to eleven A.M. on the morning after the senior prom.

As a teacher, do you view your instruction in a wider context? Do you modify your lesson plans based on the current dynamics in your classroom and within the school? Are you sensitive to the various social, emotional, and physical "conditions" that your students bring to the classroom each day? Would your students describe you as "flexible," "responsive," and "understanding"?

A good coach applies and practices new skills. Coaches present and practice new skills in a very deliberate and purposeful way. These skills are taught slowly and this instruction follows a specific, detailed sequence. The skill is rehearsed and practiced until it is mastered, and the players do not move on to the next skill until the current skill has been ingrained. Then the skills are continually drilled and reviewed to ensure that mastery is permanent.

As a teacher, do you provide sufficient drill and practice to ensure that mastery is accomplished? Many teachers feel constant pressure to "move along" in the curriculum and will begin instruction in a new skill even though some students have not yet mastered the previous skill. This common but flawed practice ignores the fact that most curricula are sequential and that success in higher-level skills is largely dependent upon the child's ability to master the lower-level skills.

A good coach constantly evaluates and assesses. Coaches are extraordinary observers and they use the daily, ongoing observations of their players to assess performance and progress. These assessments are conducted in a nonthreatening way. In fact, the player may not even be aware that she is being evaluated. The coach uses this diagnostic information to make informed decisions.

Are you a keen observer of your students? Daily "snapshots" of a student's performance can add significant and meaningful data to your knowledge about a youngster. The wise teacher looks for patterns of behavior and uses her observations diagnostically and prescriptively.

In an insightful essay in *Educational Leadership*, Richard Sagor examined the skateboarders who inhabit every community in America. These boys, often described by teachers as unmotivated and lazy students in the classroom, will go to their local skateboard track and practice their moves and tricks for endless hours. They experience a failure-to-success ratio of 100 to 1 as they attempt to learn the latest maneuver, and yet they persevere, hour after hour, day after day, tumble after tumble. They constantly attempt to master ever more difficult routines. All of this occurs despite the fact that they have no expectation of an extrinsic reward—no grades, no pay, no awards.

Dr. Sagor interviewed dozens of these young men to determine why they are able to maintain such extraordinary perseverance and commitment on the skateboard track and yet are unable to bring this motivation to the classroom. The boys' responses were insightful and highlighted the disparate "cultures" that they found on the track and in the classroom. On the track, they were evaluated solely upon their own performance, and their progress was measured only in comparison to their accomplishments on the previous day. Every skateboarder was aware of the "levels" of his compatriots, and rather than competing, they taught their colleagues, supported their efforts, and learned from one another. Compare this culture to the environment that these boys confront in the classroom, where punishment, testing, and competition are used in order to "motivate" them. Basically, on the track they are compared to themselves; in the classroom their progress and performance is compared to others or to an arbitrary expectation level.

There are several other reasons why children who are unmotivated and uninspired in the classroom persevere mightily on the playing field.

One element that differentiates the classroom from the playing field is that, quite simply, sports are fun! They can be exciting and stirring and meet the child's natural need for thrill. Unfortunately, many teachers feel that "learning" and "fun" are mutually exclusive. However, this is not the case. Although teachers should not endeavor to constantly entertain their students, a little creativity can serve to make drills, memorization tasks, and other classroom activities less tedious and more enjoyable. Fun works.

Sports also feature a constant flow of successes. Even if Melissa's team loses the game, she should be comforted by her stellar catch in the third inning and her double to left in the fifth. Teachers can structure their instruction in such a way that every child has some small victories to reflect upon at the end of the day.

Recreational activities and sports also feature activity and movement. Children are expected to use their minds and their bodies simultaneously. Classroom activities that require and emphasize this mind-body connection will be highly motivating for children, particularly those with attentional difficulties. Ironically, this high degree of activity actually enhances the child's ability to focus.

Sports require a significant amount of flexibility, creativity, and decision making. I recall watching a student of mine, Kyle, as he played pool with a group of friends. Mindful of his impulsivity and hyperactivity in the classroom, I was intrigued to see his patience and perseverance while he lined up his pool shots. He greatly enjoyed considering his options, weighing his choices, and developing a strategy. He was able to generate many possibilities and variables as he examined his next stroke. He relished the fact that there was more than one possible strategy that he could use. After I observed him in this setting, I began restructuring his classroom instruction so that he could generate options. ("Kyle, I want you to find out the capital of Kentucky. You can get the information any way you wish—ask someone, encyclopedia, Internet . . . your decision.") And I avoided fostering the tyranny of the right and only answer. (Instead of "Why was JFK a great president?" I would ask "Do you think that JFK was a great president? Defend your answer.") I was wonderfully impressed with his positive reaction to these strategies.

Another advantage that sports have over the traditional classroom is that an athletic situation provides the child with a truly multisensory experience. During a ball game, he is receiving, giving, and responding to auditory, visual, tactile, and kinesthetic input. This multisensory approach is stimulating for him and enables him to maintain his focus, attention, and motivation.

The final and perhaps greatest advantage that a sports setting has over the classroom is the emphasis on teamwork and camaraderie. Although the athletic contest is competitive by nature, the sports activities also feature teamwork, mutual support, peer encouragement, empathy, and cooperation. These five characteristics would contribute greatly to the successful functioning of any classroom as well.

In summary, it should come as no surprise that many children who appear unmotivated in a classroom setting are active and enthusiastic participants in athletic/coaching situations. Teachers can greatly enhance the motivation of their students by using some of the strategies regularly used by coaches. Leave your classroom at the end of a day and go to the gym to observe your school's coaching staff at work. It will be time well spent.

CONFERENCING

"Pupils are more willing to attend to one who gives directions than to one who finds fault."

—QUINTILIAN

The fifth C in a well-motivated classroom is for "conferencing." Many teachers fail to see the tremendous value and effectiveness in one-to-one student/teacher conferences, and they reserve these sessions for crises or emergency situations. In reality, these conferences can be used to prevent problems from occurring by enabling the child and the teacher to gain a deeper understanding of each other's viewpoints, needs, and opinions. These conversations can also be a valuable motivational tool by providing the child with ongoing and meaningful positive reinforcement. Do not reserve conferences for scolding and reprimands. Rather, use them as opportunities to support, praise, reinforce, and motivate.

By making conferencing an integral ingredient in your teaching style, you are able to develop more meaningful and effective relationships with students. These sessions present you in a more personal and approachable manner, and they allow students to ask questions or seek clarifications that they cannot (or will not) present in a more public setting. Initially, students may be reluctant to participate in these conferences because they have come to associate one-to-one discussions with scoldings or reprimands. This reluctance can be greatly reduced if the teacher handles the conference in an upbeat and supportive manner. Always treat the child—and his problems—with respect. Use these conclaves to initiate, strengthen, or maintain your relationship with students.

Teachers will often say, "I don't have time to conference one-on-one with my students. I am too busy dealing with behavior and disruptions." This is akin to the harried farmer who says, "I haven't got time to build a fence. I am too busy chasing these cows all over the fields." If the teacher (or the farmer) were to take some *preventive* steps (e.g., conferencing with students occasionally or constructing a fence), she would be less likely to be faced with continual crises (disruptive students and wandering cows). An effective teacher, coach, or parent uses conferencing as a *pro*active measure not as a *re*action to a child's behavior or performance.

In the movie *Footloose,* the minister's wife says to her charismatic husband, "There is nobody I know who can control, inspire, and entrance a large audience better than you. It's your one-to-one relationships that could use some work." So it is with many teachers. They have superior planning and management skills and can enthrall an entire class with their knowledge and their delivery. However, they feel uncomfortable and stilted when dealing with individual students in a one-to-one setting.

This may be because teachers are unfamiliar with the concept of active listening. Communication is a two-part process that consists of speaking and listening. Unless both sides of the equation are present, the communication is ineffective. Many of us who work at the front of the classroom are effective speakers, but inexperienced and inept listeners. Teachers are well advised to make a concerted effort to improve and enhance their ability to listen in order to add effective conferencing to their repertoire of teaching skills. Active listening reflects the adult's empathy, sympathy, and compassion for the student. It also communicates that the youngster is worthy of the adult's time and attention. This is a significant and very meaningful message for the child who struggles daily in school. Active listening is not a technique or a strategy. Rather, it is an attitude.

There are several variations on the active listening strategy, but these sessions generally begin with the adult asking a nonjudgmental question in order to elicit an initial response from the child. The question may be as simple as a query about the previous night's thunderstorm or the student's involvement on the soccer team. The session should have a positive or neutral beginning. Do not initiate the conference by focusing directly upon the issue at hand.

In an active listening session, the teacher plays an involved, but not overpowering, role in the conversation. Allow the child to express her feelings and opinions freely. The teacher may want to respond to the child with reflective, contemplative comments ("It sounds like you are very upset with Jeremy"), but resist imposing your thoughts, feelings, or opinions on the child. Your demeanor should reflect your desire to *understand* what the child is thinking, saying, and feeling.

Carefully monitor and control your body language during these discussions. Make and maintain eye contact with the student and sit close enough to her to ensure that she knows you are interested in her and her conversation. Avoid sitting or standing overly close to the youngster, as this can be intimidating.

During the conference, avoid assigning motives to the child or her behavior. ("You must dislike Kimmy if you were so mean to her.") Allow her to offer motives herself. Focus your comments on the child's *behavior,* not on the child herself. ("Spreading that rumor about Kaylee must have hurt her very much." Versus "*You hurt Kaylee very much* by circulating that rumor about her.")

When conferencing with a child who has special needs, the teacher must abandon some of the assumptions that she might hold if she were having a conference with an adult or a typical student. These children face the daily challenges that *all* youngsters face, but they confront these pitfalls with atypical memory, organization, language, and impulse control. As a result, the act of listening to another's comments becomes a challenge for special needs children. Their inability to follow and participate in the discussion should not be viewed as a lack of respect or concern.

Teacher-student conferences may also be negatively impacted by the inherent inconsistency that characterizes the progress and performance of these children. This inconsistency is a significant aspect of the profile of children with special needs, but may be misinterpreted as purposeful and viewed as manipulation, laziness, resistance, or lack of motivation.

Children with special needs often have difficulty understanding and responding to the reality of others. They are unable to walk in another's shoes or view a situation or event from another person's viewpoint. Of course, the ability to relate to and understand others is a fundamental ingredient in any meaningful conference or conversation. Again, the child's inability to do this is often misinterpreted as selfishness or insensitivity. Actually, it is neither.

When conferencing with a child, it is important to remember that feelings and emotions are more powerful than facts or reason. If the child is in a very emotional state, he is unlikely to be swayed by your reasoned, considered approach to the problem. Remember that your emotional state during an adult-child conference should have an inverse relationship to the emotions of the child. That is, if the child is withdrawn and reticent, the adult should be enthusiastic and animated. Conversely, if the child is angry and indignant, the adult should be calm and controlled.

When having a conference with a youngster, remember the following:

EFFECTIVE TEACHER/STUDENT CONFERENCES

- Allow and encourage the child to ask questions at any time during the conference. Conclude the session by asking if the child has any questions or concerns.
- Set an agenda for the meeting and, if the conference begins to introduce unrelated issues, remind the child of the purpose or topic of the conference and get the discussion back on track.
- Don't hesitate to be redundant. Repeat or rephrase the main points and issues of the conference. Summarize the conference at the conclusion of the meeting and ask if *your* understanding of the conference in the same as the child's.
- If the conference is in response to a child's misbehavior, describe the child's behavior in specific, nonjudgmental terms. ("You ran into Michael when you entered the classroom." Versus "You came barreling down the hallway and purposely knocked Michael down because he was in your way.")
- Many effective one-on-one conferences occur spontaneously. However, you should plan and initiate a conference if a serious problem exists or if you have observed a sudden, inexplicable change in a youngster's behavior or schoolwork.

- Charles Appelstein, Massachusetts social worker and author of *No Such Thing As a Bad Kid,* recommends the use of understandable metaphors to assist children in visualizing and understanding their behavior. ("Your disappointment and sadness about losing your bike is like a big snowball. Over the next few days, it will melt and melt until the sadness is gone." Or "You have a decision to make here, Colin. It's as if you were at a fork in the road and you had to take a right or a left.") This strategy is particularly effective for children with learning or language problems.
- If the conference is in response to a crisis or a specific incident, calmly secure the four *W*'s of the incident: Who? What? Where? When?
- Don't use questions to intimidate the child. ("I want an answer *right now!*") Give him ample time to process the question and formulate a response.
- Conferences need not be formal, contrived events. You can have an effective and meaningful conference with a child over lunch, on the playground, or walking with her down the hallway.
- The most effective one-on-one conferences conclude with decisions that feature shared responsibility. ("Okay, Trevor, it's agreed I will let you sit next to Hector at assemblies if you promise not to talk when someone is performing onstage.")
- Conferences are more effective if the adult has an identifiable goal and purpose for the discussion. The goal may be global ("to enhance my relationship with Mary Jane") or specific ("to discuss Terry's ongoing difficulties in Mrs. Duncan's art class").
- Use reflective language during a conference by merely repeating or rephrasing what the child has said. In this way, he knows that you are listening to him and that you understand his viewpoint. ("It sounds like you are pretty angry at Joe and Franklin and you feel that they treated you unfairly.") Reflective language does not necessarily indicate that you *agree* with the youngster's input, only that you have heard his concerns. By listening to a child, you can often defuse his feelings of anger and rejection.
- Active listening not only can defuse the child's anger, it also may

enable him to create solutions. By "talking the problem out," he may arrive independently at a solution. Also, if you listen politely and reflectively to a child, he is more likely to be willing to listen to your input and opinions.

- Reflective listening and responding may also help the child to identify his feelings. Children who are upset often misidentify their emotions. A calm, dispassionate adult can assist the child in recognizing his true feelings. ("You know, Aaron, I don't know if you are really *angry* at Ben. It sounds to me that you are *jealous* of the time that he is spending with Alexander. Anger and jealousy are different from each other.")
- Always begin and conclude the conference in a positive and supportive manner. Even if the session did not go particularly well, make an effort to end the session on an upbeat note.
- The location of an adult-child conference may be as significant as the content. If you want to take an authoritarian stance regarding a child's behavior, meet him in your office or your classroom. If you wish to have a more open-ended conversation, meet him on "neutral turf" (e.g., cafeteria, gym, hallway).
- Never deny a child's feelings or attempt to tell him how he feels.

CONTROL

> "The beauty of empowering others is that your own power is not diminished."
>
> —BARBARA COLOROSO

The final *C* in the six *C*'s of a motivating classroom is for "control." As will be discussed throughout this book, children have minimal control in or over their lives. They are allowed to make few significant major decisions and are given few meaningful choices at school or at home.

Because the child has a natural human need to exert some degree of control over his environment, he begins to resist the constraints placed on him by adults. This ongoing battle for control is first evidenced when the word "no" enters the child's vocabulary at two years of age, and the battle continues through adolescence. As we will discuss extensively in chapter 5, this natural manifestation of the child's need for control often meets with significant resistance from the adults in the child's life. We often fail to recognize that the child does not wish to snatch any of *our* power; rather, he just wants a bit of *his own* power. Our failure to recognize his need for control—and his subsequent failure to understand our desire to keep him safe—results in ongoing conflict and power struggles.

Adults must gain a better understanding of a child's control issues if they are to motivate the youngster to reach his fullest potential. Children, naturally, wish to do things that they enjoy and things that they do well. Further, they wish to avoid doing that which holds no interest for them or activities that they do poorly. This reflects the child's understandable need to avoid failure, anxiety, humiliation, and embarrassment.

Therefore, the child is more likely to be motivated in an environment in which he is occasionally allowed to make choices and decisions. When children are given options or choices in situations where such choices are appropriate, they are more likely to be responsive and cooperative than in situations where the adult must be the sole decision maker. Of course, these choices must be offered in consideration of the child's health and safety.

Because children have a natural need for control, they will continuously test the limits that adults have established. They will often use a testing behavior while they simultaneously watch the adult in order to gauge the degree to which the adult disapproves. They walk a tightrope between their need for autonomy and their desire for adult approval and acceptance.

Teachers would do well to create a learning environment that provides the child with as much control and power as is appropriate. These options should reflect the disparate skills, affinities, and interests that can be found in any classroom. Allow each student to enjoy success, realize progress, and be recognized and celebrated for his strengths and interests. In such an environment, the child's natural control needs are met and he does not find it necessary to embroil himself in power struggles in order to satisfy his need for independency and autonomy.

Adults must understand the fundamental difference between being *in control* and being *controlling.* We must also be aware of our own control needs and how those needs may impact our ability to deal with children. When a person feels that he has minimal control, he will ineffectively attempt to exert even greater control over others. This strategy is doomed to failure.

I recall watching a confrontation between an adolescent boy and an inexperienced teacher. The incident began innocently enough. The teacher saw the child leaving the classroom carrying a resource book that was supposed to remain in the classroom so all the students could use it. The teacher told the boy that the rules forbade him to take the book home. The boy explained that he needed the book in order to complete a homework assignment. The conversation escalated as the two presented and defended their sides of the argument. A power struggle ensued, with the boy insisting that the teacher was being unfair and the teacher demanding that the youth "put the book on the table and leave the room."

Finally, the boy slammed the book on the table and stormed from the room. The teacher angrily came out from behind his desk and followed the boy down the hallway, insisting that the student return to the classroom and "pick the book up and place it gently on the table ten times." The boy reluctantly returned to the classroom, but did not serve his "penance" to the teacher's satisfaction, and another power struggle ensued. Eventually, administrative crisis intervention was needed.

That young teacher would have been well advised to evaluate *his own* power needs. When the boy left the room, he did so after complying with the teacher's wishes and demands. He put the book on the table and left the room. The escalation that occurred after that was clearly caused *by the teacher.* The adult had won. There was no need to humiliate and degrade the child any further. While I agree that the boy's slamming of the book was disrespectful, it was not deserving of the teacher's hostile reaction. He should have discussed the issue with the boy later in the day or before their next class together. In this case, the adult's power need trumped the power needs of the student. The adult felt that the situation escalated beyond his control so he attempted to regain control by inflicting shame, embarrassment, and punishment.

Most children will treat adults with respect, consideration, and dignity if they are treated in a like manner.

In summary, any motivating class will feature the following characteristics:

CHARACTERISTICS OF A MOTIVATING CLASS

- *Relevance*: The content of the class should be, in some way, related to the child's life and daily experiences. New information should build upon previous knowledge and there should be an observable, meaningful connection to the real world. Students need to feel that schoolwork is valuable and important.
- *Control*: Students need to feel that they have some degree of control and influence over the learning activities. Children respond well to being allowed to make decisions and choices. These activities do not require the teacher to surrender her position of authority; they merely give the students a sense of independence and autonomy.
- *Balance of support and challenge*: The effective, motivating teacher continually strives to balance support and challenge. If the teacher assigns challenging work but fails to provide the support and structure that the child requires to be successful at the task, the child will not be motivated.

  Conversely, if the educator provides tremendous support for the child but the curriculum is not sufficiently challenging, the child will not be motivated.

  This interaction between support and challenge should shade every classroom decision made by the teacher.
- *Social interaction*: As much as possible, classroom activities should feature some degree of interaction between or among students.

Learning pairs, small-group work, and interactive classroom discussions provide students with an opportunity to interact and work toward common goals. This is motivating and energizing for many students.

- *Safety and security*: Children simply cannot learn if they feel unsafe, threatened, or insecure. The classroom environment must be tolerant, accepting, welcoming, and secure. One of the primary roles of the teacher is to protect the physical and emotional well-being of the students. Motivation cannot exist in an environment where children feel or fear embarrassment, humiliation, intimidation, or isolation.

3

One Size Does Not Fit All: The Eight Forces of Motivation

"Commandment Number One of any civilized society is this: Let people be different."

—DAVID GRAYSON

THERE ARE FEW psychological theories or concepts that are as widely accepted and embraced as is the work of Abraham Maslow. His pioneering research into human motivation demonstrated that each person is motivated—to varying degrees—by a series of physiological, safety, security, and belonging needs.

Each person has a unique set of motivators that inspire and lead to action. Your pattern of motivators is different from mine; my pattern is different from my wife's; and her pattern differs from that of her sister. In fact, nearly an infinite number of combinations exist. Every child in your classroom (and your family) has a unique set of factors that motivate. You will not be able to motivate all of your students by using one solitary motivational approach.

It is important to note that motivation is one of the few psychological aspects that remain consistent throughout the life span. As an adult, you are doubtless inspired by the same motivators that inspired you as a child.

For example, I am significantly motivated by *affiliation,* the need to be identified with something larger than myself. Nearly every piece of leisure clothing that I own is emblazoned with a logo from a Boston sports team. When I was a headmaster, I purchased every school-logo ball cap, T-shirt, and jacket available in the school store. I enjoy walking through a Los Angeles airport and being instantly identified as a Bostonian. I enjoy the affiliation with an organization or entity.

Upon reflection, I realize that I was affiliation-oriented as a child as well. Logo sportswear was not readily available in the 1950s, so I would buy Red Sox or Celtics patches and have my mother sew them onto my jackets and shirts. As a high school senior, I designed a "Class of '67" T-shirt that I sold to my classmates as a fund-raiser. Affiliation was—and is—a significant motivator for me. My cherished 1972 Volkswagen Karmann Ghia is festooned with bumper stickers that publicly announce my politics, my interests, my charities, my sports teams, my favorite music, and my hometown on Cape Cod.

There are eight basic motivational forces that inspire human beings to action and sustained effort. Each of us is inspired to some degree by each of these forces. But the extent to which you are motivated by each of them creates a "motivation profile" that is unique to you.

The eight motivators are:

Gregariousness	Aggression
Autonomy	Power
Status	Recognition
Inquisitiveness	Affiliation

In the following pages, I will define each of the above terms and explain the impact of each upon motivation. In an exercise of self-disclosure, I will also analyze my personal reaction/response to each of the motivators and discuss my motivation profile. You will be given an opportunity to explore and analyze your own profile as well. It is important for teachers and parents to understand their profiles because, as you will see, your preferences may impact and interfere with your attempts to motivate children.

As you read the explanation of each motivator and my response to them, be prepared to rate yourself in relation to the motivators. A score of ten would indicate that you are significantly motivated in that particular category; a score of zero would signify that you are minimally motivated; a score of five would reflect that the category is somewhat motivating for you.

GREGARIOUSNESS: THE NEED TO BELONG

The gregarious person is never happier than when he is in a crowd. He has many, many friends and enjoys these relationships. He relishes committee work and does not enjoy independent or solitary projects. He is both a joiner and a leader and invests much effort in establishing and maintaining relationships with others. He initiates and sustains these connections judiciously. Gregariousness can manifest itself positively (popularity, friendliness) or negatively (joining gangs, challenging authority).

Lavoie Profile—3

Although I cherish the relationships that I have in my life, my needs are met quite satisfactorily by my family and a small circle of trusted friends. My wife and I have shared an office together for thirty-five years and she is my partner, mentor, and best friend. I have no significant need for or interest in supplementing that relationship with large groups of people. I do not enjoy crowded venues, and although I greatly enjoy meeting new people, I do not invest much effort in establishing ongoing connections or correspondence with folks who cross my path.

Your Profile—☐

AUTONOMY: THE NEED FOR INDEPENDENCE

The autonomous person relishes opportunities to work independently on projects. Unlike the gregarious person, he dislikes committee work and is most inspired by solitary projects where the results are totally dependent upon his performance. These people are decision makers and invest significant energy in making decisions, and then making the decisions work. Although they recognize, admire, and acknowledge the talents of others, they are at their best when they tackle a project alone and, invariably, see it through to a positive conclusion.

Lavoie Profile—10

Autonomy is one of my most significant motivators. I put great energy into projects and have a history of approaching and completing these projects successfully. When I require assistance, guidance, or advice related to a project, I consult the aforementioned small but talented group of folks that make up my support system. You would greatly decrease my effectiveness by placing me on a committee.

When I left my eleven-year position as a school head, I sent an e-mail to the trustees thanking them for "*letting* me run this school." I always appreciated their willingness to allow me the autonomy that I required in order to do my job.

Your Profile— ☐

STATUS: THE NEED TO BE IMPORTANT

Many children and adults are motivated by status. For these people, their self-esteem is intricately tied to the opinions of others. The status person is greatly concerned with the viewpoints that other people hold regarding the person's performance and progress. The status person is eager to please others and can be extremely sensitive to criticism. He is greatly concerned about disappointing or upsetting other people.

Lavoie Profile—3

Like all people, I care about the feelings, opinions, and beliefs of others. I want to please the folks with whom I come into contact. However, I am unlikely to modify my feelings or opinions based solely on the input of others. For example, suppose I finished a speaking engagement and was very pleased with the audience response and the content of the session. An audience member approaches me and tells me that he was dissatisfied with the presentation. Although I would take his input into consideration, it is unlikely that I would be overly concerned or that my initial assessment would change significantly.

Conversely, if I delivered an address and felt that it did not go well and an audience member approached me and told me that he had heard me speak numerous times and that this session was the best by far, I would be grateful for his comments, but again, it would be unlikely to change my initial evaluation of the session.

Your Profile— ☐

INQUISITIVENESS: THE NEED TO KNOW

The inquisitive person has a need to learn and know. She is extremely curious and hungry for new information. This inquisitiveness is not limited to her areas of expertise or interest; she enjoys learning about nearly any topic.

The inquisitive person wants and values information. She feels uncomfortable if she believes that information is being kept from her, and she is interested in gaining social, personal, and professional information about others in her environment. She continually asks questions and enjoys informally researching topics that are of interest to her.

Children and adults who are inquisitive are able and eager to relate new experiences and information to their body of knowledge. They are interested in the *how* and *why* of rules, procedures, and lessons.

Lavoie Profile—7

I tend to be very inquisitive, particularly about topics that are of great interest or usefulness to me. I devour education journals and am eager to learn more about my chosen field. I am also interested in enhancing my cultural literacy and will be found watching a documentary on the Galápagos turtles that I may have stumbled upon while using the television's remote control. I love trivia and religiously watch *Jeopardy!* and other quiz shows.

However, I gave myself a seven because there are massive areas of study about which I know nothing (medicine, law, technology, economics) and I have little or no desire to enhance my knowledge in these areas. In order to score a ten in this category I would need to be a bit more of a Renaissance man, with an insatiable curiosity in *all* areas.

Your Profile— ☐

AGGRESSION: THE NEED TO ASSERT

A person's need for aggression is not necessarily negative or disruptive. Aggression can be channeled into positive activities (leadership, assertive personality) or negative actions (bullying, intimidating).

Aggressive people are willing (and even eager) to confront perceived injustice or unfairness. These confrontations may be socially appropriate (debate, standing up for rights, political activism) or inappropriate (disruption, challenging, contentions). Aggressive people are interested in expanding their sphere of influence and want their feelings and opinions to be recognized and responded to.

Lavoie Profile—2

I am very nonaggressive in most settings and situations. I was raised in a household that included a significant amount of tension and friction, and as a result, I prefer to avoid conflict whenever and wherever possible. For the past thirty years, I have traveled extensively, staying at countless hotels and eating in hundreds of restaurants. Throughout these three decades, I have never rejected a meal or glass of wine because it was unsatisfactory. Again, I would prefer to avoid confrontation or conflict whenever possible.

Of course, there are times when a person *should* be willing and able to stand up and defend himself. When I reflect on my life, I recognize that several of the most significant mistakes that I have made in my life were rooted in my lack of aggressiveness. A lack of aggressiveness and contentiousness is admirable to a degree, but it is important to be assertive when the situation warrants it.

Your Profile— ☐

POWER: THE NEED FOR CONTROL

The person who has strong power needs is greatly concerned with control and influence. This should not be viewed as a negative trait, but merely as a certain type of worldview. Interestingly, people who strive for power may have very strong—or very weak—self-esteem. Their need for power may have its origin in feelings of confidence and superiority, or it may be rooted in a feeling of helplessness and inferiority. Power-driven people relish responsibility and authority.

Lavoie Profile—3

I view power as a means to an end, not an end in itself. Power enables one to have significant influence in an organization and enhances one's ability to make meaningful impact and change. However, I have held positions of significant power and I never found this authority to be fulfilling or motivating in and of itself. In fact, as a longtime school headmaster, I found that unfettered power was a great and troublesome burden. I had the power to hire, fire, promote, and demote staff members. I could accept or reject student applications at my will. I did not enjoy having such significant power and influence over the lives of others.

My need for autonomy reflects the fact that I do not like it when others have limitless power over me; therefore, I do not enjoy having great control over others.

Your Profile—☐

RECOGNITION: THE NEED FOR ACKNOWLEDGMENT

Although teachers often attempt to motivate students by giving them—or threatening them with—a failing grade, very few people are motivated or inspired by failure. Most people are driven by a need to be recognized and acknowledged for their accomplishments and efforts.

On every Academy Awards evening, past Oscar recipients are invariably asked where they keep their coveted statuettes. Often, the actors will say that they built a separate wing in their home, where the award is displayed with reverence and solemnity. Still others will say that it is used as a doorstop in their child's bedroom. Actors in the first category are recognition-driven; actors in the second category are not. It is important to understand that recognition-driven people are not necessarily braggarts who are constantly preening and need attention. Some people simply have a greater need for recognition than others.

Lavoie Profile—7

There are areas of my life in which I enjoy recognition. During my speaking career, I would often receive awards, certificates, or plaques from the sponsoring organizations. I displayed them in my office and took pride in the accomplishments and affection that they reflected.

However, my recognition score is moderated by the fact that I do not seek or strive for recognition. I am not competitive and would never engage in an activity for the sole purpose of receiving recognition.

Your Profile— ☐

AFFILIATION: THE NEED TO ASSOCIATE AND BELONG

The affiliation person has a strong need to be connected with others and with organizations, movements, and institutions. These people gather great strength from the affiliations and they garner a great sense of belonging and identity from these relationships.

Children who are driven by affiliation often seek the approval of and association with teachers.

Lavoie Profile—10

As stated earlier in this chapter, I have significant affiliation needs.

Your Profile— ☐

Now review your scores and compare them to my ratings. Are our scores identical? The chances are that they are not. I have conducted this exercise with audiences of eight hundred people, and no participant has ever had a profile that matched mine exactly. Neither did their profiles match perfectly with anyone else in the audience. As I stated earlier, there is a nearly infinite number of variables between and among the eight motivational forces of gregariousness, affiliation, inquisitiveness, power, achievement, aggression, status, and autonomy.

This concept has significant ramifications for teachers and parents, and a failure to understand and embrace this concept leads directly to the most common mistake that adults make as they attempt to motivate children: *As adults, we attempt to motivate children by applying the forces that motivate us.*

There is no reason to believe that the students in your classroom or the children in your family will be motivated by the same forces that you find inspiring or energizing. In fact, the chance that *any* child in your class will have the same motivational profile that you have is minimal.

Suppose, for example, that you are a teacher with a strong need for autonomy. A student, Luke, has been extraordinarily well behaved and cooperative in recent weeks and you wish to reward and reinforce his efforts. You decide to allow him to go to the media center and do an independent research project. After all, *you* would relish such an assignment and would greatly appreciate the opportunity to work alone on a well-defined project.

But Luke is motivated by gregariousness and would find a solitary project tedious and not enjoyable. If he were allowed to work with a group of classmates, he would be extraordinarily inspired and motivated. Instead, you attempted to motivate Luke by imposing your motivational profile on *him*.

As I stated in my profile, I am driven by affiliation. As a young teacher, I would surprise my students each September by distributing T-shirts emblazoned with our class logo to each of them. I generally ordered five shirts for my personal use. This "motivational" activity seldom produced the desired results. Some students wore the shirts until the garment nearly dissolved off their bodies. Others never wore them again. The first group consisted of kids who were driven by affiliation. The second group was motivated by power, inquisitiveness, or autonomy. They had no desire to wear the shirt. I assumed, wrongly, that my students would be inspired by a force and activity that motivated *me*.

Now that I understand motivational forces, I realize that I could have greatly enhanced the effectiveness of my T-shirt venture had I modified it to meet the disparate motivational needs of my student. I could have:

- Allowed the *students* to select the colors and logo (Power, Status)
- Given extra T-shirts as a reward for progress (Recognition)
- Designated each Monday as T-shirt day, when all students should wear their T-shirts to school (Affiliation, Gregariousness)
- Asked colleagues to comment favorably to my students about the T-shirts (Status)
- Taken and displayed a photograph of the students wearing their T-shirts (Affiliation, Status)

In order to motivate *all* the students in her class, a teacher must utilize a wide variety of approaches, strategies, and techniques. The standard "star chart" or point system simply will not be effective for the majority of students.

DETERMINING A CHILD'S MOTIVATIONAL TYPE

Determining the motivational style of a child is not an exact science. It is neither possible nor advisable to slot children into "motivational categories," so that you can identify Juan as a "power kid" and Rachel as an "inquisitive kid." Student motivation is simply too complex. Each child will possess traits that are reflective of the various categories. However, when you carefully and thoroughly analyze the behaviors, traits, and temperament of a child, a pattern of preferences will begin to emerge and you will be able to use classroom activities that complement the child's motivational style. The informal assessment survey below may help.

In the left-hand column is a list of teacher comments that might be made on a report card. Using an informal scale of one to ten, score each comment for your child. If the comment describes the child very accurately, score that item a ten; if the comment does not describe the child at all, score that item a one; if the comment is somewhat descriptive, score the item four, five, or six. Once all the comments are rated in a specific category, add up the scores. When all categories are completed, compare the scores to determine which motivational drives are more significant for the child.

As you complete the survey, remember that every trait has a positive and negative side. Is the child bossy . . . or a natural leader? Is she nosy . . . or curious? Sullen . . . or reflective? Hyper or enthusiastic? Noncompliant or creative? Always try to view the traits as positive and use that strength to enhance learning and motivation.

Gregariousness

- Highly verbal
- Good sense of humor
- Self-confident
- Popular
- Dislikes being alone
- Enjoys group work, teams, committees
- Peer-oriented
- Generally positive attitude
- Outgoing; friendly
- Stylish

Autonomy

- Masters new material rapidly
- Very productive
- Good memory
- Highly verbal
- Very curious
- Enjoys independent work
- Extensive vocabulary

- Large fund of background information
- Self-motivated
- Decisive

Status

- Fears imperfection, failure
- Highly sensitive to criticism, reprimands
- Often requests confirmation, reassurance
- Peer-oriented
- Judgmental
- Fashionable
- Needs praise
- Self-critical
- Generally compliant
- Enjoys the spotlight

Inquisitiveness

- Has passionate interests
- Avid, independent reader
- Large fund of background information
- Strong memory
- Enjoys experiments
- Asks questions
- Gives unique, creative responses
- Enjoys problem solving
- Gossips
- Volunteers

Aggression

- Has strong opinions
- Wants/likes responsibility
- Argumentative
- Questions authority
- Complains
- Very persuasive

- Quick temper
- Unique sense of style
- Outspoken
- Vindictive

Power

- Enjoys being in charge
- Often involved in power struggles, debate
- Has leadership qualities
- Self-confident
- Courageous
- Decisive
- Straightforward
- Independent
- Bears grudges
- Competitive
- Persistent
- Tenacious

Recognition

- Optimistic
- Self-assured
- Industrious
- Goal-driven
- Efficient
- Highly competitive
- Vain, self-promoting
- Enjoys spotlight
- Sensitive, easily disappointed
- Enjoys performing

Affiliation

- Seeks and displays group identity
- Sensitive to the needs of others

- Skilled motivator
- Fears rejection
- Seeks adult attention
- Admires role models
- Helpful
- Cooperative
- Sensitive to disapproval
- Conformist
- Volunteers often

MOTIVATING DIFFERENT TYPES OF CHILDREN

There are some general guidelines that should be adhered to when attempting to motivate children from the eight categories. The *gregarious* child should be allowed and encouraged to interact with others. She benefits greatly from a sense of belonging and can contribute significantly to class morale and school spirit. She also enjoys cooperative learning activities and works well on committees or academic teams. Continually reinforce the idea that she is an important and valued member of the class.

The *autonomous* child relishes independence and enjoys responsibility. He enjoys working on projects and doing research. He does not depend heavily upon teacher reinforcement but greatly enjoys self-correcting activities.

The *status*-driven child is very aware of the feelings and attitudes of others and is easily embarrassed. His self-esteem is largely dependent upon the responses that he receives from significant others in his life, and he has difficulty evaluating his own performance or strengths. He needs a teacher who is enthusiastic and who celebrates children's unique strengths and affinities.

The *inquisitive* child is curious and enjoys problem solving and research. She needs to be shown that learning is an ongoing process and that most "new" information is related in some way to previously learned material. She also benefits from a curriculum that is relevant to her daily life. Help this child to establish personal goals, and then continually *reestablish* these goals as she makes progress.

The *aggressive* child wants to have her opinions and feelings heard. Give her an opportunity to express her opinions, and solicit her ideas on occasion. Use her suggestions and commend her for her contributions. She enjoys problem solving and is often quite adept at analyzing and resolving issues and situations. Remain mindful that her need for power and control is a very real need. Avoid power struggles and allow her to make choices and decisions whenever possible. The adult should assist the child in converting her aggressiveness into assertiveness that is more socially appropriate and acceptable.

The *power*-driven child needs control and influence over the activities and goals of the class. If he is deprived of power, he will seek less appropriate venues to gain control (disruption, challenging authority). He will be very responsive to responsibility. Foster his leadership skills and ask him for input about the class curriculum.

The *recognition*-driven child has a strong need to be recognized for her strengths and abilities. She benefits from receiving immediate feedback and is very sensitive to criticism, reprimands, and nagging. She often is highly self-critical and can become distraught over insignificant failures or errors. She will respond well to awards, certificates, and public recognition.

The *affiliation*-driven child wants to be identified with a collective entity and will also respond well to academic teams and cooperative learning. He wants to be identified with adults and will respond very well to a teacher's self-disclosures (e.g., discussing your family during class activities). He needs to feel that you know him and enjoy his company.

THE SIX *P*'S OF MOTIVATION

Every child has a unique pattern of forces that motivate him. Quite simply, a motivational technique that inspires a child may be totally ineffective with that child's classmate. Just as we tailor instructional methods to meet the academic needs of students, we must also use a variety of motivational techniques in order to reach and teach the children in our classes.

Toward that end, I have translated the Maslow research into six sets of teaching strategies that are designed to emphasize the motivational drives for each individual child. For example, the autonomous child will respond well to projects and prestige strategies. The recognition-driven child will respond more positively to strategies involving praise and prizes.

The following motivational approaches are aligned with each of the motivational styles we outlined earlier. The styles are:

Projects—motivate the autonomous or inquisitive child
People—motivate the gregarious or affiliation-driven child
Praise—motivates the status-driven or recognition-driven or affiliation-driven child
Prizes—motivate the status-driven or recognition-driven or affiliation-driven or power-driven child
Prestige—motivates the autonomous or status-driven or aggressive or power-driven child
Power—motivates the power-driven or autonomous or aggressive child

GETTING THE CHILD'S INPUT ON HIS MOTIVATIONAL FORCES

The following informal assessment tool may be of assistance in determining the drives that motivate each child. This minisurvey could be given to all students at the beginning of the school year and could also be administered to any students who join the class during the school year. Explain to the students that the survey is designed to help you get to know them better and to assist you as you design and plan your classes. Ask that they answer the questions thoughtfully and honestly, and assure them that there are no incorrect answers.

Read these questions. Circle TWO answers for each question. Read all answers carefully and select the TWO answers that you like best.

1. *If you did really well on your science project, what would you prefer the teacher to do?*

a. Let you carry the project to the other classrooms and explain the project to the students
b. Put the project on display in the hallway
c. Give you a small prize
d. Write a note to your parents to tell them what a good job you did

2. *When you get a good grade on a paper, what do you do?*

a. Show it to your friends on the bus
b. Hang it on the refrigerator or on a bulletin board at home
c. Ask your parents for a treat as a reward for your good work
d. Call your relatives and tell them how well you did

3. *If you found a ten-dollar bill on the playground and turned it in to the school office, what would you want the principal to do?*

a. Call your parents and tell them about your honesty
b. Announce your honesty at a school assembly and give you a certificate
c. Give you a two-dollar reward
d. Bring you down to the office to congratulate you in person

4. *You are on a roller coaster, and a photographer from a local newspaper takes your picture. The photo appears on the front page the next day. What do you do?*

a. Carry the newspaper with you to show your friends and relatives
b. Frame the picture and hang it in your room
c. Hope that the photo wins a prize as "Picture of the Week"
d. Hang out by the newspapers at the local store and hope that someone recognizes you

5. *What do you like best about your birthday?*

a. Your family has a party for you, and all your relatives come
b. You are treated special that day and your mom makes your favorite meal
c. You get presents
d. Everyone tells you that you are growing up and maturing

6. *What do you wish that your teacher did more of in class?*

a. Let you work together with your friends
b. Put your papers on display
c. Had contests with prizes
d. Told you that you were doing a good job

7. *Your dad asks you to clean the yard on Saturday and you do a really good job. How would you want your dad to respond?*

a. Give you a hug and say, "Thank you"
b. Tell you that you do a better job than anyone else in the family
c. Give you two dollars
d. Make an announcement at dinner about your hard work

8. *Think about the teacher you liked the most out of all the teachers you've ever had. What did he or she do whenever you did an outstanding job on a project or assignment?*

a. Let you sit with and work with your friends
b. Gave you certificates and awards
c. Gave you a prize
d. Gave you lots of compliments

9. *Think of your favorite grandparent, aunt, or uncle. What is it that you like most about him or her?*

a. He or she is fun to be with
b. He or she is proud of you and talks about you
c. He or she gives you gifts
d. He or she is very interested in you and listens to you

10. If you were a teacher, how would you reward a student who did a great job on an assignment?

a. Have lunch with the student
b. Have a "Student of the Day" award
c. Give the student a small present
d. Give the student a note congratulating him

INSTRUCTIONS FOR ANALYZING THE ASSESSMENT

Record the number of *a, b, c,* and *d* responses, and analyze the results.

> If there are a lot of *a* responses, the child is motivated by people.
> If there are a lot of *b* responses, the child is motivated by prestige, power, and praise.
> If there are a lot of *c* responses, the child is motivated by prizes and prestige.
> If there are a lot of *d* responses, the child is motivated by people, prestige, and praise.

Human motivation is a complex concept and we are all motivated by a variety of drives and needs. One of the primary responsibilities of a teacher is to inspire students to reach their fullest potential. As we have discussed in this chapter, each student has a unique combination of drives that will move the child to apply himself fully to his academic work. It is futile to attempt to motivate a disparate group of youngsters by using a single general approach or method. *If the child cannot learn the way that we teach, we must teach the way that he learns.*

4

The Child Motivated by Praise

"Praise consists of two parts. What we say to the child and, in turn, what the child says to himself."

—HAIM GINOTT

THERE ARE a number of active and ongoing controversies in the fields of psychology and education. There is much disagreement about issues related to effective discipline, learning styles, child care practices, and motivational approaches. However, there is one issue about which one would assume there would be universal agreement—PRAISE!

Surely, everyone would agree that we should praise our children often, loudly, and consistently.

Wrong!

There is a considerable amount of controversy regarding the use, overuse, and abuse of praise as a motivational technique. Parents and educators have become increasingly aware of the importance of self-esteem in a child's development, and as a result, adults are more mindful of praising a child at home and at school, and many children receive constant and noncontingent compliments on an ongoing basis. Many child psychology experts believe that we praise children too often and that this freewheeling and excessive use of praise can actually *decrease* the intensity of a child's motivation.

However, there are many children who need praise from significant adults in their lives. Without this praise, their motivation wanes and their self-esteem deteriorates.

So how does a caring parent or teacher decide when, where, and how to distribute and express praise to children? Perhaps the answer to that question lies in an examination of the *praise vs. nonpraise* debate.

Some opponents of excessive praise feel that verbal praise often increases a child's anxiety regarding his performance. Some recent research from Columbia University seems to confirm this concern.

In the study, some students were given lavish praise after each successful response on an oral mathematics test. These students became overly concerned about the performance of the other students in comparison to their own, were less enthusiastic as the tasks became more difficult, and—when given a choice between two tasks—generally selected a task that was less challenging and one for which the child had previously been praised. They also became rather upset when they experienced failure and received no praise.

It is important to note, however, that the administrators of these quizzes were specially instructed to provide the children with praise regarding their *intelligence* ("You are a smart young man," "You are a very bright math student"). However, when the examiner consistently praised the child's *effort* ("You're really trying, aren't you?", "You're a very hard worker"), the child's response was quite different. The students began focusing more on *learning* than on arriving at the correct answer, were more resilient in the face of failure, and remained interested and motivated throughout the task. They also challenged themselves more and explored different ways to solve the assigned problems.

Another common criticism of excessive praise is that the practice is manipulative and the child becomes dependent upon praise in order to assess and evaluate his performance. Students can become addicted to praise, according to some experts. The next time you are visiting an elementary school classroom, you will see and hear children constantly "fishing" for praise. ("Is this good, Mrs. McCue?" "Do you like my drawing, Mr. Marshall?") These students seem to have lost their ability to judge their own performance and rely totally upon an adult to assess their progress and skills. This is significant because the ability to evaluate one's own work is a critical ingredient in academic success in secondary school.

Lavish, automatic, knee-jerk praise does not consider the child's motives. For example, suppose second grader Maria forgets to bring her lunch to school. At lunchtime, the teacher observes Maureen and Tina sharing their sandwiches with Maria. Tina is doing this because she likes Maria and doesn't want her to go hungry. However, Maureen is sharing in order to receive praise from the teacher, who is standing nearby. The teacher approaches the table and praises both girls equally.

As a result, Maureen's and Tina's behaviors were reinforced and will occur more often. Tina will become increasingly *generous* and Maureen will become increasingly *manipulative*.

The "too much praise" proponents also cite studies where children who were constantly praised became fearful of the adult's withholding that praise and felt rejected when praise was not received. These children seldom attempted challenging tasks for fear that they would fail and would receive no praise. They gave fewer responses in class, took fewer academic risks, and often lacked persistence on difficult tasks. They even began looking at the adult's eyes to check for approval or disapproval. Children—particularly younger children—are very eager to please adults and will repeat any behavior that is praised. If you lavishly commend David for creating "terrific trees" on his latest drawing, be assured that trees will appear in every picture he draws for weeks.

The effectiveness of praise is dependent, of course, upon the student's desire to please the teacher. As students proceed into middle and high school, they become less and less interested in making or keeping the teacher happy and may be *more* interested in impressing and influencing their peers. Therefore, lavish public praise from a high school teacher may actually squelch a student's motivation and desire to progress.

Another study published in *Psychology Today* decried the practice of overpraising by demonstrating that preschool students became less and less motivated to try difficult tasks when they were constantly praised for doing tasks that they had already mastered (tying their shoes, hanging up their coats). They seemed to find it safer to stick with tasks that would earn them automatic praise. Eventually, they even became inconsistent at the mastered tasks because the praise they received was less meaningful. This study also demonstrated that a child's response to praise might vary depending upon the child's age, gender, and socioeconomic status. Clearly, praise is not a motivator for *all* children *all* of the time.

Alfie Kohn, author and expert on education issues, has been sounding the "too much praise" alarm for years. He finds praise to be a manipulative method to coerce the child into complying with the wishes of the adult. He feels that praise is something done *to* kids rather than *with* kids, and therefore, its results are not lasting. Praise does not increase self-esteem, Kohn argues. Rather, it merely increases the child's dependence on adults and their approval. He cites research that demonstrates that children who receive constant praise are often more tentative in their responses and answer in a questioning tone of voice ("Um, Washington?"), and they quickly abandon an idea as soon as the adult disagrees with them or questions their recommendation. The children begin to view praise as a reward, and the absence of praise as a punishment or reprimand. Kohn feels that constantly saying "Good job!" can be as damaging as constantly saying "Bad job."

Kohn makes the point that rewards and punishments are very similar. Both strategies involve manipulating a child into doing something to elicit (or prevent) a response from an adult. "If you do *that,* you get *this.*"

His most controversial tenet holds that intrinsic (internal) and extrinsic (external) motivation are inversely related. That is, when a child has more of the former, he has less of the latter. If the child is inspired to learn, he needs little praise or reinforcement. Conversely, the more external rewards he receives, the less inspired and motivated he becomes. Kohn believes that children need unconditional love, support, and encouragement. They also need feedback. But he says that praise is none of these. It is extraordinarily conditional and it provides judgment, not feedback.

The Center for Nonviolent Communication takes an even more negative stand toward indiscriminate and unceasing praise. They term praise "a *violent* form of communication" because it is part of the "language of domination that passes judgment on another." They view praise as a manipulation rather than a reward.

In the face of all this antipraise evidence, why do teachers and parents continue to heap lavish, empty praise on children? This is done in the mistaken belief that praise automatically builds self-esteem. Adults would do well to remember the following profound truth: *You cannot give anyone self-esteem. You can only create an environment where it can grow.*

However, the "antipraising" findings appear to contradict one of the basic fundamental tenets of psychology: **Behavior that is reinforced is repeated.**

This tenet holds that if an adult recognizes or rewards a behavior, it increases the likelihood that the child will continue to use that behavior. If a mother praises a child for using good manners at Grandma's, he is more likely to use those manners at his next visit to his grandparents. Conversely, if a father buys his daughter a toy in response to a temper tantrum at the toy store, she is likely to have a tantrum every time they go shopping.

I would suggest that there exists a happy medium between lavish, constant, undeserved praise and the actual withholding of praise. As legendary Green Bay Packers coach Vince Lombardi wisely stated: *Practice does not make perfect; only perfect practice makes perfect.*

Perhaps the solution to the praise dilemma is in a paraphrasing of Lombardi's statement: *Praise does not make perfect; only effective praise makes perfect.*

Many children need praise in order to maintain their motivation.

But this praise must be delivered in a natural and effective way. Further, teachers and parents must consider and use some alternatives to praise, including:

Encouragement
Interest
Gratitude
Enthusiasm

USING ENCOURAGEMENT EFFECTIVELY

Most people view "praise" and "encouragement" as synonyms. Actually, the two concepts are quite different from each other, and encouragement may be more effective and more motivating than praise.

Praise is largely conditional. It is granted in response to a child's success and withheld in response to a child's failure. Encouragement, on the other hand, is a positive acknowledgment of a child's effort or progress. It is largely unconditional and it can be given to a child even when he has failed at a task. Basically, praise is a judgment; encouragement is acknowledgment. Praise is earned; encouragement is a gift.

In order to better understand this concept, compare the following "praise statements versus encouragement" statements.

Praise

You're my best student.
You are always the first one to raise your hand.
I'm so proud of your composition!
You got the highest grade in the class.

Encouragement

You are a terrific student and I enjoy working with you.
You make a real effort to participate in class.
You really seem to enjoy writing.
You must have studied very hard for that test.

Praise uses words that judge. ("You got twenty questions *right,* Taylor. That is *terrific. I am very proud.*"). Encouragement uses words that notice. ("*I see* that you are in a good mood today . . . and you've been working for thirty minutes straight.")

Praise teaches the child to please the adult. ("I am very happy with you. Your room looks great.") Encouragement teaches the child to please himself. ("Willie, I noticed how helpful you were at Grandpa's today. You should be very proud of yourself.")

Most important, *praise can be given only when the child is successful.* ("Jeff, you did great on the spelling quiz.") Encouragement can be given even when the child is experiencing failure or frustration. ("Scott, you have really been working hard on that report. Keep it up!")

Basically, praise works. But encouragement works better. Encouragement makes the child feel recognized, significant, and truly important.

Children react very differently to praise and encouragement. Praise promotes competition by comparing one child to others. It focuses on the quality of a child's *performance* and virtually ignores his efforts or motives. When a child is praised, he feels that he has been judged or evaluated based upon how he has performed in comparison to others. Praise fosters the child's dependence upon the opinions of others.

Conversely, encouragement fosters cooperation and collaboration and focuses on the child's individual effort and progress. The child feels valued rather than evaluated. Encouragement recognizes a child's individual contribution to the common good. It promotes effort and enables the child to accept setbacks, mistakes, and failures. The child becomes more independent and motivated. Encouragement underscores that learning is a process and improvement is always possible. Anyone can criticize. It takes a sensitive, compassionate, and creative person to encourage.

In his autobiography, *Cellist,* renowned cellist Gregor Piatigorsky relates his first meeting with maestro Pablo Casals. Piatigorsky was a young man who was asked to play a Beethoven sonata for Casals.

The nervous novice played the piece, making several mistakes. Casals enthusiastically praised Gregor and animatedly gave a detailed review of the sections that he most enjoyed. The young man knew that he had played poorly and was greatly disappointed at Casals's obvious insincerity.

Some years later, the two men had become colleagues and friends. One evening, Gregor related the story of their first meeting to Casals and told the maestro how disillusioned he was by Casals's lack of candor.

Casals suddenly became angry. "I praised you for the passages that you played beautifully and masterfully," he said. "Leave it to the ignorant and stupid who judge by counting on the faults."

As former speaker of the United States House of Representatives Sam Rayburn often stated, "Any jackass can kick down a barn, but it takes a carpenter to build one."

Expressing Interest

I have been blessed with some wonderful and generous mentors in my life and career, and I have learned much from their collective wisdom.

One such gentleman was Joe Williams, the board chair of the school that I directed on Cape Cod. Joe was an extraordinarily bright and gifted man, and his opinion and his counsel meant a great deal to me. He taught me much about fiscal accountability, spreadsheets, and effective record keeping. But I learned most by watching and replicating his people skills.

Whenever my assistant would call my office to tell me that Joe was on the line, I would light up. I so enjoyed our phone conversations. One day, I tried to analyze the reason that these calls were so joyful for me. After this analysis, I came to understand. Joe provided me with a lot of praise ("The board minutes were great last week, Rick") and plenty of reinforcement ("The long-range plan is coming along nicely! The section on the physical plant is so much better now that you added the blueprints"). But, perhaps most important, Joe always showed *interest* in my life. He consistently demonstrated his interest in me as a person.

Whenever Joe called me, he obviously had school business to conduct. But he began every call by inquiring about my kids, my wife, or my activities. He was interested in *me*. And I loved it.

When I recognized the power of interest, I began using the strategy to build and maintain my relationships with family members, colleagues, students' parents, and students. People love talking about themselves.

I recall running into a young teacher on our campus. I had heard that she was doing a terrific job in the classroom and was an exceptionally hard worker. We stopped to talk for a moment. Taking a page from Joe's book, I didn't praise or encourage her. Instead, I showed a genuine and sincere *interest* in her. "I saw that you've got a new car. I love the color. Do you have a minute to take me to the parking lot to look at it?"

The young teacher was delighted. The school's director had noticed her prized new car and took the time to mention it to her! That interaction was more meaningful to her than any praise or encouragement I could have given.

Teachers and parents can use interest to foster a child's motivation and build relationships. Ask a student what he did last weekend . . . and really listen to this response. Make a point to call home from the office to ask your daughter how her first soccer practice went. If a child has mentioned that he has a new puppy, occasionally ask him how his dog is doing and use the dog's name.

You may be surprised how much impact it has when an English teacher stops by basketball practice occasionally and watches his students play. This gesture demonstrates a genuine interest in the kids as people.

Expressing Gratitude

Praise can often be described as "disguised gratitude." When a dad says, "Nice job on cleaning the garage, Franklin," he is *actually* saying, "Thanks for finishing the garage. Now I will be able to play golf on Saturday."

If you are grateful for something that the child has done, tell him. ("Zak, you really helped out with the snow shoveling. We got it done in half the time and now I can make those phone calls that I need to make. I really appreciate it.")

By expressing your sincere gratitude to a child, you underscore his role in the family and his responsibility to contribute to the common good. You are showing the child how his positive behavior benefits others.

Expressing Enthusiasm

My undergraduate teaching mentor often said, "Enthusiasm is contagious, and so is the lack of it." He strongly believed that the teacher is the most important and influential person in the classroom. The teacher sets the tone and the climate. Therefore, if the teacher is enthusiastic, lively, and animated, the students are more likely to mirror this attitude. At home, the parent who takes a spirited, vigorous approach to Saturday morning chores will find that his children approach these tasks with greater enthusiasm as well.

If you reflect for a moment upon the most memorable teachers and coaches from your school career, you will doubtless find, as I did, that they were enthusiastic about their subject area, their jobs . . . and their students.

As I look back on my school years, I fondly remember:

> Miss Malahy, my English teacher who would excitedly relate the high points of the Shakespearean plays that she had attended in Boston the previous weekend. Her animated telling made us feel that we had been there with her and—surely—that she had been thinking of us as she sat in the darkened theater. "I couldn't *wait* to tell you folks about it."

> Mr. O'Rourke, a current-events teacher who would devour *Time* magazine cover to cover at his desk during study hall, reading every single section in order. He taught us to do the same. I still do.

> Miss Bray, a geography teacher who would recline in her wooden desk chair, close her eyes, and describe in glowing detail the castles of Europe and the mountains of South America that she'd visited. The textbooks' descriptions paled by comparison.
>
> Mr. Nattinville, a young Spanish teacher who spent weekends at our local courthouse as a volunteer translator for Hispanic families. "I used my gift of language," he used to say, "to help these folks understand and access our justice system."
>
> Mr. Gilbert, an industrial arts teacher who—instead of merely sitting at his desk observing us—would work shoulder to shoulder with us at the benches, making small wooden toys for his grandson.
>
> Dr. Cunningham, a college physical education instructor/professor who ran gym laps and did calisthenics right along with us.
>
> Mr. Griffiths, a physics teacher who would sit at our lab tables with his chin in his hands, watching us as we conducted our experiments. When the experiment went well, he seemed as excited as we were!

The enthusiasm of these teachers affected us . . . and *infected* us. They demonstrated that the material they were teaching was well worth learning.

Of course, we also remember the teachers who sat passively behind their desks, droning their material at a ponderous pace, making no eye contact and, indeed, no *human* contact with their students. These teachers had lost their interest, fervor, and enthusiasm for education a long time before. They viewed students as mile markers on the teacher's voyage to retirement. Their students were bored, complacent, and uninspired. The students completed the minimal amount that they could in order to receive the grade they desired. Unfortunately, this apathetic and tedious classroom environment is all too common in our schools today.

When these bored and boring teachers are confronted by a rebellious student who voices the age-old complaint, "Why do we have to learn this stuff, anyway?" they respond with:

"You need to learn this subject or you won't be able to understand the next subject."

Or

"You need it to graduate (be promoted, move to the next grade)."

Or

"The state says you have to."

Or

"It's part of the curriculum."

Or, simply

"Because I said so."

The inspired and inspiring teachers that I mentioned—Messrs. O'Rourke, Griffiths, Cunningham, Natinville, and Gilbert, and Misses Malahy and Bray—were seldom asked the "Why do we need to learn this stuff?" question. But if they were asked, they would respond enthusiastically: "Because it is important, valuable, significant information that can help you become a more dynamic, accomplished, contributing, and *interesting* person."

Better answer.

A study reported by Penn State professor Stanley DuBelle surveyed a large group of students and asked them to identify teachers whom they would describe as "enthusiastic." These teachers were then observed to see what traits and behaviors had earned them the "enthusiastic" designation.

Not surprisingly the research showed that *body language* contributed significantly to the students' perception of enthusiasm.

These teachers tend to have:

- Fast-paced, upbeat, animated vocal delivery
- Frequent, demonstrative gestures
- Varied, dramatic body movement

- Wide, rich vocabularies with extensive use of adjectives
- Ready, animated acceptance of students' ideas, suggestions, and questions
- High degree of energy, exuberance, and vigor

Of course, I am not recommending that you become a frenetic cheerleader at the front of the classroom, particularly if you are a somewhat low-key person by nature. But in order to motivate your students, you should make a concerted effort to incorporate some of the above-listed traits into your daily teaching style.

I presented this list to one of my graduate classes one evening. A teacher who attended the session approached me after the lecture. "I'm just not an enthusiastic person. I'm not very energetic and it will look phony if I start acting animated and excited."

Perhaps. But she has doomed herself—and her students—to six hours of daily tedium, monotonous and wearisome instruction of material that will likely be forgotten by semester's end. She will also be plagued by constant misbehaviors, confrontations, and disputes with her uninspired students. I commended her for recognizing and acknowledging her shortcomings, and suggested that enthusiasm is not optional for a teacher. It is, quite simply, a necessity.

RESPONDING TO A TEACHER'S LACK OF ENCOURAGEMENT

Fortunately, the overwhelming majority of classroom teachers are kind, responsive, well-trained professionals who genuinely care about the performance and progress of their students. However, a parent might occasionally deal with a teacher who is not interested in providing the child with the inspiration he or she needs in order to be consistently motivated.

Some parents are overly judgmental about teachers' performances and do not understand or consider the myriad challenges that teachers face daily in the classroom. Other parents feel unqualified to evaluate a teacher and will allow negative situations to continue because they are reluctant to intervene. Neither of these views is in the best interest of your child.

In the most basic terms, teaching is a service industry, and service industries *can* be evaluated and assessed by the consumers. If I order a bowl of breakfast cereal in a diner and the milk is curdled and obviously sour, I do not need a degree from a culinary institute or certification from the state board of health to assess that situation. Similarly, if a child comes home from school daily with complaints about his teacher and anecdotes about troubling goings-on in the classroom, Mom does not need a graduate degree in education in order to determine that a problem exists.

That being said, it is also inappropriate for parents to be overly judgmental and negative about a child's teachers. A generation ago, teachers were expected to provide instruction in reading, writing, mathematics, science, and history. Today's teachers are expected to cover that basic curriculum, plus offer instruction in sex education, fire safety, recycling, cultural diversity, computer literacy, AIDS awareness, the Heimlich maneuver, storm preparedness, the food pyramid, good/bad touching, saving the whales . . . and prepare the students for the hours of state-sponsored testing that will determine the future of the children, and in many cases, the teacher as well. Parents must remember this profound reality: For the mother of three children, her little Joseph is 33 percent of her child-related responsibilities. However, Joseph's teacher has thirty-five children in her classroom. Joe represents about 3 percent of her responsibilities. Parents are entitled to want and demand effective and responsive educational services for their children, but they also must understand the dynamics of the parent-teacher relationship.

When a parent is assessing a teacher, this evaluation should not be based solely on personality. Rather, consider the teacher's subject-area knowledge, ability to manage the classroom, enthusiasm, professionalism, and ability to establish and accomplish goals. A teacher who has the above capabilities is generally able to motivate the students in her class. If one or more of those attributes is missing, the students are generally uninspired.

If a parent is convinced that a teacher is not providing appropriate or effective motivation for the child, the parent should make an appointment to discuss the matter with the teacher (informal, unplanned "corridor conferences" are seldom effective). Have an agenda of specific topics or issues that you want to discuss and judiciously adhere to that agenda. At the conclusion of the meeting, formally outline the specific duties and responsibilities that each party has agreed to assume.

During the meeting, be cordial and collaborative. Treat the teacher with respect and make it clearly understood that you also expect respectful treatment. Begin the meeting positively by praising her classroom or commenting on her bulletin boards.

The unmotivating (and unmotivated!) teacher will often have a tendency to "blame the victim" by highlighting the child's performance and outlining ways that the *child* should and must change. The parent should continually emphasize the concept that the current situation simply is not working, so *all* parties (child, parent, and teacher) need to take a degree of ownership and work—together—toward a solution. Again, conclude each meeting by outlining and agreeing on what each party will do in order to enhance the child's progress. ("Thanks for meeting with me, Mrs. Shields. So, I will tell Benji that he must bring his assignment booklet to you at the end of the day. You will check his booklet to be sure that he has recorded all the assignments correctly, and I will check his homework nightly and initial each assignment. Are we agreed?")

The goal of the unmotivating teacher is often to identify the child as the *cause* of the problem and identify the parent as the *solution.* ("Kyle is doing very poorly in spelling because he simply is not applying himself. You will need to review his spelling words with him daily.") The parent should present and explore some other possible reasons for the problem. (Are the assigned words at the appropriate level? Can he be given additional instruction in class? Does he have a *memory* problem rather than a spelling problem?) And the parent should generate some alternate solutions. (Can the child work with a teacher aide? Can the teacher try different instructional strategies?)

Many parents feel immediately defensive when conferencing with a teacher, because this interaction often brings back memories of our own school years. If you are going to be an effective advocate for your child, you must overcome these insecurities and enter the conference confidently and view yourself as an equal with useful information about your child. If the teacher asks you questions that you do not feel like answering, simply do not respond. However, control any anger that you may feel. Keep the tone of the meeting cordial and collaborative.

EFFECTIVE USE OF PRAISE

> "The applause of a single human being is of great consequence."
>
> —JAMES BOSWELL

The surveys, studies, and theories that have been cited in the previous pages demonstrate that praise is not a panacea to enhance student motivation and progress. Praise in and of itself will not solve your students' motivational difficulties.

However, praise *can* be of great assistance in creating an environment where motivation can flourish. When used effectively, praise can be an important ingredient in boosting a child's motivation and desire to progress. It can be particularly valuable for students with low self-esteem or students who are struggling academically. Effective praise can be a source of strength, inspiration, and motivation.

Effective praise should have several specific ingredients.

INGREDIENTS OF EFFECTIVE PRAISE

Praise should be contingent. There should be a solid, observable, and realistic reason to praise the child. The praising comment should respond directly and specifically to a behavior that reflects a child's improvement, accomplishment, or effort. ("Trevor, you got every one of these math problems correct—even the ones where you had to use the eight times table—and you kept all the numbers in neat rows. Great improvement, Trev.")

Praise should be sincere. Most children can recognize "phony praise" instantly. This insincere praise is ineffective and may cause the child to feel minimized and patronized. If the adult continually offers the child insincere praise, the child becomes desensitized to praise, and even well-earned compliments become meaningless to him. I once asked a student how his mother reacted to his much-improved report card. "It doesn't matter," he responded dejectedly. "She *always* tells me I'm great."

Praise should often be given in private. Some children react negatively to public praise. They may become embarrassed by the attention or may become the subject of ridicule from their classmates. Taking a child aside and giving him praise can be quite meaningful. Believe me, he will share your comments with the people with whom he wishes to share them.

Praise should focus on effort and improvement, not be an assessment of a finished product. Place your emphasis on the *process* not the *product.* ("Juanita, I can see that you are still having some difficulty with the long division problems, but your work has really improved. You correctly followed every step for this problem, and you would have gotten the answer right except that you forgot to carry the six. Much, much better.")

Use praise to focus the child's attention on his own pleasure and pride related to the learning process. Instead of lavishing praise and compliments on the child when he has accomplished a task, make statements that encourage him to recognize the positive feelings that accompany success. ("You looked like you really enjoyed that." "How did it feel to finish that task so successfully?")

Accompany these reflective comments with statements or questions that facilitate self-evaluation. ("How do *you* like your composition?" "What part of your drawing do you feel is best?") Self-assessment is an important and valuable academic skill.

Use appropriate body language when offering praise. Praise will be more effective and meaningful if the adult's body language mirrors and emphasizes the verbal message. Make eye contact. Smile. Move close to the child. Wink. Have feeling in your voice. Touch the child gently on his shoulder.

Effective praise should be specific. The more specific and detailed the praise, the more meaningful it will be. When praising a child, provide her with specific examples and incidents that illustrate her effort and progress.

Imagine for a moment that your principal calls you into his office. He tells you, "You're a really great teacher." Certainly you would be pleased with that feedback.

But wouldn't it be more meaningful if he were to say, "Mary, you are truly a remarkable teacher. The parents had such wonderful comments about your holiday play and we so appreciate your willingness to work with our kids with special needs. You were so kind and generous to your teaching assistant when she was having trouble at home, and the presentation that you delivered on social skills was extraordinary. You have become such a valuable member of our faculty."

The second example reflects the fact that your principal *noticed, appreciated,* and *remembered* specific aspects of your positive performance.

Praise can encourage the development of positive social and personality traits when you identify and label those traits. You can foster these values by linking them with the child's behavior. ("I saw you let Tommy take your turn on the computer so he could finish his work. That was very *generous.*" "You shook Shelly's hand after she beat you in the race. That was very *gracious.*")

Accompany praise with a description of the behavior that you are praising. So many teachers' lounges that I visit across the country feature a widely distributed poster that lists dozens of phrases that can be used to praise children—"attaboy," "way to go," "great work," "terrific."

The phrases would be far more effective if they were used as a tagline for a *description* of the child's positive behavior. ("Jamal, you completed every one of the addition problems in only ten minutes. Way to go!" "Julie, you remembered to bring your science notebook. Terrific.")

Praise is effective when it affirms and recognizes realized expectations. On the way to the museum Mrs. Havens gently reminds Mikey that he is to stay with her during the tour and that he should make a special attempt to keep his voice low. During the field trip, she occasionally acknowledges his adherence to her expectations by whispering to him, "Great job, Mikey. You are staying with the group just like we discussed."

Praise can be used to soften the blow of a criticism. Suppose Ashley submits a paper to you that appears to be 90 percent complete. Praise the 90 percent prior to pointing out the 10 percent. ("Ashley, I see that you remembered to put your name and section number on the heading, and the margins look terrific. Your handwriting looks very neat on this paper. You must have tried very hard. [*Pause.*] Don't forget to write the date on the top!")

Praise can reinforce study habits and effort. You can recognize and reinforce desirable study habits by pairing them with praise. Rather than: "Justin, you will receive your best grade yet in math this term. You are very smart." Say this: "Justin, you will receive your best grade yet in math this term. Your hard work in class and your consistent homework have really paid off."

Praise (and encouragement) will be more effective if delivered in a novel or surprising way. Early in my career I had a twelve-year-old named Steven in my language arts class. We did not have a particularly good relationship and his effort and performance in my class were inconsistent. I praised and encouraged him frequently, but my comments did not seem particularly meaningful to him.

One evening, I was correcting papers at home and read Steven's composition about his dog. It was wonderfully done, filled with lively, descriptive language. He had obviously invested a great deal of effort in the paper, and I made a mental note to be sure to catch up with him the next day to commend him for his work and encourage him to keep it up.

Upon reflection, I realized that he was scheduled to go on a three-day field trip with his science class the next day and they were departing at sunrise. I would not be seeing him for several days.

Impulsively, I went to the phone and called him at home. The conversation went like this:

"Hello."

"Hi, Steven. This is Mr. Lavoie."

"What'd I do wrong?"

"Nothing, Steven. In fact, just the opposite. I am sitting here at my kitchen table and I just read your composition about Scout. It was wonderful! You used so many of the adjectives that we discussed in class. You described him so well that I could actually picture Scout in my mind. In fact, it reminded me of a dog that I had once. I am going to put your composition in a folder that I will use to demonstrate good student writing for my class this summer. I know that I won't be seeing you tomorrow and I just wanted you to know."

"Gee, thanks, Mr. Lavoie."

That one spontaneous phone call made a significant and lasting change in our relationship. His improvement and investment in my class grew markedly. We developed a very effective working relationship and his defensive, disinterested classroom demeanor began to improve significantly.

Some twenty years later, Steven came to one of my speaking engagements when I was in his area. He approached me after the session and we had a wonder-filled few minutes discussing students and staff whom we knew in common.

At the end of the conversation, the now thirty-year-old Steven said quietly, "Mr. Lavoie, do you remember the night that you called me at home?"

Again, my call to Steven was spontaneous and unplanned. But once I recognized the effectiveness of this strategy, I used it many times with many kids over the years. I can also suggest some other unusual ways to give praise.

UNIQUE PRAISING STRATEGIES

- *Compare the child to* you: Say, "When I was a kid I was never able to draw well. I wish I could have drawn as nicely as you do."
- *Praise with a touch:* A simple touch can communicate a very meaningful message and can often be more effective than verbal praise. A simple touch on a child's shoulder accompanied by a smile can communicate appreciation, admiration, or approval. Simple, ritualized gestures (e.g., a wink or thumbs-up) can also communicate your positive feelings about a child or his work.
- *Praise the act, not the child:* Parents are often counseled to give their children unconditional love and positive regard. Although this is sound advice, children are often suspicious of and unresponsive to blanket praise. An Australian therapist, Elizabeth Hartley–Brewer, surveyed a group of teens who reported that their least favorite type of praise was their parents saying "I am proud of you." Specific comments such as "I am so proud of the job you did clearing the cellar" or "You must be so proud of that science project" are more meaningful than general ones.
- *Post-it notes:* Write a positive, praising comment to a child and post it on his desk, book bag, or locker. Once of my daughter's teachers would occasionally sneak a praising note into Meghan's book so she would find it when she began that night's homework assignment.
- *Praise partners:* Solicit colleagues to help you deliver praise. Suppose Kimmy has been working very hard to improve her spelling. Ask the principal, a colleague, the lunch lady, or the bus driver to make a comment to Kimmy about her efforts. ("Hey there, Kimmy. I was talking to Miss Becker today and she told me how well you were doing in spelling. That's terrific.")

  Kimmy will be surprised and pleased that you were impressed enough with her progress to mention it to another staff member.
- *Indirect praise:* This technique involves praising Child A to

Child B—within earshot of Child A. Cindy and Jeffery sit side by side in your fourth-grade classroom. When passing Jeffery's math paper back to him, show the paper to Cindy. "Hey, Cindy. Look at the great job our buddy Jeff did on his math. Great, neat numbers, good margins, and he got nearly every answer right! Pretty good, huh?" Then wordlessly hand the paper to Jeffery.

THE ROLE OF PRAISE IN YOUR MOTIVATIONAL ARSENAL

This chapter was difficult and challenging to write. My career has had, at its core, an abiding belief in the use of positive reinforcement for students, particularly those who struggle with the academic and social demands of school. By criticizing the indiscriminate use of praise, I run the risk that the reader may misinterpret my intent and simply cease using praise to motivate children.

Praise is an invaluable tool in the motivational arsenal of a parent or teacher. Praise can be instrumental in building self-esteem, enhancing pride, fostering cooperation, building positive adult-child relationships, celebrating unique skills and abilities, and assisting struggling children during difficult or challenging times.

Lest my point be missed, I will repeat that praise is effective *only* if delivered correctly and can, indeed, be counterproductive if used inappropriately. The impact and effect of praise will be greatly enhanced if used in conjunction with *encouragement, interest, gratitude,* and *enthusiasm*.

Adults must realize the tremendous impact that they have upon the children they teach, coach, and parent every day. Even the smallest gesture of kindness and support can have a lasting effect on a child, as my phone call had with Steven. We can all look back on our childhoods and recall an incident when a teacher, coach, or parent made a supportive comment to us that provided us with the inspiration to attempt a challenging task or persevere through a difficult time. As Henry Adams once wisely stated, "A teacher affects eternity. He has no idea when his influence will end."

Childhood self-esteem, motivation, and resilience are not constructed through major colossal victories and accomplishments. Rather, a child's self-concept is enhanced or diminished by small, seemingly insignificant day-to-day events and interactions. Children who struggle in school can often find solace and inspiration in the smallest of victories. As teachers it is our privilege to provide the child with those victories.

Whenever I feel powerless to assist a struggling child and I doubt that I can truly provide him with a motivational spark, I reflect on Jordi, and I look to a scrap of paper that has hung framed on my office wall since 1975.

Jordi was a nine-year-old tutorial student of mine early in my career. He maintained a diary for me as part of his language arts curriculum. Each day at the beginning of class, he would take his journal and write a sentence or two about his activities from the previous day. He rushed, breathless, into my classroom one spring morning. "Gimme my journal, Mr. Lavoie. I gotta write something great from yesterday."

He wrote in the notebook and handed it to me. I put it into my briefcase. That evening as I corrected that day's papers, I read Jordi's journal entry for the first time. I tore the page out, framed it, and it has hung in every one of my offices for over thirty years. Jordi's entry is a constant reminder that special education is not about breakthroughs and miracles. Rather, our mission is about small victories and plodding progress.

Jordi wrote: "Yesterdae was a relly grate dae. I almost caght a ball."

5

The Child Motivated by Power

"Power does not corrupt. FEAR corrupts . . . the fear of a lack of power."

—JOHN STEINBECK

THE CHILD WHO IS MOTIVATED by power is among the most feared and misunderstood children in our classrooms and homes. These children cause great anxiety, panic, and dread in parents and teachers. In fact, these children tend to bring out the very worst in caregivers. As a parent once said to me at the conclusion of a seminar, "It's not fair! When I was a kid, I was afraid of my parents. . . . Now I'm a parent and I'm afraid of my kids."

This inappropriate and somewhat irrational response to the power-driven child is based upon a common and quite damaging misconception. Adults feel that when a child desires power, he wants to take some of *our* power. Because we do not want to lose control of the classroom or the home, we embroil ourselves in power struggles born of our refusal to surrender *our* power. Adults need to come to understand that the child does not want any of *our* power. He merely wants some of his own.

An analogy. Suppose that you have a candle that is burning and I hold a candle that is unlit. You touch your wick to mine. Now my candle has a flame, heat, and light; but your candle continues to be lit and your flame is not diminished in any way. You have given me a flame without decreasing your own. So it is with power. It is possible, using specific techniques, to give power to a child without surrendering any power of your own. Interactions with children need not be "winner take all." We should try to convert power struggles to win-win situations.

In order to understand and empathize with the Power Child, we must first examine the nature of a child's power needs. As the child grows into adolescence, he naturally develops a need for power and control over his life. Children have virtually no power. They cannot choose their school, their home, their family, or even their names (hence the preadolescent fascination with assigning one another nicknames). As a result, many children develop an intense need for power and may attempt to gain control at home or in the classroom.

Again, adults often respond inappropriately and ineffectively to these challenges to our authority. We allow ourselves to become embroiled in unproductive and damaging power struggles. We fail to recognize that a child's attempt to secure some personal power is a natural and necessary step in the maturation process. Children need limits and restrictions—and are constantly pushing against these limits. This is their primitive way of determining where their boundaries are. We would all do well to be mindful of the sage words of psychologist Salvador Minuchin: *"Parents cannot protect and guide without controlling and restricting. Children cannot become individuals without resisting and attacking. The process of child rearing is, therefore, inherently conflictual."*

In other words, our duty as parents and teachers is to keep children safe and secure. But if children are to mature and grow, they need to oppose our restrictions and exercise their independence. Conflict and discord are the natural outcomes. Conflict is inevitable and it is the responsibility of the adult to ensure that these unavoidable clashes cause minimal damage to the caregiver, the child, and the relationship that they share.

DEFIANCE VS. NONCOMPLIANCE

There are several characteristics and behaviors that are common among children who have significant power needs. Their desire for power and control often results in resistive, noncompliant, stubborn, or oppositional behavior. Of course, this behavior causes frequent conflicts with authority figures and peers. These children are often unresponsive to traditional management techniques, and adults will find that unique strategies must be devised in order to deal effectively with the noncompliance and defiance that characterize this behavior.

It is important to recognize that there is a fundamental and significant difference between defiant behavior and noncompliant behavior. *Defiance* involves active verbal or physical resistance to instructions, directions, requests, or commands. Examples of defiant behavior might include physical aggression, destroying property, refusing to comply, running away, truancy, and lying. *Noncompliant* behaviors are more indirect and passive. This cluster of behaviors might include complaining, whining, delaying, ignoring requests, crying, or annoying others. While all of these behaviors are disruptive in the classroom and in the home, it is important for caregivers to recognize that there is a spectrum of power-driven behaviors and that defiant behaviors are more serious and disruptive than are noncompliant behaviors.

DEFUSING THE POWER STRUGGLE

In order to understand and deal with the natural conflicts that occur between adults and children, you must understand that children and adults hold different—and often conflicting—agendas. Dad wants to have a clean, uncluttered garage, so he assigns his son to tidy it. Dad's goal is an orderly garage. The son wants to complete this distasteful task as quickly as possible so he can join his friends for a game of basketball. Their two goals are competing and this creates a breeding ground for conflict. Conflicting goals impact innumerable child-adult interactions, including homework, bedtime, mealtime, and so forth. When these conflicting goals are considered, it is little wonder that power struggles are so common between adults and children.

These power struggles often involve the most cherished and deeply held beliefs of the adults. The teacher's son begins to skip school; the police officer's daughter begins to experiment with illegal drugs; the minister's child refuses to attend Sunday services. These challenges are painful for the caregiver and often result in significant conflicts that can cause irreparable damage to the relationship between the adult and child. Children will often choose battles that directly confront the parent's core beliefs, in an attempt to challenge the boundaries that have been established. Children who are disturbed or deeply troubled will use these strategies in an attempt to humiliate or defeat their parents or teachers. However, most kids are merely attempting to test and assess the limits of the world in which they live.

When you become involved in an intense power struggle with a child, you have automatically lost the battle! Adults should not argue with kids. *We* are the authority figures. The child's role is to comply with *our* wishes. If a serious power struggle occurs, the adult has failed somewhere in the process. It is the adult's responsibility to avoid, prevent, or extinguish the power struggle.

When inevitable power struggles occur, the adult should—as much as possible—select the battleground, the weapons, and the rules of engagement! Your goal is to win the *war* (the mature development of the child), and you need not win each battle. In the American Civil War, the Confederates won the great majority of the skirmishes, but the Union was the ultimate victor. The goal is to win the major battles and "keep your powder dry" in the meantime!

If you insist upon total and complete compliance, you deprive the child of a valuable learning tool: natural consequences. For example, a parent may insist that a child complete her homework thoroughly and correctly every evening. Skirmishes over homework occur regularly. The battle rages! Perhaps it would be best to back off a bit and not insist on total compliance. The child would then face the *consequences* of her failure (teacher reprimand, poor grades). This experience may contribute greatly to the child's homework performance in the future.

It might be valuable to consider the manner in which you would handle a similar situation with an adult. Suppose a friend asked to borrow your lawn mower on Tuesday. You lend the mower to him, but request that he return it to you by Friday so that you can mow your lawn for a Sunday barbecue that you are hosting. It is highly unlikely that you would call him daily to remind him of the details of the arrangement. Further, if he failed to return the tool to you on Friday, you would doubtless not scold him or give him a lecture on personal responsibility. Rather, you simply would not lend him the mower again. He would experience the natural consequences of his failure to comply with his commitment. Experiencing a natural consequence will do more to ensure a child's compliance than will hours of lecturing, nagging, or negotiating—particularly for the child who is driven by power.

Choose Your Battles

Much of what I learned about dealing with children who need power, I learned from a young girl named Michelle. She was a wonderful kid, but was extremely troubled, argumentative, and combative. She had marked difficulty with peers and would constantly challenge the authority of the adults in her life. At fourteen, she developed an adolescent-onset seizure disorder that impacted upon her ability to monitor and control her own body. Because she felt that so many aspects of her life were out of control, she developed an intense and all-encompassing desire for power. She habitually challenged every decision, direction, or command given to her by an adult. She was a student in my social studies class, and our daily arguments and power struggles became a ritual. Even the simplest instruction (e.g., "Michelle, could you please close the door for me?") became a battle royale. "Why ME? Why do I have to do everything?

I wasn't the last one to come in! Why don't you ever make Alex do anything? . . .") Michelle's need for power was extraordinarily intense!

These daily skirmishes were distracting, unproductive, and exhausting. Both Michelle and I arrived at class every day prepared for our battles, weapons at the ready. I am sure that these daily conflicts were a great source of anxiety for Michelle's classmates . . . never mind the toll that this strife was taking on Michelle, me, and our teacher-student relationship. Michelle's classmates referred to us as "the old married couple" based upon our ongoing arguments, skirmishes, and confrontations.

I was tremendously frustrated with this situation and sought the counsel of my mentor. As always, he provided me with invaluable and profound advice. "Rick," he began, "you need not attend every battle to which you are invited!"

Wise counsel. I decided to pick my fights and to confront and combat Michelle only on issues that were significant and crucial. I called a truce on the trivial confrontations that we had every day. Initially, I lost some battles that I could have won, but I eventually began to win the war.

Beyond this, I began to develop and utilize strategies designed to *give* Michelle power. I came to recognize that power and control were significant NEEDS of hers and that she would not be able to learn effectively or efficiently *until those needs were met.* She NEEDED POWER, so I gave her some. I lit her candle with mine without losing any of my flame!

I well recall one Friday afternoon when our class had just concluded. As the students began to file out of the room, I asked Michelle to come to my desk. We were alone and we had the following exchange:

"Michelle, we are going to begin our unit on New Zealand on Monday and I will be doing my research over the weekend. Is there anything special that you would like to learn about New Zealand?"

"Well, I've seen movies from New Zealand and they have a lot of cars there, but they don't *make* cars there. How do all the cars get to the islands?"

"Good question! I will look that up. Anything else?"

"Yeah. I know that they have lots of sheep in New Zealand. Does it hurt the lamb when they cut off the wool?"

"Very interesting. I will research *that,* too. Any other questions?"

"Well, my brother said that the southern part of Australia is colder than the northern part. Is that true for New Zealand, too?"

"Excellent. Those are some pretty tough assignments that you have given me. I hope that I can find all of this information!"

Michelle left the room wearing a huge smile and wished me a sincere, "Have a great weekend! See you on Monday." I had given her a mammoth injection of *power.* I would be working for her that weekend. I would be completing *her* requested "assignments."

On Monday, I arrived at my social studies class and was greeted by an eager Michelle. "I told my mom that I gave my teacher homework over the weekend. She thought that was pretty funny."

When class began I said, "Well, gang, we're going to study New Zealand this week. Michelle gave me some pretty difficult assignments to research over the weekend, but I think that I was able to find most of the material that she requested. Michelle, why don't you sit up front here so that you can help me with some of this?" She enthusiastically joined me and participated eagerly in the week's activities, discussions, and demonstrations.

She responded beautifully to the fact that I'd given her some power. But the power was, largely, on *my* terms. My candle (control) continued to burn, as did Michelle's. The ritualized power struggles began to give way to a more cooperative and supportive relationship.

This strategy can be easily modified for use at home or on the playing field. Seek the Power Child's advice or input on family issues, and whenever possible, follow his advice. ("Your cousins are coming to dinner tomorrow. What meal do you think I should serve?" Or "We have a big game tomorrow, Roger. What drills do you think we should do this afternoon?") Again, these techniques do not—in any way—detract from your power or control. You merely give a little power to the child. You are successfully and effectively meeting a significant need that the child has.

Nothing makes a person feel more powerful than to have his opinions solicited—and followed. The three most important things that an adult can do for and with a Power Child are listen, listen, and *listen.* Involve him in family discussions and accommodate his preferences when you can. Look for opportunities to give him power by giving him responsibilities, asking for his advice, or requesting his input.

Offer Minor Choices

Another strategy that worked effectively with Michelle is known as "the minor-choice technique." This approach provided Michelle with the power that she needed without impacting my agenda or goals. For example, if I wanted her to write a two-hundred-word essay on Spain, I recognized that a power struggle was nearly inevitable. ("I don't want to write about Spain. Why can't I write about France?" Or "Why *two hundred* words? I love Spain! Why can't I write *four hundred* words?")

I defused and prevented the skirmish by embedding a small choice within the assignment. ("Michelle, I want you to write a two-hundred-word essay on Spain. Would you prefer to use white paper or yellow paper?" Or "Would you prefer to write at your desk or go to the library table?") By providing her with this minor choice, she had a sense of power and control and did not challenge *my* agenda of two hundred words on Spain).

Again, this strategy can be modified for the home or playing field. ("Matty, you have to clean up the mess that you left in the driveway. Do you want to do it *now* or after supper?" "Carol, I want you to feed the dog. Do you want to give him canned or dry food tonight?")

The key to the success of the minor-choice strategy lies in the delivery of the script. The adult should clearly and simply state his instruction and follow that immediately with a two- or three-option choice that the child can make in the completion of the instruction. All of the options provided should be readily acceptable to the adult, and when the child makes the choice, he should be commended for making an appropriate and timely decision.

For example:

"Rachel, I need your help getting the deck cleared off for a barbecue. Do you want to put away the hose first or sweep off the lounge chairs?"

"I'll do the chairs."

"Good choice, Rach. Thanks for your help."

Give Responsibility

In working with Michelle, I came to realize that I was giving her minimal amounts of responsibility. I seldom asked her to run errands, attempt extra-credit assignments, or do independent work. I was hesitant to give her responsibility for the solitary reason that I believed she was irresponsible and that she would handle these duties poorly. Again, I consulted my mentor, who wisely reminded me, "In order for a child to learn how to *handle* responsibility, he must be *given* responsibility to *handle*." His advice made great sense and I began to give Michelle chores and tasks to complete on a regular basis. I was heartened by her response.

Use Proximity Control

Power Children also respond well to basic "proximity control." This simply means sitting or standing near the child at times when his behavior may become a problem (transitions, tests, in-class videos). Do not use proximity in a threatening or intimidating way. Merely stand near the child and you will often find that your closeness will have a calming effect on him.

Allow Yourself to Lose

In the spirit of picking your battles, I believe that it is appropriate to allow the child to win one once in a while. Many parents and professionals may disagree with this strategy, but I feel that you should avoid *modeling* the stubborn, obstinate behavior that you are trying to eliminate! I recall Michelle entering the dining hall one day and angrily slamming the door behind her. I told her to go back and close the door appropriately. She refused so I repeated my command. The situation was escalating and, based on my previous experience, I recognized that it would soon expand into a nose-to-nose confrontation. I said, "Okay, Michelle, forget it! Just come on over to the table and have breakfast. There is some important information that I need to give you before we go off on our field trip. Do you want some cereal?"

I was surprised and pleased with her response. She did not gloat or revel in her "victory." She smiled slightly, came to the table, and was compliant and cooperative throughout breakfast. I continued to use this strategy with her on occasion. I believe that the strategy was successful because it communicated and demonstrated a mature and purpose-driven decision on my part. Basically, I communicated, "Michelle, our breakfast and our upcoming discussion are far more important than your compliance with my command. So I have decided to forgo this battle and invest our time in a far more important activity."

Again, my goal was to eliminate her power-driven, stubborn behavior. Therefore, it made little sense to model that behavior by blindly insisting that I win every confrontation.

State Your Commands and Instructions

Adults often unintentionally invite power struggles by giving ineffective or indirect commands. For example, commands should not be stated as requests ("Janet, would you please close that door?") or favors ("Janet, would you please close that door for me?"). This indirect instruction can easily ignite a power struggle. Rather, state the command in a firm tone. ("Janet, close that door, please.") State only one direction at a time and be certain that you have the child's attention before giving the instruction. You may want to ask the child to repeat the direction before she begins the task, to be certain that she understands the instruction. This may prevent additional conflicts.

Make and Enforce Rules

Power struggles can also be reduced by establishing and enforcing a set of rules for classroom and home behavior. By setting these regulations, the adult develops an effective buffer between the child's behavior and the adult. The *rules*—not the *adult*—should be obeyed. ("Johnny, the rule is 'no running' in the classroom." Rather than "Johnny, stop running and do as I say!") When establishing rules, make them simple, basic, observable, and specific.

Good Rules:
Submit all assignments on time.
Raise your hand.
Walk in the classroom at all times.

Poor Rules:
Try your hardest.
Behave yourself.
Be polite and kind.

Rules should be stated positively. Tell the child what you *want* him to do. ("Sit in your seat unless you have permission to walk around.") Not what you *don't* want him to do. ("Don't walk around the room.")

Set Deadlines

Inexplicably, Power Children respond very well to deadlines—particularly deadlines that they establish themselves. Michelle had great difficulty maintaining the cleanliness of her dormitory room and was very resistant and combative when asked to clean it. This was another ongoing source of conflict between us. One day—quite by accident—I set a deadline for her. She had been dawdling (another common behavior for Power Children) and resisting my request and instructions that she tidy her room before heading for supper in the dining hall. Ten minutes before we were to depart, she began a half-hearted attempt to clean the room.

I told her that she now did not have adequate time to finish the room and that she should wait and clean it after supper. "I can get it clean in ten minutes," she argued.

"I'll bet you can't!" I countered.

She suddenly became a cleaning dervish and the room was inspection-ready in eight minutes flat! By meeting the deadline—and proving me wrong—Michelle gained a tremendous sense of power. It is important to note that she did not gloat or boast when she beat the deadline. She was rightfully proud of herself, but accepted her victory graciously.

Several times after this incident, I would good-naturedly challenge Michelle by saying, "I bet you cannot get those clothes hung up in ten minutes." This would trigger cooperative and goal-directed behavior on her part. Sometimes I would ask Michelle to set the deadline and she would attempt to beat her own self-imposed schedule. ("Michelle, how long do you think it will take you to finish this work sheet? Ten minutes? Okay. One, two, three, GO!") Again, beating her own deadline was a tremendous source of power for her.

The Broken Record Technique

One of the most powerful and effective strategies to use is Lee Canter's *Broken Record* technique. This approach is used when the child becomes noncompliant or argumentative, and the strategy can be used in nearly any setting with any child.

The technique is effective because it responds to and eliminates the three main reasons why a child argues with an adult: (1) to gain power and control, (2) to receive positive reinforcement from his peers for confronting the adult, and (3) to avoid the task at hand that is the source of the conflict.

Suppose, for example, a teacher makes a simple request of a child (e.g., sit up straight, remove your hat). If the child initiates an argument over the issue, he clearly accomplishes all three of the aforementioned goals: he wrests power from the teacher by not complying; he is viewed positively by his classmates for resisting the regulation; and the teacher's time and energy is suddenly invested in the *argument,* not in the academic tasks that she'd planned for that session.

Consider this teacher-child exchange wherein the adult allows himself to be drawn into an argument with a child.

TEACHER: Today, class, we are going to discuss the Statue of Liberty. This statue is located in New York Harbor. It was given to the people of the United States by the people of France in recognition—Hey, Mitch. STOP PUSHING ELLIOT!"

MITCH: I didn't push him. HE pushed ME!

TEACHER: No way. I'm not blind. I *saw* you push him.

MITCH: I just moved his arm away.

TEACHER: Hey, I know a push when I see one! That was a push!

MITCH: Well, he said something I didn't like.

TEACHER: Oh, yeah. It's NEVER your fault, is it?

MITCH: You're always on my back! You never get mad at Elliot.

TEACHER: How dare you say that! I kept Elliot after school last week for breaking the globe.

MITCH: Yeah, you and your precious globe. You went ballistic when that got cracked.

TEACHER: Well, I'll have you know that the globe wasn't mine. I borrowed it from Mr. Staples.

MITCH: O-o-o! You afraid of Mr. Staples?

TEACHER: I am *not!* He's my friend. We even go hunting together.

MITCH: Wow, you in the woods! That's something I'd like to see!

TEACHER: I happen to be a *good* hunter. Just last year I shot a buck with a 30-30.

MITCH: Bow and arrow hunting is *real* hunting. Anyone can shoot a deer with a *gun.*

And on, and on, and on, and on, and on!

It is clear that all three of Mitch's arguing goals are being met.

He is controlling the agenda, his classmates are greatly enjoying the scene, and the topic of the Statue of Liberty is being totally ignored. Game, set, and match for Mitch.

There are many reasons why parents and teachers should not allow themselves to become embroiled in arguments with children. Primary among these is that *children don't follow the rules when they argue.* Adults generally follow established guidelines when they debate. They adhere to the topic, don't insult, and don't introduce unrelated materials and issues. Children do not adhere to these conventions and, when losing an argument, will resort to any and all strategies to regain power. For example, if you were having a political argument with a colleague, you would be unlikely to suddenly make a derogatory comment about his shoes or his hairstyle. However, kids will simply change the topic in order to maintain control of the argument. In the above dialogue, Mitch changed the agenda seven times and the teacher just went along for the ride!

If this scenario sounds eerily familiar to you, the Broken Record technique can be extraordinarily useful and effective.

Consider the same scenario, but in this instance the teacher will use Canter's Broken Record technique.

TEACHER: Today, class, we are going to discuss the Statue of Liberty. The statue is located in New York Harbor. It was given to the people of the United States by the people of France in recognition of—Hey, Mitch, STOP PUSHING ELLIOT!

MITCH: I didn't push him. HE pushed ME.

TEACHER: In my classroom you keep your hands to yourself!

MITCH: I didn't push him! I just moved his arm . . .

TEACHER: (a bit softer volume and slowly): In . . . my . . . classroom . . . you . . . keep . . . your . . . hands . . . to . . . yourself!

MITCH: You're always yelling at ME! You never yell at Elliot!

TEACHER: (even softer and more slowly): In . . . my . . . classroom . . . you . . . keep . . . your . . . hands . . . to . . . yourself.

MITCH: All right!

TEACHER: The French people were very grateful to the United States for their intervention during the war . . .

This strategy is remarkably effective because it addresses the three goals that the child has for initiating an argument. In the above dialogue, the *teacher* has control, the classmates are not entertained by the student's behavior, and the teacher returns to her task in a matter of seconds.

The Power Child also benefits because this strategy does not insult or embarrass him. The teacher merely repeats the preestablished rule in an understandable and firm manner.

The Broken Record strategy will not only extinguish a specific argument, it also serves to decrease the number of future arguments because the child comes to realize that his goals (control, reinforcement, avoidance) are not met when he argues with you.

In order for the Broken Record response to be effective, the adult must be certain to use the procedure correctly. Some guidelines to follow are:

- Do not raise your voice. Instead, *lower* the volume of your voice and spread . . . the . . . words . . . out. This communicates your very firm resolve and control.
- Do not repeat a *command*—repeat a *rule*. If you tell the child to go to bed and he refuses, do not repeat the instruction using the Broken Record format. ("Go to bed; Go . . . to . . . bed; Go . . . to . . . bed.") Rather, convert the *instruction* into a *rule*. ("You go to bed at nine o'clock on school nights. You . . . go . . . to . . . bed . . . at . . . nine . . . o'clock . . . on . . . school . . . nights. You . . . go . . . to . . . bed . . . at . . . nine . . . o'clock . . . on . . . school . . . nights.")
- Watch your body language. Avoid pointing your finger at the child or scowling when doing a Broken Record sequence with a child. This greatly changes the dynamics of the interaction and can be viewed as threatening and confrontational.

Preventing Power Struggles

Often, a Power Child will share your distaste for ongoing and constant power struggles, but may not have the ability to recognize when an interaction is escalating into a power struggle or may not be able to disengage in the early stages of a confrontation. You may find it useful to discuss this matter with the child and design a signal that you can give to each other to indicate that the exchange is beginning to escalate.

Your conversation may start out like this:

"Carol, we have been fighting a lot lately and I don't think that you enjoy it any more than I do. It was embarrassing for both of us when we argued at the mall yesterday and your softball coach walked by and heard us. I've got a suggestion. Whenever we have an interaction that is beginning to get out of control, I will give you a thumbs-up signal. That will indicate that we both *need to calm down a bit in order to prevent a blowup. You can give* me *the signal as well if it is appropriate."*

Another way to prevent power struggles with the Power Child is to solve conflicts *before* they occur. For example, if the child frequently initiates power struggles at the supermarket, make an agreement with him *prior to* entering the store.

For example:

"Tom, we are going into the market to get a gallon of milk for dinner. We are in a real hurry, so we will not have time to shop for anything and you won't be able to buy any candy or gum this trip. I really appreciate your cooperation with this."

"Ben, when we go to the store, you can choose the cereal that you want, but we will just need a small box because we are leaving on vacation next Tuesday. And please don't ask for anything else while we are shopping."

By establishing the ground rules and guidelines before entering the situation, you have greatly decreased the chances of a confrontation occurring. This approach also is effective because it emphasizes cooperation rather than control. You are requesting that the child assist you rather than lording your power over him.

Adults can often avoid power struggles with children by merely providing the child with advance notice about upcoming events, transitions, or changes in plans. For example, Mom goes into the backyard and tells Molly that she must discontinue the in-progress hopscotch game in order to visit Grandma. Molly is furious and a battle ensues. Mom knew several days ago that Grandma needed help in her garden on Saturday afternoon, but she failed to share that information with Molly. This conflict would not have occurred if Mom had informed Molly on Friday that they would need to depart for Grandma's at two o'clock on Saturday. Children with significant power needs are very resentful of unannounced transitions because they feel that this reflects a lack of respect for them, their schedules, and their interests.

Don't Forget to Wipe the Slate Clean

It is important to recognize that Power Children NEED power. It is their primary motivation. They need power in the same way that *you* need oxygen—they cannot live without it. Because this is such a significant need for them, they are often obsessed with establishing and maintaining control. They may view interactions as threatening even though no threat was communicated or intended. They also have great difficulty letting go of a negative interaction. They bear grudges, and they assume that the adults in their lives do as well. A relatively minor altercation with Mom on the way to school may be a source of anger and concern for the child all day, long after Mom has forgotten that the argument occurred. The child gets off the school bus at the end of the day in an angry and sullen mood, and the mother has no idea why he is being sulky and uncommunicative.

Because the child has difficulty wiping the slate clean after an altercation, the adult must do it. Whenever I had difficulty with Michelle during the day, I would be certain to seek her out before I left work and give her a smile, a kind word, and wish her a good evening. By doing this, I communicated, "We're okay now. We had our battle, but that is behind us and tomorrow is another—and hopefully better—day." This prevented her anger from festering and contributed greatly to our relationship.

A Place of Their Own

A major battleground for child-parent conflict is the cleanliness and condition of the child's bedroom. This discord is rooted in the fact that the *child's* perspectives on the room ("a place that's my own," "a place to relax," "a place to get away") are radically different from the perspectives of the *parent* ("must be neat and clean," "must be maintained in a similar manner as the rest of the house"). This may be a battle that the parent would be well advised to avoid. The room will doubtless *never* be clean to your satisfaction. You may want to concede and surrender. Close the door and live with it. Insist that the room be sanitary, and establish guidelines regarding food, laundry, and so on, but concede the neatness factor. This sounds like radical advice, but I know many functioning families who have chosen that route, and they have been quite satisfied with the result. If you find it impossible to surrender on this issue, you may want to reflect on your *own* personal needs for power and control.

Bullying

The Power Child will often have conflicts with siblings—especially younger ones—because he will attempt to satisfy his power needs by bossing or bullying his younger brothers or sisters. This behavior must not be tolerated and should be dealt with directly.

By allowing her to exercise power over those who are younger, smaller, and weaker, you create a very unhealthy pattern of behaviors that will cause great social and emotional difficulty for her. She may develop a sense of unrealistic invincibility. Provide the younger siblings with a supportive and responsive reporting system so that they can inform parents of the bullying behavior without fear of retaliation.

PRINCIPLES FOR MOTIVATING THE POWER CHILD

Like all power-hungry children, Michelle had two main goals that were often misunderstood by the adults in her life (including me!). Basically, she wanted to be *helpful/useful* and she wanted *choices/options.* She wanted a degree of input and control. She responded well to strategies that met these needs and resisted strategies that failed to meet them. I began to ask her for help, advice, and assistance, and I gave her responsibilities and offered her options within boundaries. My colleagues commented upon how much Michelle had changed. Actually, it was *I* who had made the most significant change. I merely started to meet her needs and avoid or modify situations that quashed those needs.

Who's in Charge?

The power-driven child views the world differently from the way most children do. This child believes that every situation, interaction, and activity *must have someone in charge.* He does not respond well to cooperative activities where all duties, responsibility, and power are shared equally. He feels that a top-down hierarchy of leadership is fundamental to the success of any activity. Interestingly, it often does not matter to him *who* is in charge—as long as *someone* is. He respects power and is often willing to cede his own power if a capable and assertive leader steps forward. If someone—anyone—is firmly and clearly in charge, the Power Child feels comfortable.

This is an important and significant concept for adults to remember. If the adult leader in a group refuses to (or is unable to) take *firm* and definite control of a situation, the Power Child will step forward and seize that control. He does not do this out of anger or disrespect. Rather, he acts out of a deep need for the situation to have a hierarchical structure and a clearly designated leader. Therefore, the Power Child will often challenge a weak or indecisive adult.

This child wants two things from the adults in his life: COMPE-

TENCE and CONFIDENCE. He needs the adult to be skilled, decisive, and commanding. Absent this leadership, the Power Child will step up and fill the leadership vacuum.

Power Children are also quite perceptive and sensitive to adults who disperse fake power to them. They dislike being patronized and respond negatively to adults who throw them a bone by granting them power that is meaningless or inconsequential. For this reason, be judicious in your use of democratic approaches with these children.

Several years ago, the Democratic Classroom was all the rage in American schools. This misguided—and hugely unsuccessful—movement promoted the idea of having *students* design, implement, and adjudicate the rules in the classroom. Students as young as ten would caucus to write the classroom rules, and violators were brought before student tribunals. This approach was purported to provide students with firsthand exposure and experience in the workings of democracy. It didn't work.

Democratic principles are effective only when all involved parties share a common goal. All Americans want our country to have the best possible president. We may differ strongly upon the policies of one candidate or another, but our goals are identical—elect a leader who will govern effectively. Therefore, democracy works and elections are held.

However, when involved parties share *conflicting* goals, democratic principles are ineffective and inappropriate. For example, the government would not hold a national election to lower the federal income tax to 5 percent. In this case, the citizens' goals (pay less in taxes) and the government's goals (solvency and continuation of services) are totally opposed to each other. Democratic principles do not work in this case.

I recall observing a young teacher many years ago who was trying to create the Democratic Classroom with her students. She assigned a group of students to write the classroom rules, policies, and procedures. In this way, she posited, they would learn about democracy.

The students caucused and announced two new class rules: no

homework on weekends and double recess on Fridays. The teacher responded by saying that curriculum guidelines rendered these two rules impossible. She unilaterally vetoed both regulations. What did those students learn about democracy? Not much.

Democracy has no place in the relationship between an adult and a child. A benign dictatorship works best. As I reminded our children when they were young, "Our family is a democracy . . . and I am the president (or, more often than not, the *vice* president!)."

Respecting Boundaries

The Power Child will, by his nature, challenge the boundaries and restrictions that are placed on him by the adults in his life. If the child were to have his way, boundaries would be eliminated in favor of open-ended choices. Adults will sometimes expel all boundaries in order to satisfy the Power Child or to avoid confrontation. This, ultimately, is not in the child's best interests. Boundaries are born from respect, cooperation, and consideration and are a fundamental part of any child-adult relationships.

Power Children often mistake *courtesy* and *consideration* for *control.* They will struggle against reasonable restrictions or regulations placed upon them because they view them as intrusions on and challenges to their freedom and autonomy. Michelle once came to me irate because of her dormitory counselor's requirement that she let the counselor know where she was going whenever she left the dorm. Michelle felt that she was being treated "like a baby" and insisted that the restriction be removed. I reminded her that it is simple *courtesy* to inform the people you live with of your destination when you depart the building. As I told her, I would never rise from the dinner table at home, leave the house, and drive away without mentioning to my wife that I was leaving and where I was going. ("I'm going to the dry cleaner's and the hardware store; be back in an hour.") I explained that I was not asking my wife's *permission* to depart, only extending the courtesy of notifying my loved ones of my plans. Viewed in this context, Michelle complied with the regulation.

Promises vs. Threats

Children who are motivated by power do not respond well or positively to threats, and these attempts at intimidation often precipitate confrontations and power struggles. By threatening a child, you send the message that he has *no* power and that you have *all* of the control. Of course, this dynamic will be quite troubling to the child who has power as his lifeblood.

Power Children respond far better to *promises* than to *threats*. For example, consider the profound differences in the power messages that are communicated in these two statements:

Statement A: "Bill, if you do not get your room clean, I am not going to let you go to the pool."

Statement B: "Bill, you can go to the pool as soon as your room is clean."

Statement A presents a clear threat and challenge and indicates that the adult has total control over the situation. Statement B communicates a promise and provides Bill with significant power. The second statement makes it clear that Bill has *control* over the situation. *He* and *his* behavior will determine whether or not he goes to the pool. This establishes and maintains a positive—not punitive—dynamic regarding the situation and fosters cooperation and responsibility. The child is far more likely to comply.

Power vs. Authority

Adults often use the terms "power" and "authority" interchangeably. In actuality, these terms describe two different concepts. It is possible to give *power* to a child without surrendering any of your *authority*. Below is a child-parent dialogue wherein the adult is using *power*.

SCOTT: Dad, can I walk to the mall with Jerry?

DAD: No.

SCOTT: Why not?

DAD: Because I said no.

SCOTT: That's not a reason.
DAD: It's reason enough. I'm your father.
SCOTT: But Jerry's dad is letting *him* go.
DAD: I said no.
SCOTT: Well, I'm going anyway!
DAD: If you do, you will be one sorry young man.

In the dialogue below, Dad uses *authority* rather than power.

SCOTT: Dad, can I walk to the mall with Jerry?
DAD: That's not a good idea, Scott. There are no sidewalks on the highway and I wouldn't want you to take a shortcut through the woods.
SCOTT: It's not fair.
DAD: I'm sorry that you feel that way, but I need to make sure that you are safe.

By using authority instead of power, clashes can be avoided. Remember that power struggles are always counterproductive and always serve to distort the child's view of power. If the child wins the struggle, he feels that he won because of the omnipotence of power; if he loses the struggle, he feels he lost because of power. Authority emphasizes cooperation, reasonableness, and preventive strategies. Power emphasizes control, emotionality, and reactive strategies.

STRATEGIES FOR MOTIVATING THE POWER CHILD

Give Him Responsibility

Giving the Power Child responsibility can do much to satisfy his need for power and, simultaneously, enhance motivation. Give the child power by leaving him in charge on occasion. Make him responsible for taking phone messages, babysitting, or starting dinner. Grant him some authority and be certain to commend and thank him when he handles the responsibility well. Although he may initially resist these new "burdens," he will eventually come to appreciate the responsibility and grow more confident.

Let Her Help Others

The Power Child can also gain power by assisting others and doing volunteer work. We live in an unfortunate social climate, wherein community service is being used as a punishment for white-collar crime. This is truly unfortunate because it gives children the impression that helping out or giving back is a form of punishment. In actuality, providing assistance to another person is a source of satisfaction—and power. Encourage the child to assist elderly neighbors, community organizations, or even family members. This may do much to satisfy her need for power.

Express Interest Instead of Praising

Power Children—unlike most other youngsters—often do not respond well to praise. When an adult communicates approval of a child's behavior, it is the *adult* who wields the power because he is evaluating and assessing the child's performance. However, you can meet the child's need for power by expressing *interest* in his activities and hobbies. For example, if he has a particular interest in NASCAR, you may want to clip articles or photos that you run across and give them to him. This places him in a power position because this is an area in which he has superior knowledge.

Give an Allowance

Parents can feed a child's power needs by providing the child with a regular allowance. This empowers him to make spending decisions and increases his sense of autonomy and independence. Saving money also helps the Power Child learn to delay gratification. This is often difficult for the child with significant power needs.

There are several common mistakes that parents make in regard to allowances. First, the parent should allow the child to spend his allowance *as he wishes.* Initially, the child will make mistakes and make impulsive purchases that are not well considered. He may spend the entire allowance on the day that he receives it, leaving him with no spending money for the remainder of the week. The child will learn from these experiences and will begin to develop more effective consumer habits.

The major mistake that parents make regarding allowances is attaching the weekly stipend to the child's successful completion of household chores. The child is required to *earn* his allowance, and failure to satisfactorily finish his assigned tasks results in the allowance being withheld. This is an extraordinarily ineffective strategy, particularly for the child with significant power needs.

The child is a member of the family. As such, he has *rights* and *responsibilities.* He has the *right* to share in the family's financial resources and he has the *responsibility* to do chores and errands that contribute to the common good and support the successful day-to-day functioning of the family. But these rights and responsibilities are largely unrelated and should not be linked in a cause-and-effect way. If the distribution of the allowance is determined by the child's completion of chores, the child becomes an *employee* of the parent. The only motivation the child has to help out around the house is his allowance. As a parent, your goal is to have the child help out because it is the appropriate thing to do. Further, during the child's birthday week, when he receives ample cash from adoring grandparents and family members, he is likely to refuse to do his chores because, frankly, *he doesn't need the money.*

Basically, the child should get an allowance. Also, the child should do assigned chores. But one should have nothing to do with the other.

Respect His Agenda

Another way that parents can meet power needs is to respect the puzzling and perplexing agendas that are often held by children.

Your eight-year-old may begin to collect bottle caps; your twelve-year-old suddenly refuses to be seen with you in public; your fourteen-year-old announces that she is a vegetarian. These are all attempts to seize a degree of control over their lives. Resist the temptation to cavalierly dismiss these behaviors or tell the child that her actions are silly or pointless. Accept and support these behaviors and recognize them as normal and natural steps in the maturation process.

Avoid Using Peer Pressure

One ineffective strategy to use with a Power Child is peer pressure. By saying "Why can't you sit quietly like Peter?" or "Why can't you keep your room clean like your sister?" you are creating a power vacuum for the child, and she will respond negatively. She cannot control or influence anyone's behavior but her own, and she will—understandably—resent being compared to another child.

Let Her Generate a Solution

Encourage the Power Child to generate solutions to problems. In this way, she will feel that she has input into the situation, and she will be more likely to comply. For example, if Mom and the child have a disagreement about her weekend plans, the mother might say, "There must be a way that we can compromise on this so that we *both* get what we want. Why don't you think about some workable solutions and we will discuss this again after dinner." This approach is quite effective for the child with strong power needs.

Be Willing to Negotiate

When adults deal with the Power Child, they must be willing to negotiate on some issues and situations. Again, it is ineffective to meet stubbornness with stubbornness or inflexibility with inflexibility. There are myriad benefits to negotiation. Among them are:

- Reduces power struggles
- Increases likelihood of cooperative and committed behavior on the child's part
- Reinforces limits and boundaries
- Reflects willingness to listen to and consider child's opinions and feelings
- Provides a positive model of flexibility
- Reinforces valuable real-world skills of negotiation, bargaining, and mediation
- Strengthens the adult-child relationship

Of course, not all issues and situations are negotiable. ("Mom, Frankie has a box of fireworks that his uncle gave him. Can I buy some to use at my birthday party?") Issues that impact upon health and safety are generally nonnegotiable. Any issues that are contradictory to the family's values or that present great inconvenience or expense are also ineligible for negotiation. But there are many day-to-day issues that *are* eligible for give-and-take bargaining.

Use Teachable Moments

The teachable moment is another wonderfully effective strategy to use with children who need power (particularly adolescents). Teachers (and parents) must recognize that there are many unplanned, unscripted opportunities in a day during which the adult should depart from the regimented schedule in order to provide instruction in a skill that was not part of the planned agenda. *Good* teachers use their lesson plan as a road map that guides them along the route in a sequential and predictable manner. However, *great* teachers use their lesson plan as a *compass* that points out the general direction in which the lesson will go, but that also allows for occasional departures from the main route onto interesting and valuable side roads.

I remember entering a teacher's classroom to observe his lesson as part of his evaluation process. The teacher beamed as I walked in, for he had a dynamic and valuable lesson planned for that day. On the blackboard, he had drawn a multicolored, detailed facsimile of a bank check. It had required a tremendous amount of time and energy on his part, and he was delighted that I chose that particular day to observe and evaluate him. He confidently began his lesson by informing the students—a very challenging and power-hungry group of fifteen-year-old vocational boys—that he would be teaching them the valuable skill of check writing. He pointed out the blank where the date was to be recorded and he wrote "Nov. 17."

The students were confused and clamored to know what "Nov." meant. He explained that it was an abbreviation for the month of November. They became more confused—but more engaged. They told him that they were unaware that the months could be abbreviated. He informed them that nine of the twelve months have widely accepted abbreviations and that the months can also be represented by the numerals one through twelve, corresponding to the month's order in the year. The boys were fascinated. They explained that they all had difficulty completing their time cards at their part-time jobs because they had been unable to write the date in the small area allotted for that purpose. They had been smuggling their time cards out to their girlfriends in the parking lot so that *they* could complete the required data.

The teacher, with a lump in his throat, erased his beautiful check facsimile and conducted a thirty-minute lesson on the appropriate abbreviations of the months. The students were attentive and cooperative throughout the lesson. When the students departed, the teacher approached me and apologized for abandoning his original lesson. I assured him that his decision to take advantage of the "teachable moment" was an extraordinarily wise one and reflected solid instincts and a genuine responsiveness to the needs of his students! Not only did he provide the students with valuable information and knowledge, his willingness to respond to their interests and needs provided them with an incredible injection of power! Their cooperative behavior demonstrated their recognition that he had responded to them in a positive way. Now, *that's* good teaching!

Handling Poor Decisions

Another dynamic involving power-driven children is their need for control—on their terms. This craving for control can cause them to make counterproductive and irrational decisions. When I worked in an ice cream shop in high school, a little boy insisted that his dad buy him a jumbo cone. The father told him that a jumbo was too big, but that he would buy him a medium cone. The boy stated that if he could not get a jumbo, he didn't want anything, and he left the shop empty-handed. His need to control the situation caused him to make a very poor decision. The dad would have been well advised to explain to the boy that this decision was a poor one, and to encourage the boy to accept Dad's compromise.

When a Power Child makes a poor decision or receives a punishment, the adult should avoid gloating or rubbing salt in the wound. ("Well, if you had accepted the medium cone, then you would have some ice cream like your sister." "If you had done your homework last night like I told you to, you wouldn't have gotten into trouble with your teacher today.") Rather, react to the situation with a degree of sadness in your voice and demeanor. ("I'm sorry you didn't have any ice cream, Joey. I know that you really love it!" "It's too bad that the teacher got angry with you about your homework. You must have had a tough day.") This approach (even if you must feign sadness) is more effective than gloating and is far less likely to escalate into a power struggle. Saying "I told you so" to a Power Child is akin to throwing down the gauntlet and inviting him to battle.

GROOMING LEADERS

When adults discuss children who have significant power needs, the conversation generally focuses upon the negative, challenging, confrontational, and combative aspects of these children. But it is important to remember that a need for power and control can also be a positive and productive trait. Children who have strong power needs tend to have leadership potential and are often skilled decision makers. If power needs are adequately met by the adults in a child's life, the child can direct these needs toward independence and self-reliance. These are particularly valuable skills for the child with special educational needs.

Many people who have a strong need for power also want to be *leaders* in order to secure power and influence. However, they may have personality or temperament traits that prevent them from achieving leadership positions. The argumentative, contentious child is unlikely to be elected class president or to be appointed as a leader by teachers, coaches, or other adults in his life.

Therefore, it is beneficial to teach leadership skills to the child and to foster these traits at home and in the classroom. If the child can achieve a leadership position, he will have a socially acceptable outlet for his power needs.

Most children do not understand the nature of leadership and often hold significant misconceptions about the dynamics of leadership. For example, children generally believe that the leader must be the *best* or the most accomplished in their chosen field of endeavor. However, most Major League Baseball captains (voted for by their teammates) are mediocre utility ballplayers. They are admired and elected for their leadership skills, not their athletic prowess.

Another common misconception held by children is that leaders have unlimited freedom and can do whatever they want. Not true. Anyone who has held a leadership position will tell you that leadership must be accompanied by great accountability and that the leader's behavior and performance is observed, monitored, and assessed by all. In fact, a person actually *surrenders* much of his freedom when he assumes the mantle of leadership.

Provide the Power Child with instruction on leadership skills. It is important that he understand that compassion is the hallmark of good leadership. He will be effective in leadership positions only if he treats his subordinates kindly, respectfully, and generously. He must come to embrace the concepts of teamwork and collaboration, and learn to listen to others and respond to their opinions and needs. In order to be an effective leader, the child must use negotiation and compromise and must be able to make and implement long-term and short-term plans. An effective leader needs vision, determination, and persistence. The Power Child may assume that, as the leader, he can do and say anything he pleases. By providing him the opportunity to learn the true nature of leadership, he is more likely to have successful experiences in leadership positions later on.

The child's power needs should not be thwarted or deleted. Rather, they should be guided and directed. When a river overflows, it is pointless to attempt to halt the rushing waters; rather, the torrent is diverted and redirected to a place where it will do no damage, and may actually do some good.

6

The Child Motivated by Projects

"I have never met a student who wouldn't do his work. But I've met plenty who wouldn't do yours!"

—SUSAN WINEBRENNER

MANY OF MY COLLEAGUES in the teaching profession are not particularly good consumers. We tend to be a bit trendy and we eagerly embrace any teaching strategy that is marketed as "new and improved." Unfortunately, some educators define progress as: Accepting what is new *because* it is new, and rejecting what is old *because* it is old.

This approach ignores the fact that some new, innovative approaches are ineffective, and some old, classic strategies continue to be useful and beneficial.

There is one educational strategy that has been embraced, rejected, embraced, rejected, and embraced over the years. When I was trained in the 1970s, we referred to this strategy as "learning units"; it fell out of favor in the 1980s, and the method returned in the 1990s known as "thematic teaching." Whatever it is called, it is a cross-curriculum strategy whereby instruction in math, science, history, and the language arts is presented using a topic of interest to the child.

Although some students may find such an intense immersion in one topic a bit overwhelming, many youngsters find this strategy exciting, stimulating, and highly motivating. They are willing and able to invest themselves fully in assignments that they may have previously perceived as dry or boring (e.g., math computations, grammar instruction) because the tasks are related to an area of particular interest (e.g., baseball, dinosaurs).

A distinct advantage to this approach is that it demonstrates to the child the connections and interrelatedness among the various areas of the curriculum. Students often view academics as a collection of unconnected, disjointed subskills that have no relationship to one another. As a result, the child seldom uses the grammar skills that he learned in English class when writing an essay for his history teacher; he may not realize that the scientific method that he learned in biology can also be applied to the problem-solving activities in his civics class. When the teacher uses a single, overarching topic to present the curriculum, the student is able to see that skills mastered in one setting can and should be applied in other settings.

The *Project Method* offers students a challenging and structured approach to learning. This strategy allows teachers to present complex and challenging material in a manner that ensures total student involvement in a focused, supportive classroom environment. Children who have a history of school failure are often inspired by the Project Method. As one child told me, "We are studying about space travel but I'm also learning how to read better and do harder math." The inherent structure in this method is particularly useful for the child who has difficulty ordering and organizing his environment. When the child has minimal internal structure, it is incumbent upon us to provide him with a well-defined external structure in order for him to progress to his fullest potential. The Project Method provides this much-needed structure in full measure.

Sally Smith, founder and executive director of Washington, D.C.'s renowned Lab School, is a pioneer in the use of project-based education. Her Academic Club Methodology is currently being used in schools across North America. In her book *Live It, Learn It,* she explains some other advantages of the Project Method when dealing with struggling or unmotivated learners:

Projects increase a child's focus on task. Children with learning problems need clear, established boundaries in order to perform to their potential. They simply cannot handle too many options or choices. They become confused, anxious, and increasingly indecisive when faced with making a choice from a wide collection of options. The wise mom knows that it is unproductive to say to an ADD child, "You can wear any sweater you choose." Rather, the mom will say, "Which sweater, Emily? The red one, the blue one, or the one with the horse on the front?"

Projects allow and encourage children to focus their efforts and energies on well-defined tasks. This enables the children to establish and meet priorities, and it enables them to organize themselves. Directions and assignments must be detailed and precise.

Projects provide an opportunity for the child to experience and enjoy success in nonlanguage areas. Because projects include assignments in a variety of disciplines (art, music, etc.), the child can receive a self-esteem boost by participating in these activities. This success can serve to offset some of the frustration that the child experiences in the language-oriented assignments.

Projects can highlight the child's strengths. Sandy, who is often rejected or isolated by her classmates because of her social and academic deficits, excels at drawing and art. When the class, or individual students, is working on the art assignment in their project, Sandy becomes a much-sought-after consultant and expert. ("Sandy, can you show me how to draw a horse?")

Projects foster memorization. Current research tells us that memorization is fostered if the learner is provided with specific "triggers" that initiate the memorization process. For children with language disabilities, these triggers are seldom the spoken or written word. Rather, a picture, a song, or a piece of art may spark their memory. Projects provide countless opportunities to tap the child's memory resources.

BRAINSTORMING

Students who enjoy working on projects often also enjoy brainstorming activities. Brainstorming is a strategy that has its origins in the business world. In the 1960s executives found that this free-flowing method was an effective way to generate several workable ideas or solutions in a brief amount of time. These ideas would then be organized and evaluated, and the most effective and workable of the ideas would be identified and enacted.

The brainstorming process as it relates to the classroom is based upon two premises:

1. Most new material is related to existing knowledge.
2. Students learn most effectively and efficiently when they are actively involved with ideas, materials, and peers. Learning is an active—not a passive—process.

Students do bring knowledge and information into the classroom. This information may well be random, disorganized, or inaccurate, but it does exist. When conducting teacher-training seminars, I often illustrate this by asking for a show of hands from people who know nothing about golf. I bring a group of five of the responders to the front of the room and we conduct a brainstorming activity about golf. Invariably, these volunteers do, indeed, have information about the sport. Within three or four minutes they are able to generate fifty or more isolated facts about golf: eighteen holes, Tiger Woods, Pebble Beach, Jack Nicklaus, putter, iron, Scotland, PGA, and so on. These folks may not be golfers or regular viewers of televised golf tournaments, but they *do* have knowledge of the game.

Select a topic that you know "nothing" about (France, NASCAR, knitting, sumo wrestling) and reflect upon it for a moment. You will find that you actually have a fairly extensive amount of background information on this topic. Again, that information may be splintered and disjointed, but it *does* exist.

Unfortunately, most teachers present information in self-contained units that fail to recognize or highlight the fact that most new information is an extension of existing knowledge. ("We are finished studying the Civil War. Put those handouts away. We will now study the Reconstruction.")

The second premise of brainstorming emphasizes learning as a dynamic, active process. Today's students have become accustomed to being passive spectators as a result of their intense exposure to television, movies, and video games. Activities that encourage youngsters to become intensely involved in the creation, gathering, and organization of ideas are very useful in motivating these passive learners. As the students become involved in this creative process, they also take more ownership of the material. As they exchange ideas with others, they develop their social emotional skills on a parallel course with their academic skills. In a free-flowing brainstorming activity, points of view are exchanged, ideas are analyzed, and *all* participants (even the teacher) become active, involved learners. This noncompetitive activity emphasizes teamwork, mutual support, sharing, and collaboration. Many students are reluctant to volunteer responses in class discussions because they fear that the teacher will pose a follow-up question that the child cannot answer. Brainstorming activities eliminate this concern.

The rules of a brainstorming activity are relatively simple:

STEPS IN A BRAINSTORMING ACTIVITY

- The leader announces the topic and is in charge of keeping order by calling on respondents.
- In random order, participants call out their ideas, suggestions, or input. This encourages risk taking.
- Each idea is accepted and recorded on a wall chart or blackboard for all to see.
- Offbeat or half-formed ideas are accepted and encouraged—no suggestion is to be criticized or rejected. This encourages creativity, originality, and unusual ideas that may have a kernel of truth. Inaccurate responses serve to point out commonly held misconceptions; half-formed ideas may trigger elaborations or ideas from others.

- Encourage participants to "piggyback" or elaborate on others' ideas. This promotes careful, attentive listening; elaborating on the ideas of others is a compliment, as it accepts and appreciates the original contribution.
- Establish and adhere to a time limit (two to five minutes) NOT an "idea limit" ("Let's generate twenty-five ideas"). An "idea limit" stifles creativity and originality.

Brainstorming activities can be used for several classroom purposes:

- To review a just-completed unit or course of study (Civil War, weights and measures, library skills, etc.)
- To solve a problem (deciding on destination of class trip, stopping classroom pilfering)
- To introduce a lesson or a concept
- List of associations: "What do you think of when I say 'Texas'?"
- Ways to _____: "How many ways can you think of to weigh a cow?"
- Uses for _____: "What uses could we find for old shoes? Broken eyeglasses?"
- Characteristics of _____: "What are the characteristics of the Rocky Mountains? Abe Lincoln?"
- Everything you know about _____: "What do you know about World War II? John Kennedy? Pearl Harbor? Punctuation?"
- List of questions: "What questions would you ask of one of the characters in the book we just read? Of Ben Franklin? Adolf Hitler?"
- Definitions: "What is a definition of 'citizenship'? 'Courage'?"

A popular alternative to traditional brainstorming consists of "split formats" that require responses in two related categories. For example:

"Let's generate some things that we know about John Kennedy and some things that we would like to know about him in these two columns." Then organize the responses into categories—early life, family, war years.

"In these two columns, let's generate things that are the responsibility of the federal government and things that are not."

By using these formats, the teacher is able to informally diagnose the students' level of knowledge and interest areas in order to design future lessons. For example, if most of the student responses involve JFK's war exploits, the teacher knows that they will be highly motivated if she focuses on that aspect of the president's life.

DESIGNING PROJECTS

Teachers will find that a significant percentage of students will respond positively to the use of projects in the classroom. Below is a list of activities that may be useful in generating and creating projects in your program.

Have the child write a/an:

- Advertisement
- Newsletter
- Slogan
- Drama
- Job description
- Telegram
- Essay
- Résumé
- Advice column
- Journal
- Alternative title for an author's title
- Case study
- Riddle
- Bibliography
- Petition
- Fairy tale
- Cheer
- Letter to the editor
- Commercial
- Flyer
- Quiz

- Skit
- Ballad
- Monologue
- News report
- Biography
- Survey
- Recipe
- Song
- Editorial
- Poem
- Vocabulary list
- Limerick
- Word search
- Crossword puzzle
- Interview
- Eulogy
- Travel brochure
- Diary
- Announcement
- Dialogue
- Trivia question

Have the child design a/an:

- Bulletin board
- Painting
- Puzzle
- Sculpture
- Award
- Chart
- Prototype
- Time line
- Collage
- Mobile
- Banner

- Comic strip
- Board game
- Maze
- Diorama
- Book cover
- Model
- Diagram
- Flow chart
- Place mat
- Poster
- Time capsule
- Shadow box
- Scrapbook
- T-shirt
- Costume
- Demonstration
- Family tree
- Mural
- Card game
- Flip book
- Cartoon
- Game
- Dance
- Map
- Greeting card
- Puppet
- Terrarium

Have the child perform a/an:

- Puppet show
- Play
- Cheer
- Song
- Commercial

- Dance
- Debate
- Demonstration
- Dialogue
- Monologue
- Eulogy
- News report
- Pantomime
- Skit
- Choral reading
- Experiment
- Press conference
- Interview

There are nearly limitless possibilities and variations that can be used to generate hands-on projects that can serve to greatly enhance the motivation of many children in the classroom.

When preparing and implementing in-class projects, it is important to emphasize process rather than product. Students need to understand that the process in a multistep project is as important as the finished product. In fact, the process may well be more important than the completed project itself because that is where the majority of learning takes place. However, most teachers assign a project grade this way:

Note cards . . . 10% of grade
Outline . . . 10% of grade
Rough draft . . . 10% of grade
Final draft . . . 10% of grade
Completed project . . . 60% of grade

Donna Goldberg, author of *The Organized Student,* recommends a different approach. She suggests that each step in the process, including the finished project, receive an equally weighted grade (e.g, 20 percent). This underscores the importance of the *process* in a long-term project. Closely monitor the child's progress throughout this process to be certain that he understands the various steps to be taken. Encourage the students to ask questions about the process. If you wait until the due date to discover the students' problems, *their* problems become *your* problems.

Several years ago, I worked with an adolescent with significant motivation difficulties and learning problems. He was very unproductive in his classes and seldom completed his assignments. However, he was a very independent-minded young man and enjoyed working on long-term projects. He was a National Football League fan and an ardent supporter of the New York Giants. I asked if he would agree to work with me on his science, math, and language skills if all of our work was related to his beloved Giants. He skeptically agreed.

I prepared a list of twenty-five independent and semi-independent assignments related to math ("Compute the square footage of Giants Stadium"), science ("Research the aerodynamics of an NFL football and discuss why its unusual shape was chosen"), language arts ("Write a letter to the Giants requesting season ticket information"), and map skills ("On this map, place a star on each city that currently holds an NFL franchise").

I allowed him to examine the list of assignments and gave him permission to eliminate five of them. This gave him a sense of power and ownership of the project. We then negotiated and assigned due dates for each task and discussed the criteria that I would use to grade each assignment.

His performance on the project was extraordinary. Each assignment was submitted punctually and completely and reflected great care and effort. The finished project was placed in a binder, which he showed to his teachers and parents with uncharacteristic pride.

Higher Order Thinking Skills

Students who enjoy and are motivated by projects are often capable of critical thinking and independent functioning. Without sufficient challenge, the child will find the project tedious and boring. When designing projects, the teacher should make sure some assignments will use higher-level thinking skills.

Critical thinking skills include considering alternative points of view, examining ethical considerations, judging ambiguity and authenticity, testing assumptions, differentiating between fact and opinion, and creating solutions.

The project-oriented child is capable of (and greatly enjoys) independent learning. If the teacher does not respond to those abilities, and fails to provide the child with independent learning opportunities, the student can become frustrated and unmotivated. Conversely, the child who is provided with these opportunities can be a capable, self-directed, lifelong learner. He becomes self-reliant, curious, and confident.

When providing independent work for the student, the teacher should remember that the child will continue to need structure and support from an adult. Teachers often use teacher assistants or librarians to assist the student with the research aspects of the assignment. Again, these professionals should be urged to emphasize the *process* of the project, not merely the finished product.

CREATING CONTRACTS FOR INDEPENDENT LEARNERS

If a teacher wishes to have a student work on a long-term independent project, it is advisable to design a contract that clearly outlines the content and time line for the project and delineates the youngster's responsibilities in detail. The contract should be read, understood, and signed by the teacher, the student, and the parent. Students who are motivated by projects are generally delighted by this formality and fanfare.

The contract should outline the assignment in detail ("John will identify the most populous city in each of the fifty states and create a chart that presents the list of cities and their populations in alphabetical order"), the criteria for assessment ("The list will be evaluated based upon accuracy, completeness, and neatness"), and the global objective of the assignment ("This assignment provides experience in Internet research and compilation of data").

The student should be responsible for documenting the time spent on each assignment and providing the teacher with information about the relative difficulty of each task. The assignments should involve the language arts (reading, writing, speaking, listening), study skills (note taking, research), social skills (interviewing, surveying), and critical thinking skills (analyzing, synthesizing, reviewing, summarizing). This list of action verbs may be helpful as you devise assignments for the project-oriented student.

Defend	Decide
Predict	Conclude
Distinguish	Choose
Summarize	Appraise
Compare	Recommend
Demonstrate	Criticize
Dramatize	Locate
Solve	Identify
Illustrate	Select
Build	Categorize
Survey	Explain
Experiment	Give examples of
Organize	Create
Construct	Inquire

Children who are motivated by projects generally demonstrate the following characteristics:

- Enjoy experimentation, exploring
- Emphasize quality over haste
- Enjoy research and "finding out"
- Do not like time constraints
- Become absorbed in projects and are enthusiastic

- Enjoy working independently
- Are very inquisitive; ask questions frequently
- Are effective problem solvers
- Often lose track of time (absentminded professor)
- Are motivated by praise for their creativity and problem-solving skills
- Respond very well when teachers accept and embrace their suggestions

When the above characteristics are considered, it becomes clear that the Project Child will become easily bored and uninspired in a curriculum of endless series of work sheets and seat work. This child wants to be actively involved in long-term projects where she can explore, create, and investigate.

In order to motivate this child, the teacher must recognize, reinforce, and stimulate the child's natural curiosity and provide her with creative outlets and opportunities to explore. Her traits of inquisitiveness and perseverance will be invaluable as she continues her academic career and moves on to the world of work. As a school administrator, I always valued the faculty member who could prioritize and accomplish multistep projects. Their curiosity, attention to detail, and ability to problem-solve made them invaluable members of our staff.

7

The Child Motivated by Prestige

"All children wear a sign that says, 'I want to be important NOW!' Many of our problems with today's youth arise because nobody reads the sign."

—REVEREND JESSE JACKSON

"Being able to showcase our talents, and to have them valued by important people in our lives, helps us to define our identities around that which we do best."

—MARK KATZ, author of *On Playing a Poor Hand Well*

THERE ARE CHILDREN IN EVERY CLASSROOM who are motivated by prestige; they need to feel important. Of course, all children have this need to some degree, but for this subset of children, prestige and recognition are fundamental to their motivation in the classroom.

Many people have a profound need to demonstrate and display their accomplishments, like the sports hero whose home features every trophy, award, and plaque that he has received since Little League, or the Ph.D. who insists that his child's playmates refer to him as "Dr. Baker." Our society can be quite judgmental about these people and may view them as egotistical or as show-offs. These accusations are unfounded. It's normal to be motivated by a public display of one's achievements. We may also know of people who have minimal need for recognition, and who in fact find awards meaningless and even embarrassing. A well-known movie actor is rumored to have used his Oscar statuettes as doorstops, and a legendary Major

League Baseball player once gave his All-Star ring to a fan. Obviously, these gentlemen were not motivated by prestige.

It is important to remember that you have both kinds of children in your classroom. Some of your students will long for and cherish the paper certificate that they receive for a month of perfect attendance. Others will discard their award like yesterday's newspaper. The assumption that all kids *love* awards is simply unfounded.

Interestingly, many children who are prestige-driven are actually quite difficult to motivate. Because they have such a deep and abiding need to receive recognition, they are reluctant to take chances or to attempt tasks that may be beyond their reach. They fear that they will fail if they attempt difficult tasks, so they function at a level that ensures their success and results in rewards and recognition.

Lawrence Greene, director of California's Developmental Learning Centers, wisely calls this level of performance the *comfort zone*. The child attempts to maintain an academic and social level that he can control. This level becomes a "sanctuary" wherein the child is guaranteed success and prestige. This does not mean that the child is lazy; he is merely creating a world where he is safe and is the recipient of recognition and prestige. These children develop strategies that allow them to remain safely in their comfort zone and rarely enter into or explore greater challenges. Again, the child should not be punished or criticized for this. It is quite normal for any human being to stay in his comfort zone.

Only when the child's reluctance to emerge from his comfort zone becomes constant and unbending does this become problematic. When the child absolutely refuses to move beyond his zone, the teacher must gradually decrease the frequency of the recognition that he receives and require greater performance in order for the child to receive recognition. This is a gradual, and at times painful, process but one that is necessary in order enhance the child's motivation.

PRESTIGE AND IDENTITY

Teachers and parents often misinterpret the behavior of the child who is prestige-driven. The adult may feel that the child is self-involved, arrogant, and superior. The child's need for recognition is viewed as a need to flaunt her superiority. In actuality, the child's need for recognition may be reflective of her feelings of *inferiority.*

Many children who are motivated by rewards and prestige may have fragile and poor self-esteem. Of course, many children with learning disorders have poor or distorted self-esteem due to their constant struggles in school, their inability to make meaningful social connections, and their repeated failures and frustrations in the classroom.

Before examining the impact that self-esteem has upon the child who is prestige-oriented, we should clarify the terms that we use to identify a child's feelings about himself. People often use the terms "self-esteem," "self-concept," and "self-image" interchangeably. Actually, these three terms refer to three unique concepts.

Self-concept refers to the child's identity and answers the question "Who am I?"

Self-esteem refers to the value that a child places on himself and answers the question "What am I worth?"

Self-image refers to the child's opinion of how others view him and answers the question "Do other people like/respect me?"

Because the three concepts listed above are *feelings,* the child expresses them in the way that he acts and behaves. You cannot simply *ask* the child if he has a positive self-esteem. You must observe his behavior and the manner in which he acts in the classroom, at home, and in social situations.

A child with high self-esteem feels capable of influencing the behaviors and opinions of others in his environment. He is able to communicate his feelings and emotions and approaches new situations with confidence. He is not easily frustrated, and he willingly accepts responsibility because he feels that he is capable of completing tasks correctly. He generally deals effectively with mistakes or failure and keeps these setbacks in proper perspective.

Conversely, the child with low self-esteem often criticizes himself, seldom volunteers in class, and may become overly dependent on the teacher. His behavior may reflect an inappropriate need to please and be accepted by others. He will likely have great difficulty making decisions and have a low tolerance for frustration. He avoids new or challenging situations and may feel that he has minimal control over his own progress or performance.

Self-esteem is both a *cause* and a *consequence* of school success. The child who feels good about himself generally succeeds, and this success enables him to feel even more positive about himself and his capabilities. Conversely, a child with low self-esteem approaches tasks tentatively and with the expectation of failure, and often does poorly on the task. This failure confirms and enhances his frustration and feelings of inferiority.

Basically, self-esteem underlies our every behavior. It impacts our desires, goals, values, creativity, and ability to think about and process information. Self-esteem plays a crucial role in every behavior and in every decision that we make.

Although self-esteem is a crucial concept throughout the life span, it appears to manifest itself in a variety of ways as the child grows and matures. For example, in early childhood (preschool) the child's feelings of self-worth are determined largely by his ability to please the adults in his life. Young children often have an inflated and unrealistically positive self-esteem ("I'm Superman") because of the constant verbal reinforcement that they receive from the adults in their lives and their lack of exposure to failure or frustration.

In middle childhood the child's view of himself is largely determined by his ability to succeed at school tasks. Success in school enables and encourages him to take calculated risks in other areas of his life (e.g., swimming lessons, T-ball) because he assumes that he will succeed. If the child faces chronic failure in school, he begins to anticipate failure in other areas of his life and he becomes increasingly reluctant to attempt new or challenging activities.

In adolescence, the youngster begins to understand the value of *traits* (e.g., kindness, generosity, honesty) and begins to recognize that performance and progress are not the sole indicators of success and worth. Some adolescents may feel good about themselves even though they are not succeeding in school. However, teenagers with chronic learning problems tend to be unable to compartmentalize their strengths and weaknesses, and their school failure causes significant difficulty with self-esteem. Children with positive self-esteem are able to compartmentalize. ("So I'm not doing well in math—I've got plenty of friends and I'm a great swimmer.")

Again, many children who are prestige-driven also have poor self-esteem. It is important to consistently tell and remind this child that he is liked and respected by the adults in his world, regardless of his success in school. Avoid comparing him or his performance to others. He can control only *his own* behavior, so comparing his performance to the performance of others is both futile and unfair. Take care to reject the child's *behavior*—not the child himself—when reprimanding him.

Correcting the Prestige-Motivated Child

When working with a child who is prestige-driven, it is important to recognize that the youngster is very easily embarrassed. This hypersensitivity is caused by the fact that the child's view of herself is intricately tied to the opinions that her classmates have of her. Even a seemingly benign public reprimand or scolding (e.g., "Sarah, would you mind quieting down so that I can hear myself think?") can cause great embarrassment for the child. The teacher may forget about the comment moments after it is made, but it may be a source of angst for the child for several hours. As much as possible, provide any criticisms or rebuke in private and out of earshot of other children.

Teachers and coaches must remain constantly mindful of the embarrassment factor for the Prestige Child. Being the last one picked in a game or activity can be devastating for her. Avoid placing the child in this position by picking the names from a hat or establishing permanent teams. Again, no child enjoys being embarrassed in front of others, but the Prestige Child can be emotionally devastated by this humiliation.

Another characteristic of the Prestige Child is her high degree of sensitivity to corrections on tests, homework, and written assignments. The child may become so fixated on the few questions and problems that are marked "incorrect" that she may overlook the fact that she got the great majority of the answers correct and has, indeed, made good progress.

When correcting this child's behavior, the adult should make an effort to begin and conclude the meeting in a positive way. The reprimand or criticism should be sandwiched between positive and supportive comments.

For example:

"Ethan, I have seen you show real sensitivity in this class since September. When Josh broke his leg last month, you were the only one of the boys who helped Josh carry his books and get to lunch every single day. The other kids got tired of helping, but you stuck by Josh for the entire month. I was very impressed by this, and even Josh's mom mentioned your kindness to me.

"But I am concerned by the way that you have been treating the new boy, Aaron. You have been hassling him on the playground and you purposely tripped him in the cafeteria yesterday.

"I will not tolerate this. Your behavior toward Aaron is simply unfair and unacceptable. If you choose not to befriend Aaron, that's fine with me. Just stay away from him.

"Ethan, I know that you are capable of better behavior. You have shown yourself to be a kind and mannerly boy. I expect to see that type of behavior when and where Aaron is involved."

By using this format, the Prestige Child is far more likely to be responsive to your instruction and message.

Be mindful of the use of sarcasm with the Prestige Child. Again, an offhanded, mild put-down that would not impact upon most children can be devastating and hurtful for this child.

Perfectionism

It is important to reinforce with the child the fact that errors and mistakes are a fundamental and inevitable aspect of the learning process. Characteristically, the Prestige Child overreacts to failure of any type. Explain to him that learning can occur only when mistakes are identified and analyzed. I once told a math student of mine, "I cannot begin to teach you *until* you have made a mistake. If you continue to solve all the problems correctly, I have no idea when and where to begin my instruction. Once a mistake is made, I can review and explore the error and determine what your needs are. No mistakes—no instruction."

The adult can also use role modeling to demonstrate the appropriate response to failure. I once had a student who consistently overreacted to his mistakes and errors. Even the most minor error or miscue on his part was viewed as a disaster. In point of fact, he was far more demanding of himself than were his parents, his teachers, or his coaches. I discussed this issue with him often and continually urged him to "lighten up" and to try to be his own best friend. I reminded him that he was far less forgiving of his mistakes than were his teachers. He once tore a paper up because he got one math problem incorrect. I asked him how he would feel about his math teacher if *she* destroyed one of his papers because of one error. He agreed that this would be inappropriate, but he continued to overreact to every error, misstep, or miscue that he made.

I was quite frustrated by my failed attempts to impact his perfectionism. He was in my seventh-period tutorial class and one morning I approached him in the hallway. "Remember that Robert Frost poem I told you about? The one that we couldn't find in the library?" I asked excitedly. "Well, I found it! I was in a used bookstore last night and I found an anthology that contained the poem. I brought it to school today and I *can't wait* to read it to you seventh period. You'll love it."

I ran into him several times in the hallways that day and each time I reminded him about the poem. We both entered the seventh-period class with great excitement and anticipation and took our seats. With a colossal fanfare and ceremony, I opened my briefcase to retrieve the much-anticipated anthology. The briefcase was empty.

"Oh, darn!" I said. "I guess I forgot the book at home. Oh, well. We have plenty of other things that we can do. Let's take a look at the essay that you have been working on. . . ."

The boy looked at me incredulously. I had made a mistake. But life goes on. I did not become upset, angry, enraged, exasperated, or irate. I didn't curse or swear. I didn't lose control or let it set a negative tone for the seventh-period class. I just went on. There are some magical moments in the life of a teacher when you know that you have made a breakthrough. That was such a moment. From that day on, the boy demonstrated a far more realistic view of errors, mistakes, and oversights. We *all* make them. The key to success lies in the way that we react to them.

Awards and the Prestige Child

This child is motivated by rewards, awards, certificates, plaques, testimonials, commendations, and tributes. Unlike the Power Child or the Project Child, she cares desperately about the opinions of others and is greatly motivated by public recognition of her successes.

This child will be motivated by anything that can be magnetized to her family's refrigerator. Look for opportunities to present awards and commendations to her. Using desktop publishing, a teacher can design and distribute a limitless supply of these trophies. You can grant awards and certificates for:

- Achievement
- Outstanding effort
- Cooperation
- Class participation
- Positive behavior
- Initiative
- Effort
- Attendance
- Volunteering
- Acts of kindness
- Helpfulness
- Accomplishment
- Assistance
- Punctuality

Provide and create audiences for the Prestige Child's work by having her read her writings aloud in front of the class or by allowing her to show her projects to others.

Leadership

Similar to the Power Child, the Prestige Child has a strong need to be a leader. However, many children have significant misconceptions and misinformation regarding the nature of leadership. I have conducted numerous leadership seminars with school-aged children and never cease to be amazed by the misunderstandings that many students hold about leadership. They simply do not understand the basic tenets of leadership and do not appreciate the traits or behaviors of effective and efficient leaders. The Prestige Child who does not understand the underlying principles of authority will be greatly frustrated in his attempts to secure and maintain positions of leadership.

Among the most common leadership misconceptions held by students are:

STUDENT MISCONCEPTIONS ABOUT MOTIVATION

Leaders are lucky. They don't have to listen to *anybody*. In actuality, a good leader must listen to *everybody*. An effective leader must solicit and consider the input from constituents at all levels of the organization.

Being a leader means that you are the *best*. In reality, being a true leader means that you are the best at getting *others* to be at their best. The leader must be an ongoing source of information and inspiration to his colleagues, but he is not necessarily the most skilled or the most talented. A principal is the leader of a school and is in charge of the classrooms, curricula, cafeteria, and physical plant. However, he need not be the top teacher in the school. It is not necessary that he be able to cook macaroni and cheese for two hundred or fix a leaky toilet. He doesn't need to be the best; he needs to consistently bring out the best in his staff.

Leaders can do anything they want. In fact, leaders have a sacred responsibility to protect and defend the best interests of the organization and its various constituents. If these interests are to be served, the leader must continuously and seriously consider all actions that he takes. The high visibility of his position requires the leader's behavior to be exemplary because he serves as a role model and a representative of the organization. In effect, the leader *loses* autonomy and freedom when he becomes a leader. Leaders are well advised to remember this sage advice: "Those who are in the highest places and who have the most power have the least liberty—because they are the most observed."

The leader needs to know everything. In actuality, the leader cannot know everything, but must serve as a resource for her colleagues and must know how and where to secure information that is needed by others. One of the most valuable phrases in leadership is "I don't know the answer, but I know where to find it."

The leader needs to do everything for others. One of the main functions of a leader is to teach others and enhance their independence. In the words of the ancient Chinese proverb, "If you *give* a man a fish, he eats for a day. If you *teach* a man to fish, he eats for a lifetime."

Being a leader is cool. You get lots of glory. This is true to a degree. But the leader who eagerly basks in the glory of victory must be equally willing to shoulder the blame when errors or misjudgments occur.

The frustration of leadership is that you are not judged or evaluated solely on your own performance. Rather, you are judged by the performance of your colleagues and staff. When a National Football League team has a poor season, the coach—not the players—gets fired.

If the Prestige Child aspires to achieve and maintain a leadership position, he must come to understand and embrace the true nature of leadership and authority.

Below are some classic quotations about leadership from some of history's greatest and most accomplished leaders. Use them to explain, foster, and promote leadership skills with your students.

- Compassion is the basis of all leadership.—Arthur Schopenhauer
- A rock pile ceases to be a rock pile the moment a single man contemplates it, bearing within him the image of a cathedral.—David McGannon
- Managers are people who do things right; leaders are people who do the right thing.—B. Nanus, business leader
- In order to lead people, you must stand behind them.—Peter Drucker, author
- Great humility should come from others having faith in you.—Dag Hammarskjöld
- The reward of the general is not a bigger tent, but responsibility and leadership.—Oliver Wendell Holmes Sr.
- Leadership does not mean choosing sides, it means bringing sides together.—Jesse Jackson
- You can delegate authority, but you cannot delegate responsibility by delegating the task to somebody else. If you picked the wrong person, the responsibility is *yours*—not his.—Robert Krause, author
- Of a true leader, when his job is finished, his work done, they will say, "We did this ourselves."—Lao-tzu
- I start with the premise that the function of leadership is to produce more leaders, not more followers.—Ralph Nader
- Example is leadership, leadership is example.—Albert Schweitzer
- A leader is not a person who loves to control others, but someone who carries water for his people so that they can get on with their work.—Robert Townsend

FINDING AND USING ISLANDS OF COMPETENCE

Here is a language quiz for you. In the English language there is only one nine-letter word that has only one vowel. Can you think of it? It is a word that is crucial to the success and progress of Prestige Children. The word is "strengths."

The most effective way to motivate the Prestige Child is to find and celebrate her specific areas of skill, affinity, and strengths. These children who feel so inadequate in many areas of their lives must come to realize that they have significant power and potency in some areas of their development that can and should be recognized and rejoiced over.

My friend and colleague, noted author Dr. Robert Brooks, refers to these skills as "islands of competence" in his book *The Self-Esteem Teacher.* He believes strongly that parents and professionals must search out these areas of a child's ability and competence. Further, these skill areas should be noted and celebrated. This provides the child with an anchor that enables him to truly believe in himself, his competencies, and his future.

Dr. Brooks describes these skills as "islands in a sea of self-perceived inadequacy." He uses this analogy to remind parents, teachers, and coaches of the hope and respect that we must hold for young people who struggle daily with academic and social problems. Each of these children has areas of strength and competency. It is our responsibility to find these areas and highlight them to the child and his peers. By experiencing success and progress in these strength areas, the children begin to develop greater confidence in other areas as well. Much in the way that failure breeds failure, success breeds success. Progress and praise in one area leads to increased effort and self-assurance in other areas.

Early in my career, I served as a supervisor at a summer residential camp in central Massachusetts that served children with learning disabilities. The youngsters were involved in intensive remedial courses in the morning, and the afternoon featured traditional camping lessons and activities such as horseback riding, swimming, archery, and crafts.

In September, I received a telephone call from a Red Cross swim instructor from Ohio. He told me that he had been working with two boys with learning disabilities and had been unable to teach them to swim. These same boys went to our summer program for six weeks and returned home as intermediate swimmers. He wanted to know what specialized instructional program we'd used in order to teach swimming skills to kids with learning disorders.

He was disappointed in my response. I told him that we used a standard Red Cross learn-to-swim program taught by certified Red Cross instructors. The reason that the boys were successful at our camp was simply their improved self-esteem and confidence. They had a history of failure in reading and other academic areas. They came to our program and received highly individualized remedial instruction. Suddenly, they were progressing. They were moving forward. They were learning to read and write. They began to feel more confident and self-assured. Self-confidence in one area spilled over into another. ("I never thought that I would be able to learn how to read, but now I am reading! I never thought that I could learn how to swim either. . . . Hmmm. Maybe I'll give *that* another shot!")

For the first time, they entered the pool *feeling that they would succeed*! Their newfound success in reading had greatly enhanced their confidence and this had generalized to another setting. Again, success breeds success.

When dealing with the Prestige Child, the teacher must serve as a talent scout. You must search for his island of competence, and once you have found it, you must spotlight it and celebrate it. I advise parents that if your child's solitary strength is his ability to use a Phillips-head screwdriver, every Thursday before he returns from school, Mom should go around the house and loosen every screw she can find. As soon as the boy gets off the school bus, she should hand him the screwdriver and say, "Go to it, champ, because *nobody* tightens screws like you do!"

Although the above strategy is somewhat tongue-in-cheek, it illustrates Dr. Brooks's islands concept. Every child has interests, strengths, and affinities. For the Prestige Child, adults must discover these strengths and highlight them at home and in the classroom. By doing so, the child begins to gain confidence and self-assuredness. But perhaps more important, the success in his strength area begins to generalize to other areas of his life.

Lest you believe that the islands concept creates an artificial cocoon for the child, let us consider the adult world for a moment. Each of us is allowed to work daily within our island of competence. As adults, we are permitted and encouraged to select a profession or an occupation that matches our skills, strengths, and interests. The person with math skills will gravitate toward accounting or engineering. The person with an affinity for writing becomes an author or a journalist. As adults, we are *specialists* and tend to select an area of specialty that makes maximum use of our strength areas and downplays our areas of weakness.

Students have no such option when in elementary, middle, or high school. Children are expected to be *generalists.* They are required—by the nature of the curriculum—to be proficient in language, math, the sciences, and history. They are not allowed to specialize until college. This is questionable, I believe, for *all* children but is particularly problematic for the Prestige Child. She languishes daily in her ocean of failure and frustration, and desperately needs to find success and solace in her islands of strength.

As you search for your child's islands of competence, use the child herself as your primary guide. Ask her what her strength areas are. How does she spend her spare time? What activities make her happiest? When does she feel most fulfilled and successful? What sorts of activities make her feel relaxed? What is she most proud of? When does she feel most knowledgeable and important?

There are many interest inventories available on the Internet or from educational publishers. These questionnaires are designed to determine the child's hobbies, passions, and affinities. The questions on these surveys are often somewhat dry and clinical. Supplement these questionnaires with "outside the box" questions such as:

- If you had an extra ten dollars, how would you spend it?
- If you had an extra thousand dollars, how would you spend it?
- What is your favorite part of the day?
- If you had one wish, what would it be?
- When do you feel the most relaxed?

- If you could meet a famous person, who would you like to meet?
- What magazines do you read?
- What is your favorite store in the mall?
- What would your perfect three-course meal be?

These questions are enjoyable for the students to answer, and the answers are often insightful and enlightening.

Parents, former teachers, and siblings can also be valuable resources as you search for the child's strengths and affinities. Dr. Brooks reports that some school systems begin each child's educational planning meeting with a discussion of the child's particular islands of competence and of the methods that can be used to spotlight these strengths. The children in these systems are in extraordinarily good hands.

GIVING RESPONSIBILITY TO ENHANCE PRESTIGE

> "Never help a child with a task at which he can succeed."
>
> —MARIA MONTESSORI

One effective way to provide the Prestige Child with the status that he needs is to give him responsibility. If the child feels that he is making a valued and valuable contribution at home and in the classroom, he is likely to be highly motivated. These children enjoy the status of having others dependent upon them. This makes them feel important, valuable, and indispensable. They have a strong need to be needed. Many children with special needs are greatly dependent upon parents, teachers, siblings, and others. It is extraordinarily meaningful and motivating for them to have the opportunity to have *others* dependent on *them*.

Early in my career, I had a student in my class named Christopher. He attended the residential school where I was employed. He was often disruptive in class and was extraordinarily self-centered.

He often bullied younger and smaller students and made cruel comments about the idiosyncrasies or failings of classmates.

I tried innumerable techniques to increase his sensitivity, but none of the strategies made a meaningful or lasting change in his behavior. At the time, I was coordinating an after-school program in which I accompanied a group of students to a state hospital in the area. Our students worked one-on-one with male residents of the hospital who had profound mental impairments. These men's severe disabilities prevented them from living or working in the community. Each Thursday, our students would travel to the hospital and work with the residents for two hours. They completed simple craft projects together, but the underlying purpose of the visit was to provide these lonely, solitary men with a couple hours of companionship and attention. Some very remarkable relationships developed between the residents and our students, and the men would often sit by the windows for hours every Thursday afternoon, looking for the arrival of our distinctive yellow van.

Chris was particularly disruptive in class one Thursday, and I told him that he should return to my classroom at the end of the day to make up the time that he had wasted.

"You can't make me make up the time today," he said smugly. "You gotta do that hospital thing you do."

He was right. He had me. Impulsively, I said, "Well, then you'll come with us this afternoon."

On the van ride, Chris complained loudly and often about the situation. He cited the United States Constitution several times, regaling me and his van mates about the American tradition of banning "cruel and unusual punishment," and reminded me that he knew a lawyer in his neighborhood.

When we arrived at the hospital, I assigned Chris to work with Hubert, one of the older residents. Hubert was in his late fifties and was morbidly obese, a result of his half-century-long sedentary lifestyle. He had huge meaty hands, and arthritis made his large fingers particularly painful and difficult to manipulate. He had limited language but had a great laugh and a putty face with limitless exaggerated facial expressions. Another boy had been working with Hubert to make a simple pillow, but the boy had had to leave the after-school program because of a schedule conflict. This left Hubert with a half-finished pillow and no Thursday afternoon partner.

Chris looked horrified as he sat next to this mountain of a man. Hubert took the pillow, needle, and thread from the plastic Walt Disney World bag where he stored his few precious possessions. I explained to Chris that he should make three stitches for Hubert as a demonstration because Hubert often forgot the process from one week to the next. He should then have Hubert make three stitches, followed by Christopher making three, and on and on. This procedure allowed Hubert to receive continual reminders of the process. The strategy also ensured that the pillow would be completed by June, as Hubert's stitches often took him ten minutes to complete because of his physical limitations.

Reluctantly, Chris began the process. I observed the two closely throughout the two-hour visit. Initially, Chris was reluctant to sit too close to Hubert and never touched the man's hands to guide him as he stitched. Chris seemed repulsed by the entire situation. I thought, *Well, at least Chris will behave himself in class on* Thursdays *from now on.*

About an hour into the session, I heard Hubert's hearty laugh from across the room. Chris and he were reared back in their seats and howling in laughter—together. By the end of the session, they were smiling at each other and Chris was gently guiding Hubert's hand as he stitched. Chris completed nine stitches that day and Hubert completed six. As we left, Chris gently touched Hubert's shoulder, but he did not respond to the man's guttural question, "Coming again?"

When we boarded the van, I asked Chris if he wished to return to the hospital next week. "No way!" he responded. "I've done my time. I'm done." It seemed that the human moments he and Hubert had shared were fleeting and temporary.

The following Monday, Chris approached me in the hallway. "Mr. Lavoie," he began, "if you don't have anyone to work with Hubert this week, I guess I could go. I'm not doing much else that day."

That Thursday—and for fifteen Thursdays—I watched Chris and Hubert work, smile, and laugh together. Chris was a natural. Patient. Calm. Supportive. Reinforcing. Gentle. I even began to see some of those traits generalize to Chris's behavior in the classroom, in the dormitory, and on the playing field. A colleague asked me, "What's with Chris? He's been great lately. What medication is he on?"

One dose of Hubert; apply once a week.

The final Thursday session was on the final day of school in June. As anyone who has worked in a residential school can attest, the final day of school is a very special one.

Last-minute packing, impromptu parties, and great collegial fun are the hallmarks of the day, and students look forward to the final evening with great anticipation. Our festivities begin with a special dinner at six P.M.

At the end of the hospital visit, the students were putting the finishing touches on their respective craft projects and bidding farewell to their partners. The good-byes were a bit rushed because it was nearly four o'clock and we had an hour-long ride back to school and needed to prepare for the long-anticipated farewell dinner with the other students and staff.

All the projects were done and the students were preparing to board the vans. Only Chris and Hubert were not finished, and the other boys began to hassle Chris and remind him of the tight schedule that they had to follow. Chris, who would normally react harshly to their reprimands, remained focused on the task and continued to work patiently with Hubert as they completed the final stitches. It was 4:10 . . . 4:15 . . . 4:25 . . . 4:30.

Finally I interrupted. "Chris, we need to get moving. You'll have to finish up now or we will all miss the dinner back at school."

"We have four more stitches, Mr. Lavoie. Just four more. Hubert has one of his to do, and then I do the final three. Give us a few more minutes."

I watched as Hubert slowly and methodically completed his stitch. Chris grabbed the pillow and nimbly completed two stitches and began the third and final one.

Suddenly, he stopped. He gently handed the pillow to Hubert. "This is the last stitch, Hub. This is *your* pillow. *You* ought to finish it." We watched together as Hubert labored over the final step. His face beamed as he placed the cherished pillow into the Disney bag.

Rarely had I seen a more sensitive, insightful, selfless, and compassionate gesture from one human being to another.

That evening after dinner, I stopped by Chris's dorm room. I told him that I would never forget what I saw him do that day and asked him why he responded so positively to our Thursday afternoon sessions.

"Hubert needed me, Mr. Lavoie. No one else ever needed me before."

The need to be needed provided Christopher with the status and prestige that he was unable to find in the classroom or on the playing field.

This need can be met by assigning the child classroom chores. The Prestige Child will likely be very willing to complete these chores and they can even be used as rewards. ("Chad, if you get your homework done three days in a row, I will let you clean out the classroom fish tank.") Unlike Power Children or Prize Children, Prestige Children take great joy and pride in completing responsibilities that please and assist parents and teachers. The completion of these tasks enables the child to feel important.

The astute parent can design and assign household chores that can accomplish two purposes. These specialized chores can meet the child's prestige needs while simultaneously teaching and reinforcing specific perceptual or conceptual skills.

For example, if the child needs reinforcement in the area of *sequencing,* assign her chores that require a significant amount of cyclical planning (e.g., setting the table, preparing shopping lists, planning meals).

Again, the assigned tasks and responsibilities must be meaningful and important. The child must feel that she is making a substantial contribution to the family and the classroom. This valuable involvement will do much to boost the child's sense of pride and accomplishment.

Because the Prestige Child often does not receive adequate status from his peers, he may gravitate to younger children because he receives automatic eminence by virtue of his age and experience. I once worked with a Prestige Child in a middle school who invariably chose to play with children in the fifth grade. It seems that he was viewed as a "loser" by his middle-school classmates, but the fifth graders greatly admired him merely because he attended the "big school." He regaled them with tales about lockers, dances, cafeterias, meals, and assemblies and was a hero in their eyes. He received the prestige from the younger children that he did not receive from his classmates. His parents were concerned about his new friends and felt that he should limit his relationships to kids his own age. Because he was handling this social situation quite appropriately, and was not bullying or intimidating the younger students in any way, I urged Mom and Dad *not* to intervene. He was receiving a much-needed self-esteem boost from the fifth graders, and these relationships were fulfilling his need to feel important.

In fact, Dr. Brooks recommends that buddy systems be designed within schools that allow and encourage students to serve as mentors for younger students. I consulted with a school where each sixth grader was partnered with a kindergarten student and the children would work on craft or recreational activities together. The program was extraordinarily effective. It was mutually beneficial in that it provided the younger children with guidance, assistance, and assurance, and simultaneously provided the older student with prestige, status, and a self-esteem boost.

PRESTIGE AND ACHIEVEMENT

The Prestige Child is obsessed with achievement and can become upset and discouraged when she fails to achieve a task or when she fails at an assignment. Because of her prestige needs, she may misunderstand or misinterpret the meaning of achievement. She may believe that achievement means total success . . . 100 percent . . . A+. Anything less than that may be perceived as failure. The child views "achievement" as synonymous with "perfection."

The adult should attempt to change the child's perception of achievement.

Achievement = Learning
Effort
Improvement
Completion

If the child learns, tries, improves on, or completes a task, he has achieved. I used to keep this list laminated under my blotter in my office. Whenever a student came to me discouraged about his lack of achievement, I would take out the list and use it as a basis for discussion.

"Nathan, you are upset because you received a B minus on your math test. You studied very hard and you felt that you could have gotten an A. You feel that you achieved and accomplished nothing. Well, let's take a look at the list. Did you *learn* anything when studying for the test?"

"Well, yeah. I never knew how to invert fractions before."

"Good. So you learned something. Did you *try hard* to prepare for the test?"

"Wicked hard! I didn't even play basketball with my brother the other night. I studied the math for an extra hour!"

"Great! Then you accomplished terrific *effort*. Did you *improve* in any way?"

"Yes. I got a C on a previous test. So I guess that I improved."

"Way to go . . . and did you *complete* the test?"

"Yeah. There were twenty problems and I finished them all."

"Terrific. I guess you didn't get the grade that you hoped for but you surely *achieved* a lot. Keep up the good work."

Everyone needs to feel important, but for Prestige Children, this need is particularly significant. They depend heavily on feedback from others and are easily embarrassed. They need consistent encouragement and opportunities to showcase and celebrate their talents. Teachers and parents should remember that the Prestige Child is easily discouraged and is often unable to evaluate his own skills and performance without the assistance and guidance of an adult. This child may also have difficulty establishing and maintaining peer relationships because his classmates are unable to understand and meet his prestige needs.

8

The Child Motivated by Prizes

"Our purpose in life is not to get ahead of other people, but to get ahead of ourselves."

—M. J. BABCOCK

WITHOUT DOUBT, the most commonly used motivational approach in America's schools is the classroom-wide reward system. This strategy involves the use of charts and checklists that record student performance and progress. The success and growth of each student is rewarded by predetermined prizes or privileges. The procedures of the reward system clearly states how a child can gain or lose points and how those accumulated points can be "spent" in order to gain the aforementioned prizes. Some reward systems are designed to promote individual progress while other systems have students working toward prizes for the entire class (e.g., a pizza party).

It is uncommon to walk into an American classroom without seeing a wall containing the intricate rules and regulations for the teacher's reward system. Throughout the day, students comment intensely on the system. ("Do I get a star for doing this?" "How come Brenda got two stars and I got just one?" "How many more stars do I need to get a homework pass?")

Of course, many of the students in the class truly love the reward system. It provides them with tangible rewards for accomplishing tasks that they would have been willing and able to do for free! Most students who respond well to classroom reward systems are intrinsically motivated. They enjoy doing schoolwork and are relatively accomplished academically, so the tangible rewards that they receive are a delightful bonus. However, if the reward system were to be discontinued, their motivation would not wane significantly.

Let's consider for a moment the students who do *not* enjoy or delight in the reward system. These are students who struggle with academics through no fault or choice of their own. Their limited academic skills often cause them to fall behind the others in the pursuit of prizes. They feel frustration and anxiety about the reward system, and therefore, it does not have the desired effect of enhancing the child's motivation. In fact, it may well have a negative impact upon their ability and willingness to apply themselves. As a result, the tone and climate in the classroom is damaged as well.

As we discussed in chapter 4, a reward system relies on two basic (and perhaps *faulty*) premises:

Premise 1. All behavior can be observed, measured, and evaluated. By rewarding and reinforcing an improvement in behavior, the behavior will continue to grow and develop.

Premise 2. When a student fails to make progress, it is due to a lack of motivation and effort. If given adequate incentives, he will apply himself and make progress.

The first premise stems from the work of the behavioral psychologists of the mid-twentieth century. Their endless experiments with lab rats, pigeons, and other species clearly demonstrated that behavior could be changed and improved by rewarding each step of progress toward the goal. By using this strategy, rats negotiated complex mazes, dogs salivated at the ringing of bells, and chickens shot Ping-Pong balls into hoops.

The success of these experiments was widely touted and practitioners soon began applying these concepts to the treatment of human beings, particularly children. For decades now, teachers have attempted to modify, adjust, improve, and manipulate student behavior by using these methods. ("If you're good, you get this. If you're not, you get that.")

Throughout my career I have disallowed the use of school-wide incentives or demerit programs in the schools that I have run and in the schools where I've consulted. Further, I view individualized reward systems with great suspicion, misgivings, and skepticism.

We can do better.

The key weakness of the first premise lies in the experimenter's relationship with the lab rat, the dog, or the chicken. The experimenter cares about only one thing—that the rat learn how to negotiate the maze. He has no interest or investment in how the rat feels about the task or the experimenter. The experimenter does not care about the rat's self-esteem, his future plans, his sense of independence, or his new dependency on the lab bell to control his performance. Once the maze task is mastered, the rat ceases to exist in the researcher's mind. The experimenter is interested in only one thing—measurable progress on a short-term task.

I am not stating that children who are placed on reward systems are treated like lab animals. But as practitioners, we must remember that the entire premise of reward systems is based upon the behaviorist's belief that motivation can be fostered by the application of reward/punishment strategies.

However, the second underlying premise of reward systems is probably the most important and the most damaging. Any sort of reward or incentive strategy makes the basic assumption that the child is cognitively, perceptually, and developmentally able to accomplish the assigned task, but is simply unwilling or unmotivated to do so. If he is given some sort of incentive to complete the task, he will.

For children with diagnosed neurologically based learning, language, and attentional problems, this is simply unfounded. The child's inability to complete the task may well be a result of his neurological deficits, and no amount of coaxing, cajoling, wheedling, inciting, or rewarding is going to enable him to do it.

For many years early in my career, I conducted the F.A.T. City (Frustration, Anxiety, and Tension) workshop with groups of parents, teachers, and caregivers. The workshop, which later became a best-selling video, enabled adults to experience a learning disability first-hand through a series of simulations and activities. One of the tasks required them to identify a photograph that had been altered to "trick" the neurological system. Even though it was a photograph of a common and easily identifiable object (a cow), the photo was impossible to recognize until you were provided with a series of hints that allowed your visual system to perceive it.

When I conducted the workshop, I would routinely carry a hundred-dollar bill with me and I would promise to give the bill to anyone who could identify the picture. Over the ten years that I conducted the workshop, I never gave away the bill! Certainly, the participants were *motivated* to identify the photo, but not even the offer of a hundred dollars—or a thousand, or ten thousand—could enable them to do so. Even the greatest reward cannot enable a person to accomplish a task of which he is incapable.

Suppose someone held your home and your family for ransom and told you that they would be returned only if you could—immediately—count to one hundred in Swahili, recite the entire collection of Shakespeare's sonnets in correct chronological order, or scale the outside of Chicago's Sears Tower. Certainly, you would be highly motivated, but you would be unable to complete the tasks.

Again, reward systems assume that a student does not perform because he doesn't want to. This faulty premise ignores the fact that the child's progress and performance may be hindered by learning, language, and attentional disorders.

There is a good deal of available research that refutes the widely held belief that reward programs are an effective strategy to motivate children.

The various studies had the following findings:

RESEARCH ON REWARD SYSTEMS

- Rewards can divert attention from the actual task; the reward becomes the goal, not the successful mastery of the task.
- Rewards can discourage risk taking.
- When a reward is withheld, children often view this as a form of punishment.
- In order to ensure the receipt of a reward, students often select tasks of minimal difficulty when provided with a choice of activities.
- Rewards can actually undermine a child's interest and motivation related to a task.
- The progress made by students in a reward program is often temporary and short-lived.
- When the reward system is discontinued, the student's motivation wanes significantly.
- Reward systems can impact negatively on both winners and losers. The child who fails publicly in a reward system faces embarrassment, humiliation, rejection, and isolation. Interestingly, the winner may also have some negative self-esteem effects because she may come to feel that her value is rooted solely in her ability to be superior to others. She may become overly anxious about maintaining this status.
- Optional learning environments are characterized by emotional safety, positive social bonding, low stress, control over one's learning, and hope. Reward systems may be the antitheses of these traits.
- Reward systems do little to assist the child in being a creative, self-directed, independent learner. In fact, this strategy may decrease his ability to monitor and assess his own performance by making him totally dependent upon the input and evaluation of his teachers.
- The competitive nature of reward systems can negatively impact the relationships and cooperation between and among students.
- Rewards are often used as the sole incentive for students to master a curriculum.

- By giving tangible rewards to students on a regular basis, the teacher is fostering and enhancing their *extrinsic* motivation. They view the new knowledge as a means to an end ("If I memorize these math facts, I can pick a prize from the prize chest"), rather than as an end in itself. Their natural curiosity is also stunted because they have no reason to pursue additional information. They simply want to master the minimal amount of material required to receive the reward.

These studies make a compelling argument in favor of reexamining our national fascination with reward systems. If this approach discourages risk taking, causes classroom discord, deflates creativity, and has only a temporary impact, perhaps we should look for more effective and lasting strategies, or at least look to improve reward systems in a way that makes their results more effective and lasting.

First, we should examine the reasons why reward systems are currently so popular. To be candid, *reward systems are easy to implement.*

If a child is not completing his homework consistently, it is a great deal of hard work to investigate, identify, and repair the problem. Are the assignments too difficult? Does he have a short-term memory problem that causes him to forget the material that he learned earlier in the day? Does he have ineffective study skills? Is he having difficulty at home?

A much simpler "solution" is to place all of the responsibility on the child by devising a reward system that will respond to him only when he meets expectations.

Reward systems are also an effective alternative to creating an exciting, inspiring, motivating curriculum. If a teacher cannot create a math curriculum that stimulates her students, they are unlikely to invest themselves in studying and mastering the material and will likely become disruptive and inattentive. So the teacher will create artificial motivation by connecting the child's progress in the curriculum to some sort of reward system. As a result, the child participates and cooperates in order to win a prize, but his interest in math is fleeting and secondary.

QUESTIONABLE PRACTICES RELATED TO REWARD SYSTEMS

There are many common reward practices that are simply ineffective, or in some cases counterproductive. For example, many teachers use "homework passes" as a reward for students. One of the best-selling items in any teacher supply store is the pad with the word "homework" circled in red and with a line through it, the international symbol for "no." These passes are given to "deserving" students as rewards and can be redeemed in order to excuse a student from doing a homework assignment of his choice.

I believe that this practice sends some very disturbing messages to the child. First, it implies that homework is bad and that you need not do homework if you are good. It says that homework is like a punishment; no homework is a reward. In reality, homework should be a significant and integral part of the curriculum. It is a very effective vehicle designed to review and reinforce skills and concepts learned in class. Well-planned homework also enhances the child's study habits and organizational skills. By using homework as a punishment, the teacher communicates that homework is less important and valuable than it actually is.

Second, by telling the students that any homework assignment of their choosing can be eliminated, the teacher is, in effect, saying that the homework assignments are not a critical part of the curriculum and that a child can be successful in that curriculum without completing the homework assignments.

Another reason why reward systems are often ineffective is that they are overly complicated. The rules and regulations related to the system are intricate and beyond the student's ability to fully understand. These teacher-made systems often feature a complex labyrinth of points, demerits, bonuses, and exemptions. It is unlikely that a child will invest himself in a system that he does not fully understand.

Many reward systems feature payoffs that are in the distant future. The child must wait several weeks before the reward is granted.

Many children who struggle with learning have great difficulty delaying gratification, and a system with a long-term reward would not be particularly motivating. These students benefit from immediate feedback and reinforcement.

Many reward systems fail because the rewards offered are inappropriate or of little interest to the child. A ten-year-old once described the elaborate reward system that his teacher had designed, "If I do my homework for two weeks and if I don't get into any trouble at recess, the teacher will give me an eraser shaped like a race car. I can get a bag of ten of those at the Dollar Store."

Still other reward systems are rendered ineffective by the use of demerits. One teacher issued a checkbook to each student and an account of two hundred "dollars." Whenever a child misbehaved or failed to do an assignment, she was required to "write a check" to the teacher from her account. The amount of the check correlated to the severity of the infraction. At the end of the month, the student could "spend" her remaining funds on trinkets at the classroom store. At the beginning of the semester, Audrey had a particularly difficult week and depleted her account to ten dollars. Going forward, there was little incentive for her to participate positively in the class. Most youngsters with a history of learning problems do not operate effectively when behind the eight ball.

The most significant mistake that is made with reward systems is to rely on the system—in and of itself—to effectively monitor and modify the behavior and academic performance of the students. The effectiveness of any sort of reward system lies in its connection to a well-planned, responsive curriculum and the creation of a classroom climate that provides the students with structure, acceptance, support, and challenge.

Rather than continually giving tangible rewards to students, the teacher should attempt to create a classroom environment that provides the students with academic work that is slightly above their individual mastery level. Provide them with assignments that are challenging but not overwhelming; imposing but not impossible; difficult but not demoralizing. Include occasional review work that allows the child to experience success. In your mind, substitute the word "celebrate" for the word "reward." Develop a teaching style and an interactive approach in the classroom that rejoices in, recognizes, and reinforces students' success, but does not feel obligated to *reward* students' success. Allow success and progress to be their own reward. Acknowledge and recognize the child's efforts and progress, but focus on the learning, not on the reward.

I believe strongly that educators should examine and rethink our ongoing love affair with reward systems. Under these systems, rights (e.g., recess) come to be viewed as privileges to be earned, classroom climates become chaotic, students develop attitudes of entitlement, and academic progress is temporary. There is a significant body of research that indicates that these reward systems are ineffective and counterproductive . . . and yet they continue to enjoy widespread popularity in our classrooms.

EFFECTIVE REWARD SYSTEMS

Although classroom and school-wide reward systems appear to be minimally effective and can create a culture that is hostile, competitive, and divisive, there are steps that a teacher can take that can make tangible rewards a motivator for most students most of the time.

First, grant *intermittent, unpublished* rewards. Occasionally, bring in baked goods for a treat, have a popcorn party, or take a surprise in-school field trip to a favorite spot in the building. Explain that the treat is being given because "you all have worked so hard." The students will come to appreciate these occasional bonuses, just as a spouse would appreciate a surprise bouquet or an unexpected gift. Perhaps your class has a favorite activity (peer tutoring, videos, art projects, listening to music during seat work) that you could use as an occasional, unannounced reward. These favored activities generally involve social interaction between and among the students. These occasional, unplanned rewards were a staple in American schools—and an effective one—until the onslaught of reward systems in the 1980s.

Second, reward the students by providing them with an audience for their work. Everyone loves an audience. Allow them to read their essays to a class of younger children. Ask the principal (or secretary, janitor, or support staff) to come to your class to observe the students' work and comment on it. Post their work on a bulletin board in the hallway. Compile a collection of their compositions and send the class literary magazine to *all* the parents. These strategies can be extraordinarily reinforcing and motivational for students.

Third, divide large tasks (e.g., research papers, lengthy essays, science fair projects) into several distinct steps. Assess the child's performance on each individual step in the process. Recognize, reinforce, and reward his progress. Do not wait until the conclusion of the multistep process before recognizing his efforts. This intermittent reinforcement will do much to maintain the child's motivation throughout the process.

Fourth, select rewards that are meaningful to the individual students. Grant these rewards intermittently and spontaneously. ("Sean, you worked so hard on that science experiment today. I'd like you to stand at the front of the line for lunch.") Other simple, but meaningful, spontaneous classroom rewards include:

- Sitting with a friend
- Eating lunch with the teacher
- Selecting a story to have the teacher read to the class
- Sitting at the teacher's desk
- Passing out supplies
- Delivering notes to the office
- Watering the classroom plants
- Receiving a phone call at home
- Choosing a classroom game
- Drawing on the whiteboard
- Selecting a piece of music for the class to hear
- Taking home a class game for the night
- Helping in the cafeteria
- Raising/lowering the flag

- Inviting a guest speaker or entertainer
- Submitting extraordinary work to the local newspaper
- Decorating the bulletin board
- Operating the projector
- Getting a drink
- Spending free time in the art corner
- Looking at magazines
- Using the computer
- Making up a question for an upcoming quiz
- Doing a puzzle
- Running an errand
- Using a special pen or paper
- Playing a trivia game
- Caring for the class stuffed animal on the child's desk
- Filing
- Passing out paper
- Tending the aquarium
- Taking roll
- Maintaining the calendar
- Reporting the daily weather
- Composing the "Thought for the Day"

All of the suggestions listed are enjoyable but also have a social or academic objective. These activities are preferable to rewards that simply exempt students from academic work (e.g., a homework pass, extended recess, free time).

A fifth method that is effective in rewarding and motivating students involves making learning a fun and enjoyable experience. Charismatic teachers are willing and able to inject a degree of play into their curricula. We would do well to remember the sage words of psychologist Leo Buscaglia: *"It is paradoxical that many educators and parents differentiate between a time for learning and a time for play without seeing the vital connection between them."*

Gamelike formats can make academic material more interesting and stimulating. Presenting activities in the form of games such as

Jeopardy! Match Game, and *Concentration* can be an effective and highly motivating way to review class material. This fast-paced instruction often stimulates a child who tends to be poorly motivated. These games should not be highly competitive but should involve some gamelike strategy and a great deal of luck.

Reward systems are most effective when the child has input about the rewards that he will receive. Some teachers use a "reward deck" that consists of a stack of index cards containing various classroom rewards. If a teacher wishes to reward a child for extraordinary effort or performance, she gives the deck to the student and allows him to select his reward. You can add an element of mystery to the strategy by fanning the deck and having the child select a reward at random.

Rewards that are granted occasionally and intermittently can have a positive and lasting impact upon student motivation, but not if they are given as part of an elaborate, formal, structured system of rewards, demerits, rules, and regulations.

One technique I recommend to teachers is called *"Get a Chance to Take a Chance."* This strategy is a modification of the traditional "If you do your homework for five days in a row, you can select a prize from the prize closet" approach. This technique rewards a child's positive performance with the *opportunity* to receive a prize, and is comparable to the lotteries that are sponsored by many state governments. Buying a lottery ticket does not ensure that you will win the payout, it merely ensures that you will have an opportunity to win it.

The strategy is conducted like this: "Jake, if you do your homework satisfactorily for five days in a row, I will take you up to the gym and you can shoot five baskets. If you make three out of five, we will have a snack in the cafeteria."

Basically, you establish the contingency (e.g., "do your homework," "finish your classwork"), set up a task that involves an element of chance (e.g., cut cards, flip coins, shoot baskets), and identify a reward.

If the child is successful in the game of chance, he receives the reward; if he is unsuccessful, encourage him to meet the criteria again next week and assure him that this will give him another opportunity to "get a chance" to receive the reward. You may want to increase the contingency for the next week (e.g., "complete homework six days in a row").

This technique derails the direct connection between positive performance and receiving a prize.

Another effective reward system, if conducted carefully and sensitively, bestows group rewards. This strategy grants the entire class a reward for cooperative behavior or performance. For example, the teacher may establish a contingency that involves all members of the class (e.g., arriving on time for class ten days in a row; good recess behavior for fifteen days; successful desk inspections for two weeks). If the contingency is met, the class receives the reward. This technique often encourages the students to cooperate with one another and assist classmates who are having difficulty completing the task. One teacher told me that she would write the reward on the blackboard—"Ten minutes of extra computer time"—and, with great fanfare, would erase one letter of the reward whenever the students met part of the contingency. When the words were completely erased, the reward was given.

Care must be taken to assure that individual students do not become scapegoats if they fail to complete the task and prevent the class from receiving the prize. Carefully monitor the performance of any children who may have difficulty with the task and provide them with assistance or assign them buddies who can help. Some students who are particularly troubled may even try to sabotage the activity and cause their classmates to lose the reward.

These group rewards should always consist of educationally oriented activities. When selecting a reward or a reinforcer, the teacher or parent should be certain that the reward she has selected meets three important criteria:

> *Approval:* Does the adult approve of the reward? Do you feel comfortable that the reinforcer is appropriate?
>
> *Accessibility:* Is the reinforcer available to you in the event that the child earns the reward?

Attractiveness: Is the reward appealing to the student? Will the child be motivated to receive the reward?

Rewards need to be carefully selected if the intention is to increase children's motivation. There is an oft-repeated story that demonstrates how rewards or reinforcers can be used to decrease motivation.

An old man lived next to an empty lot where neighborhood boys enjoyed playing baseball from sunup to sundown. This loud activity was very disruptive for the old man, who was unable to get any peace and quiet during the day.

Being a retired psychologist, he devised a plan to make the lot an unattractive location for the boys' games.

He approached the boys and told them that he liked watching them play and hearing them enjoy themselves. He told them that if they came back the next day, he would give them each a dollar. The boys were delighted.

He did the same thing for three days in a row. On the fourth day, he told them that he could give them only fifty cents. The boys were a bit disappointed and upset, but they agreed to play. On the fifth day, the old man told them that he could give them only a quarter. Again, the boys unhappily agreed to play. On the sixth day, the old man's offer was a dime. The boys refused to play and never returned to the lot.

The story illustrates how an enjoyable activity can be made unattractive by offering an inappropriate reinforcer.

A young teacher at a school where I consulted was having great difficulty with the students' use of foul language. They seemed to feel that the language they used with their friends in the locker room, on the ball field, on the basketball court, or on the street corner was perfectly acceptable for the classroom. They continually "dropped the F-bomb" within the context of their classroom conversations and discussions.

The teacher tried several strategies to eliminate the behavior, with minimal success. As a last resort, she established a "cussing cup." She placed the cup on her desk and informed the students that they would be required to put a quarter in the cup every time they used the F word. At the end of the semester, the monies would be used to fund a class pizza party.

The day after she established the policy, she had an ugly in-class confrontation with a student. She told the student to leave the classroom and report to the principal. As he departed, he stopped at her desk, reached into his pocket, retrieved three quarters, and dropped them into the cup.

He turned to the teacher and said, "F*** you, f*** you, and f*** you!" Then casually exited.

There were two glaring mistakes made by the teacher in this situation. First, by using the "fines" to fund a class party, she was giving positive reinforcement (pizza) for negative behavior (swearing).

Second, she established a consequence that was not sufficiently averse or undesirable. For that student, at that point in time, it was well worth seventy-five cents to curse out the teacher in front of his peers. Further, she was left with few options regarding additional consequences because the student had *paid his fine,* as agreed.

Turning Work into Play

Rewards are designed to make schoolwork more enjoyable; in effect, to *turn work into play*. However, a poorly planned reward system can have a reverse effect and can turn *play into work.*

In a classic Stanford University study cited by author Alfie Kohn, researchers observed students in a preschool classroom. Whenever the children had completed the assigned work and had free time, they were allowed to go to one of the three tables to use the materials there. One table contained toy cars and trucks, the second had stuffed animals, and the third table featured a variety of art supplies.

The researchers identified nine children who frequented the art table at every opportunity. These kids obviously enjoyed drawing, sketching, and coloring.

The nine children were divided into three groups. The first group was brought into an office and each was asked to draw a picture.

When they were finished, the examiner thanked them and commented very positively upon the drawings.

The second group was then ushered into the office and each child was asked to draw a picture. When they were finished, the examiner made very positive comments about their drawings and gave each of them an attractive personalized certificate.

The third group entered the office and the children were shown the certificate and were told that they could receive a certificate if they drew a "nice picture." The children each completed a drawing and each was awarded a certificate.

The researchers then observed the children to determine which group of students returned to the art table during the free time. The results were intriguing.

The first group of students, who received verbal reinforcement but no tangible reward, always returned to the drawing table when they had free time.

The second group, who were given the certificate *after* they'd completed their drawings, also returned to the table whenever they had free time.

Interestingly, every time the experiment was replicated, several children in the third group *simply stopped going to the art table.*

What accounts for this reaction? In effect, the researchers took an activity that brought the children spontaneous and genuine enjoyment and converted it into work. Rather than turning *work* into *play,* they had turned *play* into *work.*

Adults tend to make this conversion when working with children. A cartoon in the *Phi Delta Kappan* magazine several years ago showed a group of children on a zoo field trip. While a large group of students was observing the elephant with their teacher, two boys had wandered off and were standing in front of the giraffe cage. One boy said to the other, "Don't let the teacher catch us looking at this or she'll make us write a composition about it."

Whenever a child demonstrates an interest in or affinity for an activity, the adults in her life often begin to place well-intentioned pressure on the child. For example, a five-year-old sees a commercial for an upcoming performance of *The Nutcracker Suite* and comments, "Ballet looks like fun." Mom reacts by enrolling the child in a five-session-a-week ballet school and purchasing several hundred dollars' worth of dance outfits. This frontal assault causes the child to lose all interest in the activity. Perhaps Mom should merely have bought her daughter a used tutu and allowed her to dance around the kitchen. Again, the mother managed to turn *play* into *work.*

Adults must also take care to ensure that they are reinforcing the behavior that they wish to reinforce. For example, suppose Petey procrastinates on his chores and fails to clean the garage for several days. On Friday night, Dad realizes that the garage must be cleaned for Saturday because the new water heater is being installed. Desperate, he tells Petey that he will give him twenty dollars to do the job on Friday night.

What behavior is Dad reinforcing? Cleaning the garage? Cooperation? No. He is reinforcing and rewarding *procrastination.*

It is obvious and widely accepted that many children do respond positively to reward systems, but teachers and parents must remain mindful of several subtleties regarding the use of formal reward systems.

Reward systems, *in and of themselves,* will not result in lasting and enhanced motivation. These systems must be supplemented by:

- Opportunities for students to make choices and decisions
- Positive, sincere, constructive feedback
- Supportive interpersonal student-teacher relationships
- Celebrations of the child's progress and effort
- Meaningful, motivating tasks
- A variety of creative, effective instructional techniques
- A degree of autonomy and responsibility for learning

Unless these characteristics exist in a classroom or home setting, any reward system will prove ineffective.

Reward systems generally motivate students who are confident and competent in the area or skill being covered. If the child feels that she is unlikely to earn the reward, her motivation will be limited and short-lived.

In order to maximize the effectiveness of a reward system, keep the program simple, allow students input regarding the rewards to be received, and continually decrease the value of the rewards or increase the requirements that must be met in order to receive the rewards. Continually work to eliminate the extrinsic motivation of the reward and replace it with the intrinsic motivation of self-satisfaction.

Reward systems are generally more effective when applied to skills and tasks that are:

1. New
2. Nonstimulating or boring
3. Feared by the child
4. Related to an ingrained behavior or habit

Of course, there are times when a teacher must present material to children that is boring, tedious, and repetitious. You can make the material more stimulating by making one of three adjustments in your presentation.

- *Establish a goal.* Set individual goals for each child. The goal may involve the number of facts that the child memorizes ("Bill, let's see if you can memorize twenty-five state capitals by Friday") or the speed with which the child can recite the facts ("Belinda, let's see if you can recite the fives times table in sixty seconds").
- *Relate the material to a more appealing activity.* Explain to the student that mastery of the tedious material is necessary in order to accomplish a more significant goal. ("Roger, I know that these vocabulary drills are a bit boring, but you must learn the formal chemical names before we can begin the laboratory experiments.") The facts will seem more interesting if learned in a context.
- *Introduce a social component.* Establish study groups, gamelike activities, or study buddies that allow the students to master the tedious material within an appealing social context.

Effective Reward Systems at Home

Parents should also be aware of the effective use of reward systems at home. A positive, effective reward is one that reflects the parents' recognition and appreciation of the child's efforts and accomplishments.

There are basically three types of rewards that parents should use in order to recognize and sustain a child's efforts.

> *Social rewards* are intangible and may include praise, parental attention, or other verbal reinforcements.
>
> *Material rewards* include prizes, money, or other tangible payment.
>
> *Privileges* might involve a sleepover, a trip to an amusement park, or a later bedtime.

The awarding of these rewards may be a surprise or can be agreed upon in advance. However, surprise rewards are often more effective and are less likely to create "reward obsession." As the child masters the desired behavior (e.g., making her bed, cleaning his room), these activities become self-reinforcing and the need for *your* reinforcement diminishes. Begin to *acknowledge* the behavior without necessarily *rewarding* it.

Beware of placing too much emphasis on material rewards. Children may begin to equate love with rewards. Conversely, when material rewards are *not* given, the child may feel unloved. Youngsters become overly dependent on material gifts, particularly money. I once consulted with an affluent family who continually gave money to reinforce and reward their children, but seldom gave encouragement, verbal support, or praise. Quite understandably, the children began to see money as an expression of love.

Mom was crestfallen on Mother's Day when her nine-year-old twins joyfully gifted her with a brightly colored envelope with "Happy Mom's Day" scrawled across it. The envelope contained a ten-dollar bill.

Social rewards, however, sensitize the child to the feelings of others and teach him much about affection, acceptance, and human interaction.

Reward systems are rarely successful in making long-term changes in children's behavior and seldom motivate students in a lasting and meaningful way. Teachers and parents should avoid becoming overly dependent upon this strategy as a means to increasing and enhancing motivation.

Whenever I see a teacher or parent who uses rewards as the primary or sole source of motivation, I am reminded of an anecdote from Herbert Lovett, who served as a director of a Boston group home for adults with severe cognitive impairments. A new client was being oriented into the program. The thirty-year-old was having lunch with a resident who was nearly twice his age and who had been living at the group home for a decade.

The older man was overheard to say to his new friend, "Don't let the staff know that you like ice cream. If they know that you like it, they will make ice cream part of your reward program and you will have to work in order to get any. But if they don't know that you like it, you'll get it for dessert every night . . . just like all of us."

This telling anecdote not only illustrates how easily reward systems can be manipulated, it is a poignant reminder of the dysfunctional and one-sided relationships that caregivers develop with their clients or students. Should a person be required to *earn* dessert . . . or recess . . . or free time . . . or television time? I think not.

9

The People-Oriented Child

"Your students may not remember what you taught them, but they will remember how you made them feel."

—ANONYMOUS

As any experienced coach or teacher will attest, establishing a positive and constructive relationship with a student is a critically important ingredient in motivation. However, there are some students who thrive on the attention and respect they get from—and the affiliation with—a teacher. For those children, it is absolutely necessary that the child have a positive relationship with the adult caregiver. Absent this relationship, the child is unlikely to be motivated to reach her potential. It is the adult's responsibility—and, ultimately, in the adult's best interest—to establish an ongoing environment of mutual respect, trust, and empathy with the student. Although the people-motivated child thrives on these relationships, she may be unable to initiate and maintain this interaction because of poorly developed social skills or difficult past experiences.

In his extraordinary book *What Do You Do with a Child Like*

This? teacher and author L. Tobin observed, "Many children have the unfortunate ability to generate in adults the *exact opposite* emotional reaction than the child needs."

As teachers, we must remain mindful of the hallmark of the helping professions. When we deal with students, patients, or clients, we must always remember: Before they care how much you know, they must know how much you care.

Teachers who attempt to establish a rapport with students by dazzling them with their knowledge, background, and experience will be sorely disappointed. Of course, content-area expertise is an important trait for a teacher. But an earned doctorate and twenty-five years of teaching experience are of little interest to a student. However, the history teacher who occasional asks Sandy about her drama club rehearsal or who attends Gabriel's basketball games will be well on his way to establishing a positive and constructive relationship with his students.

In a 2001 Ohio University study and in similar research at Brigham Young University, educators asked students to list the traits, behaviors, and characteristics of their favorite teachers. The most popular teachers had several interpersonal skills, including:

TRAITS OF POPULAR TEACHERS

Popular teachers are interested in making a connection with students. Students cited the teacher's sense of humor, willingness to share personal information, and positive attitude toward class members.

Popular teachers are enthusiastic. Students can sense the teacher's excitement about the subject matter, the class, and the students. Enthusiasm is contagious . . . and so is the lack of it.

Popular teachers are punctual and prepared. Students reported having great respect for teachers who take their profession and their responsibilities seriously. Teachers who begin and end their classes on time and prepare assignments for the entire period are held in high regard. Students claim that they can easily tell when a teacher is unprepared and "winging it."

Popular teachers are concerned about their students. These teachers regularly communicate that they care about the students' success. They offer encouragement and support when they are needed. Students, again, cited that they greatly appreciated when a teacher was friendly and approachable.

Popular teachers are polite. Interestingly, the majority of students mentioned that they admired and appreciated a teacher who was courteous and polite in their daily interactions. These teachers were not condescending and treated students with genuine respect. Students were particularly attracted to teachers who did not embarrass children in front of their classmates.

Popular teachers provide individual help and assistance. These teachers willingly and courteously provided individual explanations and instructions when needed and encouraged students to request clarification or assistance when necessary. Students were not belittled or embarrassed when they requested extra help.

Popular teachers use a variety of activities and approaches in class. In order to keep the material interesting—and the class *interested*—these teachers used a number of unique and stimulating techniques to present, review, and assess the curriculum. They did not rely on a single approach such as lecturing, videos, or test-study-test.

Popular teachers do not overuse the textbook. As one student put it, "My teacher uses the text for homework and to supplement his daily lesson. But he's not a slave to the text. Most of the class time is devoted to his knowledge of the subject and his presentation of other sources."

Popular teachers are organized. Students respect a teacher who brings structure to the classroom and makes her expectations clear. Students have little patience or regard for teachers who are scattered and unfocused. They expect the teacher will maintain accurate and updated records (e.g., test scores, attendance). However, students fear rigidity and appreciate an occasional departure from the daily routine and a surprise or two once in a while.

It is interesting to note that a teacher's expertise and mastery of the subject matter were not viewed as particularly valued traits when students assessed their teachers.

Initially, students with a history of learning problems may have negative feelings toward a teacher. It is important that the adult not take this rejection personally. The student's reluctance to initiate a relationship is doubtless rooted in past negative experiences with other adults. They have come to believe that adults are not trustworthy or dependable because teachers have betrayed or disappointed them in the past. They may anticipate that you will be distant and even hostile.

When one considers the above, it is easy to see how some teachers develop a defensive and insular attitude toward their students. An oft-heard exclamation in a teachers' lounge is: "I don't care if they don't like me. Teaching isn't a popularity contest." *Au contraire.* Teaching indeed *is* a popularity contest in many respects. Rarely does a child enter his history class with a burning, unquenchable desire to learn about the causes, battles, and consequences of the Crimean War! But if this material is presented by a competent, caring, and charismatic teacher, the student's motivation to learn is increased measurably. For the people-motivated student, this need is magnified. The teacher who does not attempt to build a rapport with the students invites resistance, confrontation, and malaise. If you wish them to invest in you and your curriculum, you must invest yourself in them as well. If you treat them as the enemy, then they will, indeed, play that role.

If a student is challenging, difficult, or hostile, teachers often develop a distant and detached relationship with him. The adult interacts with the child only when scolding, reprimanding, or correcting him. As a result, the child quite naturally begins to view the adult as a source of negativity and hostility. His relationship with the teacher becomes one more in a long line of unproductive relationships with authority figures. However, by demonstrating occasional kindness, understanding, compassion, and empathy toward a troubled student, this process can be reversed. Be kind. Smile. Compliment. Be patient. Centuries ago, Plato reminded us to be understanding to all because every person you encounter is on a difficult journey. This is hard to remember when dealing with a hostile or disinterested student. Be mindful of the sage counsel: *"The pain that a troubled child causes is never greater than the pain that he feels."*

Needless to say, teachers and caregivers must maintain a professional distance when dealing with children in their charge. You should not attempt to become the child's friend. A friendship between an adult and a child is an impossibility. By definition, a friendship is a relationship based upon *equality,* and in an adult-child relationship, there is no equality with regard to age, experience, power, or influence. The twelve-year-old youngster does not need a thirty-year-old pal—and if you need a twelve-year-old buddy, you should look for another line of work!

We must consistently maintain the delicate balance between being caring, concerned, and competent, and being manipulative or receiving unhealthy gratification from the teacher-student relationship. Children who are people-oriented are quite vulnerable and suggestible. Their intense desire to please others and to establish relationships will often shade their decisions and interactions. We have all heard of situations where teachers or coaches have taken advantage of their relationships with needy children. Such relationships ruin careers and cause long-term damage to the child.

In the event that a child develops a crush on a teacher, the adult should take definitive steps to deal with the situation. Do not assume that the crush will simply disappear over time. The teacher should be extremely careful with any physical contact she might have with the smitten child. A teacher's simple pat on the back might be interpreted as a physical overture. Sternly, but kindly, tell the child that his behavior is inappropriate if he becomes overly forward or familiar. Clarify the teacher-student boundaries. In some situations, you may want to ask a teacher who is the same gender as the child to intervene and speak to the youngster.

It is always advisable to tell a colleague about the situation. This may protect you if the relationship should become more troubling.

Avoid being alone with the child and do not give him notes or accept notes from him. Maintain your teacher role at all times.

That being said, it is entirely appropriate to take an interest in a child by inquiring about his hobbies, activities, and affinities. Interest is often more effective than praise.

Many extraordinary teachers take the time (or *make* the time) to hold a brief informal conversation with each student at least once a week. This conversation may be related to classroom concerns, but it might also be an opportunity to learn a bit about the child's interests and activities *outside* the classroom. These need not occur in the classroom. A chance meeting in the hallway or the cafeteria provides an opportunity for these rapport-building interactions. (*"Hey, Joaquin. How are the play rehearsals going? Mr. Breakman told me that the sword-fight scene looks great."*)

If these inquiries are conducted in a natural and welcoming manner, students view them not as intrusive but, rather, as reflective of your genuine interest in them. These small investments of your time will pay great dividends for you and the child. Students often reciprocate by expressing a healthy interest in *you* and your activities. (*"Did you lose electricity during last night's storm, Mr. Middleton?" "I like your new car, Mrs. Marshall."*) The student comes to view you as a person, not as the enemy. As an added bonus, you begin to develop a positive reputation among the student body. (*"You'll like Mr. Keane. He really cares about kids."*)

THE ETHICAL TEACHER

As your rapport with the student grows, his trust in you increases along a parallel course. He may begin to confide in you and view you as a source of information, insight, and inspiration. This is generally a positive dynamic, but a cautionary note must be sounded here. Nearly every teacher or coach has been confronted with a situation where a child wanted to confide in the adult, but wished to have a commitment of secrecy before divulging his problem. (*"Ms. Carnig, if I tell you something, do you promise that you won't tell anyone else?"*)

There is but *one* appropriate response to that inquiry: *"Jenny, because I don't know the nature of your problem, I simply cannot make that promise. I promise you this: I will stick by you for as long as it takes to resolve the problem. But I can't guarantee that the resolution won't require that I consult with or notify someone else."*

Invariably, the child will refuse to share her secret. But just as invariably, she will return to share it with you later. Consider the following scenario that occurred to a young, well-intentioned teacher I know.

BRENDA: Miss Henry, if I tell you a secret, do you promise not to tell anyone?

MISS HENRY: Of course, Brenda. You can trust me. Whatever you share with me will go no further.

BRENDA: Well, I am the last kid off the bus every day, and when I'm alone with the bus driver, he shows me dirty pictures and sometimes touches me.

What do you do *now,* Miss Henry? Break your promise and notify school authorities? Allow this behavior to continue? Confront the driver yourself? Those are three unattractive options. But Miss Henry placed herself in this difficult position by making a promise that could not be kept.

There are several other ethical considerations related to adult-child relationships that teachers must consider when dealing with students.

AN ETHICS PRIMER

- *The teacher's primary responsibility is to the student.* As professionals, teachers are required to make dozens of decisions every day. Some of these decisions are minor ones, and others are critical and can have a lifelong impact upon a child.

  As teachers make these decisions, they often feel pressure from colleagues, superiors, and students' parents. Beyond this, one must consider the budget, time, and financial constraints that are realities in schools today.

But the ethical teacher must remain mindful that her *primary* responsibility is always to the student. If the wishes or demands of a parent or a colleague are in conflict with the genuine needs of the child, the teacher has an ethical responsibility to make the decision that is in the *child's* best interest.

- *The teacher must recognize and respect each child, and treat each as an individual.* Every child in the classroom has a unique profile of needs, strengths, affinities, and interests. The teacher must plan and implement lessons that reflect, celebrate, and adjust to these differences.
- *The teacher must encourage maximum student growth by responding to the total needs of the child.* Teachers often develop a one-dimensional view of a child based upon the nature of the teacher's relationship to the student. That is, Zachary is assigned to Mrs. Murphy's sixth-period science class; she tends to view him solely as her "science student." She must also remember that Zachary is a son, a brother, a nephew, a grandchild, a neighbor, a friend, a cousin, and a teammate. All of these roles are important to the overall development of the child. There may come a time when Zachary's role as Mrs. Murphy's student comes in conflict with some other roles in his life. For example, an extended soccer practice or a surprise visit from Grandpa may interfere with Zachary's ability to complete his science homework. Mrs. Murphy must consider Zachary's *total needs* and be willing to be flexible and accommodate for those needs.
- *The teacher must recognize and respect the student's right to privacy and confidentiality.* The teacher must never discuss a student in any identifiable manner with anyone outside the school community. It is highly unethical, for example, to discuss a child with another child's parent.
- *The teacher must never use her relationship with a student or a parent to foster personal or financial advantage.* It is unethical for a teacher to enter into any sort of formal or informal financial agreement with a child or the parent of a child currently in her class. This would include loans, borrowing goods, or bets.

- *The teacher has an ethical obligation to protect the student from embarrassment and disparagement from anyone.* Teachers have a responsibility to defend children from humiliation at the hands of classmates, other staff members . . . or the teacher herself.
- *The teacher must take all steps humanly possible to protect students from conditions that are harmful to learning, safety, and health.* During school hours, teachers play the formidable role of in loco parentis. They are responsible for protecting the children in their charge from any situation that could endanger their progress, health, or safety.
- *The teacher must not discriminate against any child or family based upon race, creed, national origin, gender, sexual orientation, socioeconomic status, or social background.*
- *The teacher must serve as a positive role model to students in regard to integrity, work ethic, honesty, responsibility, and respect for others.*
- *The teacher must use aversive measures (punishment) ONLY when repeated trials of other methods have failed.*

R-E-S-P-E-C-T

"We only learn from those whom we love."

—JOHANN WOLFGANG VON GOETHE

By establishing and maintaining appropriate and active relationships with the students, teachers will doubtless increase the youngsters' motivation. An added bonus is that these relationships are fundamental to preventing classroom disruptions, misbehaviors, and conflicts. Students are naturally invested in pleasing a teacher whom they genuinely like and respect.

Mutual respect is the key to an effective adult-child relationship. Nearly thirty years ago I developed the workshop entitled F.A.T. City that was mentioned in chapter 8. The seminar was the subject of an award-winning video that is distributed worldwide. Although the video is nearly twenty years old, it is still a staple in most teacher education programs and has been generously referred to as a "classic" in the field of staff development. Its continued popularity and wide distribution is a great blessing for me, but it is also a source of puzzlement. Why do people continue to watch and respond so strongly to the video?

Perhaps the secret lies in the aforementioned mutual respect. For years, before producing the video, I did the workshop "live" with teachers and parent groups in my community. My sons would often ask me where I was going "all dressed up" after dinner, and I would respond, "I'm doing F.A.T. City tonight."

One evening at supper I told the boys that I would be going out to "do F.A.T. City" that night, and our eight-year-old, Christian, asked, "Dad, what *is* F.A.T. City? What do you do there?"

I invited him to accompany me to that evening's seminar. His five-year-old brother, Dan, decided to join us and they agreed to sit quietly in the back of the room while I conducted the workshop.

As I did the seminar that evening, I kept looking at my boys, whose eyes were wide and whose jaws were agape. I completed the workshop, packed up my materials, and began our drive home. Both my sons were very quiet and pensive. After a while, young Dan piped up, "Dad . . . THAT'S what you do when you go out at night? You yell at people?"

From the mouths of babes! The reason that the video continues to resonate after two decades is actually quite simple. In the workshop I do things to adults that we do not do to adults—although we cavalierly do those things to children. In the workshop, I embarrass the participants, tear up their papers, reprimand them publicly, and belittle their efforts. It is somewhat shocking to watch an adult treat another adult in such a callous and shabby manner. But children are mishandled that way daily in our classrooms.

Fortunately, the overwhelming majority of America's teachers are warm, caring, and sensitive individuals who would not humiliate or publicly shame a child. However, if a child is assigned to a teacher who *does* treat students in an impatient and curt manner, the youngster's school experience is filled with frustration, anxiety, and tension. To a child in this situation it matters little that most of the teachers in the school are very understanding. The child is at the daily mercy of an adult who simply does not "get it."

Suppose I were delivering a lecture to several hundred teachers and parents. During the introduction, the master of ceremonies asks that all audience members turn off their cell phones. In the middle of the seminar a participant's phone begins to ring. What are the chances that I would cease the lecture and loudly confront the offender with a scolding and a rash of rhetorical questions? ("Well, I guess the rules don't apply to YOU, do they? Oh, no! Because you're just a little more special than the rest of us and you don't need to be bothered with rules, do you?")

What would the reaction be? The audience member would angrily leave the auditorium, doubtless followed by any of her friends or colleagues in attendance. Further, the representatives of the sponsoring organization would surely voice their displeasure with my rudeness.

An adult would never publicly humiliate another adult in this manner. Treating a child in that way is equally inappropriate. If you wish to have the respect of a child, you must give the child respect. Children will not give you respect merely because of your position. You need to gain their respect the old-fashioned way. You need to *earn* it!

There are many small but significant things that a teacher can do or say in order to build an effective working relationship with students.

ENHANCING STUDENT/TEACHER RELATIONSHIPS

- Make eye contact with students when they speak. Look away from your cluttered desk and look directly at the child who is asking you a question after class.
- Listen closely to them and use body language to let them know that you are interested in what they are telling you.
- Use their names—often—in conversations and discussions. Include their names in written correction. ("Nice work, Franklin." "Wonderful essay, Diana.")
- Meet 'em and greet 'em at the door at the beginning of class.
- Avoid using sarcasm.

- Don't carry grudges. If you and a child have a dispute, it's *your* responsibility to wipe the slate clean.
- Remember and acknowledge their birthdays.
- Move naturally around the classroom during lectures or discussions.
- Bring in a treat on occasion.
- Do a teacher show-and-tell whenever you conduct a student show-and-tell.
- When a child returns from an absence, inquire about her health and help her catch up with the class.
- Encourage growth and progress by providing opportunities for success.
- Use administrators, colleagues, and parents to *reinforce* positive behavior—not merely to punish inappropriate behavior.
- At the end of a successful class, immediately thank the students for their effort and cooperation.
- Reinforce good behavior and motivation in writing by jotting down a brief note to a student.
- Call the child's home to share *good* news occasionally.
- Be a talent scout by discovering and celebrating students' skills and affinities. ("Gee, I don't know why our plants died over the weekend. Maybe our resident flower expert, Jeremy, can tell us!")
- Communicate your confidence in the child by assuming success, not failure. ("These fraction problems are tough, Zak, but I'll bet you can solve them.")
- Drop by their soccer games; attend their play in the evening; praise their yearbook.
- Acknowledge their out-of-school lives. I once sent a sympathy card to a student who had lost his beloved grandfather. The card was addressed to the child, not his parents or his family. He later commented to me, "My parents got about a hundred sympathy cards when Grandpa died. I got one. From you." That simple gesture and an investment of two dollars completely changed my previously shaky relationship with that child.

- If the child is experiencing unusual life circumstances (recent divorce, sick sibling, cut from ball team, no prom invitation), modify and adjust your demands and expectations for the child.
- Minimize warnings, threats, and nags.
- Never, *ever* express disappointment in a child. The disappointment expressed by an important adult in a child's life is often too heavy a burden for the child to bear.
- Notice and comment on a student's new hairstyle, clothing, or book bag.
- Show them a picture of your new dog.
- Give them plenty of opportunities to move around the classroom.
- Praise in public, criticize in private.
- Have no tolerance for bullying, harassment, or humiliation of students—by anyone, including you.
- Catch 'em being good.
- Use punishment as the last—not the first—resort.
- Provide students with several ways to demonstrate their skills and knowledge. Use all four language arts to evaluate and assess their progress (reading, writing, listening, speaking).
- Model appropriate behavior. If you want them to be attentive, focused, polite, organized, and creative, be sure these traits are included in your teaching style.
- Learn and focus on each child's affinities, strengths, and interests.
- Allow students to create, design, and renegotiate assignments to make them personally meaningful.
- Ask students (and parents) to complete interest surveys to determine the interests, hobbies, and affinities of students.
- Join students for lunch.
- Make a home visit. When I ran a residential school on Cape Cod, I had a speaking engagement in Kentucky. One of my students' parents invited me to dinner at their Louisville home. I had an opportunity to see my student's bedroom, meet his siblings, and pet his beloved dog. I was never able to look at the child the same way again. That two-hour visit to his "home base" gave me immeasurable insight into the student, his personality, and his needs.

- Post every child's work. If you are an elementary school teacher, divide that huge classroom bulletin board into twenty-five sections and assign each student his own personal section. Each Friday, have each child select the assignment that he is most proud of from the week and have him post that work sheet on his section of the bulletin board. In that way, *every* child has a paper on display *every* week.
- Make an effort to end each lesson or class on a positive note by doing an activity at which the child or the class will be successful. Perhaps you could reserve the final five minutes for a review of previously mastered material. Students benefit greatly from this reinforcement, and because they conclude the session on an upbeat note, they are more eager to return for and participate in the next class. Children tend to remember the last five minutes of any experience, so make a special attempt to end the class in a positive way.
- Respect the fact that we *all* are entitled to hold our own opinions and feelings, even if those opinions differ from others. Children become understandably resistant when adults fail to validate children's feelings or opinions. We often totally deny or discredit feelings.

    MOM: John, put on a sweater.
    JOHN: But I'm hot.
    MOM: No, you're not. Put on a sweater NOW!

- If a child is likely to receive a poor grade in your class, contact the child and his parents *before* you give the low grade. A poor report card should never come as a surprise to the student or to his parents.
- Compliment students on their extracurricular and out-of-school accomplishments.
- Give students credit and praise for their ideas or comments by attributing ownership of ideas during class discussions. ("Remember when Paul said yesterday that he thought the author would surprise us in the next chapter? He was right. Good job, Paul.")

- Remember that every child has areas of strength and competence. Focus on those strengths.
- Every child in your classroom needs to be respected, acknowledged, appreciated, accepted, and supported. *Every* child.
- Be willing to admit when you have made a mistake or if you do not know something. This enables students to understand that mistakes are a normal and necessary part of the learning process.
- Be cautious of labeling your students (e.g., "the strong one," "the smart one," "the funny one"). Each of your students is an exciting, unique, and multidimensional person.
- Never display or highlight a child's work without first getting his permission. Some children respond poorly to public praise.
- Teach students how to give and receive compliments.
- Be willing to share your feelings and emotions with your students. If a story or a video touched you, tell them. Share personal experiences.
- When a child does something that annoys you, try to remember that he is not doing it *to annoy you.*
- Kneel next to a child when talking to him. Communication will be more effective at eye level.

In order to motivate children, you must establish a positive, sensitive rapport with them. The ideas listed above might help you establish and maintain this rapport. Below is a list of behaviors that have a *negative* effect on rapport:

- Sarcasm
- Failing to respond to a child's sadness
- Shouting, yelling, commanding
- Threatening
- Continually pointing out mistakes and errors
- Rudeness
- Pushing, pulling, shoving, or manhandling a child
- Disrespect
- Failing to protect or defend a child

- Being overly judgmental
- Humiliating a child by using his work as an example of incorrect or poorly done work
- Nagging

HELPING THE PEOPLE-ORIENTED CHILD MAKE FRIENDS

Students who are people-oriented need to have positive and enjoyable relationships with their peers. Unfortunately, many children who experience academic learning difficulties also experience difficulties in the social arena. In fact, 70 percent of children with learning disabilities report having "major difficulty with peers," when only 15 percent of nondisabled students experience "major difficulty."

For many years, professionals believed that the social isolation experienced by children with learning problems was an indirect consequence of the learning disability. It was believed that the learning problem caused school failure and that this failure, in turn, caused social isolation or rejection. We now recognize that the social problems experienced by these children are the *direct* result of the learning disorder. Learning disabilities actually *cause* social rejection in many cases. Even if a child is enrolled in a responsive, individualized academic program and is progressing well in school, he still might have significant problems with peer and adult relationships. If the child is motivated by interactions with and approval of others in his environment, this lack of social competence can have an impact upon his progress and performance in the classroom.

The classroom teacher can, should, and must play an important role in the child's development of social competence and friendship skills. I have lectured on this topic for many years and have often found teachers resistant to helping children develop peer friendships. Teachers often voice the opinion that their responsibilities involve the teaching of academic skills and that it is the role of the *parents* to foster and promote social skills. As a teacher once said to me at a seminar, "My job is to teach reading, writing, and spelling . . . and there is barely time for *that.* If the child doesn't have any friends, I'm afraid that's Mom and Dad's problem."

Many teachers now take a far more enlightened view of this issue. They recognize that the child who is isolated and rejected by his classmates will likely not be responsive or receptive to instruction, and his academic progress will be greatly compromised. A teacher recently told me, "I used to think that social skill instruction was not in my purview as a classroom teacher. I now recognize that a child who is preoccupied with the fact that no one is going to sit with him at lunch or who is concerned that he will be bullied at recess, is going to function very poorly in the class that morning. I now realize that it is in his best interest—and mine—to help him make friends. He will be a better, more responsive student as a result." Pediatrician and author Mel Levine reminds us that the foremost dreaded words in the world of childhood are, "Sorry, this seat's taken."

The classroom teacher can facilitate the development of classroom relationships in a number of ways. First—and, perhaps most important—the teacher must consistently demonstrate that *she* likes, accepts, and enjoys the individual student who is being isolated and rejected by his classmates.

I am often asked to consult with schools regarding an individual student who is being isolated and rejected. I begin the process by meeting privately with the students who are tormenting the child. I remind these students that I have neither the power nor the interest to punish them in any way. Rather, I ask them, in a very nonthreatening way, to identify the behaviors or traits that annoy them and are the basis for their rejection of the child. Invariably, the students respond, "But, Mr. Lavoie, even the *teachers* don't like him!"

As teachers, we need to understand that our verbal or nonverbal rejection of a child is readily observed and replicated by the children. When you demonstrate that you do not like a particular child, you are in effect placing your imprimatur on the students' feelings for him. You are giving tacit approval to their rejection or isolation of the child. As I often reminded my faculty, "You can dislike a child if you wish to, but you can't dislike a child on company time!"

By demonstrating that you enjoy a child's company and that you genuinely *like* her, you greatly increase her "social stock" among her peers and often cause her classmates to reexamine their feelings about the rejected child. ("Well, if Mrs. Richardson likes Elizabeth so much, maybe she's not such a bad kid after all.") Of course, you want to avoid treating the child like the teacher's pet. That can serve to make matters worse. Simply demonstrate that you enjoy the child by talking, walking, or laughing with her within view of the other children. Give the isolated child high-status responsibilities and chores in order to show your acceptance of and affection for her. Encourage her to publicly demonstrate her skills and interests.

Another technique to improve the child's social standing involves emphasizing her personal islands of competence, as discussed in chapter 7. Find an area of skill and interest that is unique to that child. Perhaps Mark has an extensive knowledge of meteorology or Gretchen has little-known talents in cooking. Celebrate these affinities in a very public way. Have the students read *Robinson Crusoe* and let Mark make a presentation on the nature of tropical storms. Ask Gretchen to make some tapas to supplement the class study of Spain. By spotlighting the affinities and interests of an isolated child, he becomes a more attractive partner.

Collective rewards are another effective strategy to foster peer relationships. Teachers often develop the unfortunate habit of issuing collective punishments. ("The last time we went to the media center, Joseph was fooling around and knocked over an expensive projector. So we are not going to the media center for a week.") This common strategy of punishing the group for the behavior of an individual is inherently unfair and certainly has a negative impact upon the offending student's relationship with his classmates. Most likely these students have been punished for Joseph's misbehaviors for several years as they've progressed through the grades together.

Collective rewards are an effective alternative to this strategy. Rather than *punishing* the entire class for Joseph's misbehaviors, try *rewarding* them when Joseph behaves appropriately. ("Class, I think we can all agree that Joseph was terrific on yesterday's field trip and he worked very hard to stay with the group and listened carefully to the museum guide. I am so happy with this, I have decided to give the whole class ten minutes of extra computer time this afternoon.") This strategy can have a remarkably positive effect on the manner in which his classmates view Joseph.

Another way to promote social acceptance is to make the isolated child more appealing by giving him something the other kids want. For example, suppose your students truly enjoy the Friday chores of watering the plants, returning the books to the school library, and cleaning the whiteboards. Appoint Joseph as the "foreman" of the Friday crew. ("Class, I know that you enjoy doing the Friday chores and I keep forgetting to schedule the crew to get that done. Joseph, I would like you to be the foreman of the crew. Every Thursday, please give me the names of six children whom you would like to assist you.") Someone will be nice to him at least on Wednesday. Small steps.

If a child has a particular medical, social, or learning problem that will impact significantly on her day-to-day performance, it may be beneficial to discuss this with the entire class. Some teachers have found it useful and beneficial to have the child participate actively in the discussion. I once observed a fourth grader explaining his diabetes to a group of spellbound classmates who later asked very probing and sensitive questions about the child's illness. ("Does it scare you?" "Will you outgrow it?" "Does it hurt to draw your blood?") His teacher reported that the child's courage and candor resulted in a marked and lasting improvement in his social standing among his peers.

During these discussions, point out that *all* of us have unique differences that make us individuals. But emphasize that we are all far more alike than we are different, and that these differences should not be feared or ridiculed. Further, explain that there will be no tolerance for humiliating or embarrassing one another. Deliver this part of the message in a nonthreatening and supportive way by addressing the fact that such behavior is cruel and that cruelty is simply unacceptable. Emphasize the fact that acceptance of differences is a mark of maturity.

Discuss ways that the students can assist their classmate. ("It's helpful if you talk slowly when you are talking to Heather." "When John has trouble with his temper, let me handle it. It is unfair and embarrassing to stare at him when he is having a bad time. Just go about your business.") Some children will become overly solicitous to the child and will provide an overabundance of help or assistance. Encourage the child to do the things that she can do independently. Discuss the concept of dignity.

Some schools use peer partners or buddy systems to facilitate social acceptance of isolated children. These strategies can be effective if students are selected and matched with careful and sensitive forethought. Be sure to recognize, praise, and reinforce *both* students in the pairing, not just the nondisabled child. These paired activities should be monitored closely at the outset.

Teachers tend to construct intra-class groupings based upon the academic skills of the students by placing students with similar skills in the same group. In order to facilitate student relationships, occasionally base your groupings upon the children's *interests*. For example, group students together based on their interests in sports, music, or movies. As a result, you will create groups that are heterogeneous (diverse) in their academic skills but that share a passion for a specific activity. These diverse groupings can work on projects in a very dynamic way. These activities can be conducted in a club format and often enable students who would normally never interact to share time and knowledge with one another.

Understanding Friendship

When attempting to facilitate and promote friendships, it is important for parents, teachers, and coaches to understand the nature of friendship among children and preadolescents. The Council for Exceptional Children has identified the following themes among childhood friendships:

> *Intimacy, affection, and loyalty:* Children desire friends who can be trusted. They want their friends to share thoughts and feelings

sensitively, and they demand loyalty from them. They need to feel that the friend will keep confidences and shared secrets. They also expect that the friend will not criticize them to others and are deeply hurt when this occurs. Children expect the friend to view the relationship as a true commitment. Most childhood friendships that dissolve are destroyed by a perceived lack of commitment by one of the parties.

Similarity and proximity: School-aged children have a tendency to develop friendships with others who share similarities with themselves (gender, age, race, IQ, social status). As the child grows older, these traits become less important and he establishes friendships based upon similar interests and attitudes. As adolescence emerges, friends begin to seek conformity by dressing similarly and listening to the same music.

Mutual activities and shared interests: Childhood friendships often develop during school or extracurricular activities. Children who are involved in such activities (e.g., sports teams, stamp clubs, chorus, drama) have common interests and values and often are quite compatible as social partners.

Reciprocity and support: Beyond loyalty, children must share a degree of mutual respect and affection for each other if the friendship is to be lasting and meaningful. There needs to be a degree of equity between the two friends and a willingness to assist, guide, or comfort each other as necessary.

The teacher should carefully observe the interactions of the students in an attempt to find a child who may be a good "friend match" for the isolated student. Be sure to observe the youngsters in formal classroom settings and less structured settings as well (e.g., recess, hallways, physical education). If you see that two students seem to be developing a relationship, seat them together or allow them to work as a pair in classroom activities. Perhaps you could even contact the parents of the isolated child and suggest that they may want to promote and nurture the relationship by setting up a playdate between the two children. It may seem strange for adults to be so deeply involved in the social life of a child, but in the case of the isolated or rejected child, this intervention is both appropriate and necessary. School life is difficult for *any* child who is isolated by his peers. But if the child is people-oriented, this rejection is particularly painful and will impact upon his motivation in and outside of the classroom.

I once saw a poster in a school's teacher's lounge that read:

> COMING TO SCHOOL EVERY DAY CAN BECOME A HOPELESS TASK
> FOR SOME CHILDREN UNLESS THEY SUCCEED AT WHAT THEY DO.
> WE TEACHERS ARE SENTRIES AGAINST THAT HOPELESSNESS.

Sound counsel, indeed.

10

Implementing the 6 *P*'s in the Classroom

"As we grow as unique persons, we must learn to respect the uniqueness of others."

—ROBERT SCHULLER

IN ORDER TO ENSURE that all students are motivated to reach their fullest potential, the teacher must use strategies that address the six forces that promote and maintain student motivation: Projects, People, Praise, Prizes, Prestige, and Power.

This can be done by consistently using the following motivational techniques. These strategies tend to enhance the motivation of *all* children, but are particularly effective for the subgroup of children listed in parentheses. By utilizing these techniques on a regular basis, the teacher will be able to meet the motivational needs of all students.

TEN EFFECTIVE TEACHING STRATEGIES

1. *Teach enthusiastically.* (People, Power)

   The teacher should bring great enthusiasm and energy to her teaching. A high-energy approach is far more likely to motivate and inspire children because it demonstrates that the lesson's content is important and valuable. This approach also reflects that the teacher takes her duties seriously.

Students expect two things from their teachers: that they be *confident* and *competent.* Enthusiastic teaching reflects the teacher's self-assurance and skill.

2. *Focus on strengths.* (People, Praise, Prizes, Prestige, Power)

    Many teachers, parents, and coaches believe that children can be motivated through failure. ("If you don't study more often, you will fail this course." "If you don't improve, I am cutting you from the team.") Motivation is built on strength, not on weakness. By focusing on deficits and threats, the adult triggers defensive behaviors that seldom produce motivation or meaningful change.

    A strength-based approach recognizes and celebrates the talents, interests, competencies, and affinities of each student. By focusing on these strength areas, the connection and relationship between the student and the teacher is enriched and intensified.

    The child's strengths should be incorporated into the day-to-day curriculum whenever possible. Assign roles and responsibilities that highlight his strengths and interests. ("Class, the principal asked us to make a presentation to the faculty council about our recent field trip. John, you can draw the posters. Angela, I'd like you to write the handout and Ethan can type it. Bethany, let's have you make the presentation.")

3. *Recognize, reinforce, and celebrate success, effort, and progress.* (Praise, People, Prizes, Prestige)

    Although it is not necessary (or advisable) to *reward* each success, you should make an effort to recognize and acknowledge each child's success and progress. Children will generally repeat behavior that is reinforced and recognized.

4. *Encourage and promote creativity.* (Projects, Power)

    Avoid fostering the tyranny of the right answer. Allow students to make modifications and adaptations in assignments that allow for individuality. ("Mr. Middleton, instead of drawing a picture of the White House, can I make a collage or diorama?") Reinforce creativity and originality as enthusiastically as you reinforce success and progress.

5. *Promote cooperation—not competition—within your classroom.* (People, Prestige, Power)

   Children will be more productive and motivated in a classroom that is harmonious and safe. Teach students to work together and provide them with opportunities to do so. Conduct activities that allow students to get to know one another. Encourage them to support, praise, and compliment their classmates and to participate in project teams, study groups, and buddy programs whenever possible.

   Avoid creating situations where students are in direct competition with one another. In such a setting, students begin to view their classmates as obstacles to their own progress.

6. *Establish long-term and short-term goals for and with the students. Monitor and assess the progress toward these goals.* (Projects, Prestige, Power)

   At the beginning of each school term, set goals for the class and discuss these objectives with the students. ("This term we should complete our study of the Civil War and Reconstruction. We will begin the unit on civil rights at the end of next month. We will also be working on individual essays for the town-wide history essay contest.") These goals should be posted and referred to often during the semester in order to measure the students' progress toward the goal.

   Although you may not be able to establish goals for each individual student, you should meet with the students who are having difficulty and assist them in establishing observable short-term goals ("I will volunteer at least three times per class discussion"; "I will increase the accuracy and punctuality of my homework") and long-term goals ("I will improve my grade on the final exam"; "I will read one related book independently for extra credit"). Meet with the child occasionally to discuss her progress toward the goal.

7. *Whenever possible, provide the students with opportunities to make decisions and choices.* (People, Power, Prestige, Projects)

   There are several reasons to provide students with the opportunity to make choices, and this strategy greatly enhances student motivation. When a child plays a role in making a decision, he feels more ownership of both the decision and the results. His sense of belonging and responsibility increases.

   The key to the success of this strategy is to offer choices that are equally acceptable to the teacher. ("Rachel, you need to demonstrate that you understand the battle of the Alamo. You can do that by writing a make-believe news story about the battle, by making a diorama of the mission building and battleground, or by making a time line of the battle. Which do you choose?")

   An additional benefit of this strategy is that the student deals with the positive and negative consequences of her choices and develops greater faith in her decision making abilities.

8. *Demonstrate that you genuinely care for your students and their progress.* (People, Power, Prestige, Praise)

   An effective teacher demonstrates her concern for her students by providing them with an organized, well-planned curriculum and with an accepting and welcoming classroom environment. Students are continually able to succeed and progress.

   The key to motivating children lies in mutual respect between the adults and the students. A teacher can demonstrate her respect for students by getting to know their needs and their interests. Needless to say, the goal is *not* to become friends with the youngster. Rather, the goal is to present yourself as a compassionate, responsive guide who holds great interest and investment in each student's progress. Make each child feel she is valued, recognized, and an integral part of the class.

   Teachers should be willing and eager to share themselves with their students by telling stories about their own backgrounds, particularly tales of mistakes that they have made during their academic career. These stories often give comfort to the struggling student and make the teacher seem more human and approachable.

9. *Promote peer relationships.* (People, Prestige)

   For many years, the field of education felt that the ideal, ultimate learning experience would be a one-to-one setting consisting of one student and one teacher. Recent research demonstrates the fallacy of this belief. We now understand that students learn not only from the teacher, but also from one another. An effective teacher recognizes this and provides students with an opportunity to work together and celebrates cooperation and collaboration.

   Teachers should provide a comfortable, accepting classroom environment for *all* students and should be intolerant of bullying, intimidation, or humiliation of any sort. Students should be taught to accept and embrace the opinions and feelings of others.

10. *Provide opportunities for every child to realize success.* (Power, Praise, Prestige, Prizes)

    Success is the only strategy that promotes long-term, lasting motivation. If a child is deprived of success, he will doubtless be unable to sustain his motivation.

    The effective teacher injects success into her curriculum and her lesson plans daily. If the teacher places significant emphasis on the strengths and interests of the children, they are able to enjoy success and make meaningful progress. The teacher must continually seek out opportunities to expose students to these successful experiences.

    These exposures to success provide the child with the inspiration and drive to work harder toward her goals. An oft-heard exclamation in teachers' lounges and school conferences is: "If she'd only try harder, she would do better." In fact, the opposite is true. In actuality, If she only *did better,* she would *try harder.*

Part II

IT TAKES A VILLAGE TO MOTIVATE A CHILD

"The responsibility for producing an educated citizenry is too important to be left to educators. Education is everybody's business."

—THOMAS J. BROWN

11

The Role of the Parent in Student Motivation

"The smallest school in America is the family."

—JOHN GARDNER

"Teachers need to teach kids how to learn; parents need to teach kids how to work."

—MEL LEVINE, MD

WHEN A CHILD APPEARS TO BE unmotivated in school, the parent often feels helpless to assist in any meaningful way. After all, the parent is at home or in the workplace during the hours when the child is in class. Surely, Mom and Dad cannot be expected to accompany the child to school and provide him with the assistance and guidance he needs in order to work to his fullest potential in the classroom.

Of course not. But parents *can* play a significant role in initiating and maintaining the child's motivation. By working as partners with school personnel, parents can do much to enhance the youngster's motivation and performance. A major study conducted by the National Association of Secondary School Principals reached the following conclusion: "The responsibility for children's educational development is a collaborative enterprise among parents, school staff, and community members."

Quite simply, the daunting task of motivating today's students is too big—and too important—a job to leave to one group. Only by working together in a spirit of collaboration and cooperation can we ensure that children will exert maximum effort and reach their fullest potential. Nearly every major school effectiveness study published in recent years has cited parental involvement as a critical ingredient in the success of school programs and student progress. It truly *does* take a village to raise a child.

If your child has a learning disorder, it is critically important that you play the dual role of parent and advocate. School is a daily struggle for him, and the classroom is a maelstrom of failure, frustration, confusion, and chaos. He needs his parents to be a source of strength and support. He cannot be made to feel that he is on his own as he faces his daily struggles. He must believe that his parents are his biggest fans and, further, that they will be willing and able to assist him effectively when his struggles become overwhelming. Without such support it is unlikely that the child will be able to commit his time and energy to academics.

Unfortunately, many parents find that this advocacy role places them in an adversarial position with school personnel. As I visit school districts throughout North America, it is disheartening and often frightening to see the lack of trust and camaraderie that has developed between parents and teachers in many communities. The landmark special education legislation of the 1970s was intended to build bridges between families and schools. Regrettably, this well-intentioned movement has built walls instead.

PARENTAL CONSUMERISM

Many parents feel isolated from their school systems and may find schools to be unwelcoming and reluctant to accept parent involvement. Parents need to develop a "consumer" attitude toward schools. You are a taxpayer. Further, you are entrusting the school with the most precious commodity in your life—your child. Therefore, you have a right—and a *responsibility*—to be involved in the school. You are entitled to ask questions and be informed of your child's progress and performance. You should expect that you will be listened to and that your input will be given serious consideration. By the same token, teachers and other school personnel are entitled to the same respect and cordiality. Without this spirit of collaboration, the child is unlikely to realize the progress and growth that all parties wish for him.

I have met many parents who take a somewhat perverse pride in the combative relationships that they have developed with their children's schools. One mom proudly boasted, "The school is terrified of me. When I come in the front door, the principal sneaks out the back door."

Although this mother's intentions may be pure, her behavior will ultimately have a deleterious impact upon her child. I would remind her of the African proverb: *When elephants fight, it's the grass that gets trampled.*

Two one-ton elephants meet in the jungle and a battle for supremacy ensues. They bang heads repeatedly for an hour. There is often no obvious victor and so they walk away, unscathed, and ready to fight another day. The thick bony structure in the front of their skulls has protected them from any lasting injury. But in the meantime, every shrub, every blade of grass, and every piece of vegetation in the area is trampled and gone forever. So it is in the life of a child. If the adults in his life are fighting, it is *the child* who suffers.

As I mentioned earlier, parents should recognize that they are *consumers* of products and services provided by schools. By practicing the basic tenets of sound consumerism—as you would at a restaurant, car dealership, or appliance store—you will likely forge a productive and effective relationship with your child's school and the personnel who walk its halls.

Consumer Rule #1—Consumerism includes cooperation.

A good consumer recognizes that consumerism is a mutual, collaborative process. Therefore, treat others with respect: You catch more bees with honey than with vinegar.

Consumer Rule #2—If it sounds too good to be true, it probably is.

If school personnel make promises, predictions, or commitments that seem to be overly ambitious, ask for detailed clarification.

Consumer Rule #3—Get sound advice before *you buy.*

It is unlikely that you would purchase a new car or major appliance without first researching your options and discussing the purchase with others.

Talk to your neighbors and the parents of your child's classmates to seek their advice on ways to get appropriate services and assistance for your child. Create formal and informal networks among these parents. Remember, however, to keep these networks positive and constructive. Whenever parents attempt to create a "shadow government" within a school system, the home-school relationships deteriorate rapidly and significantly.

Consumer Rule #4—Save your receipts, warranties, and instruction manuals.

A good consumer maintains orderly and complete records. Parents should maintain a file of report cards, assessments, notes from meetings, phone calls, home-school e-mails, and so on. The school will certainly keep a detailed file on the child's progress and performance. As an advocate for your child, you should do likewise.

Consumer Rule #5—Never sign a document or a contract that you do not fully understand.

Parents should carefully read any school document that requires a guardian's signature. If you do not understand any part of the document, you are entitled to ask for explanations and clarification.

Consumer Rule #6—Read and follow directions carefully.

A wise consumer knows that *he,* just like the seller, has duties and responsibilities in a transaction. The product will work effectively only if the consumer fulfills his role by carefully following the instructions provided with the product.

Parents must be certain that they fulfill their part of the bargain made with the school. If Mom agrees to assist the child with his homework by checking his assignment sheet nightly, it is important that she fulfill this responsibility.

Consumer Rule #7—Decide what you want (and how much you can afford to spend) before you go shopping.

Most purchasing mistakes are made when a shopper goes into a store with no particular purpose in mind and makes impulse purchases. Invariably, she will purchase items that she does not need or cannot afford. A wise consumer goes to a store looking for a specific item in a specific price range. That way, she is unlikely to succumb to impulse buying or sales pressure.

When a wise parent goes to her child's school for a meeting, she should know—very specifically—what she plans to request at the meeting and what she hopes the results of the conference will be.

Consumer Rule #8—Always know your options, rights, and the appeal process, in the event that a product is defective or unsatisfactory.

As a savvy consumer of educational services, a parent should always be aware of his rights and the rights that his child possesses under the law. Know the personnel hierarchy at the school so you will know how to direct your appeal if you do not agree with a situation or a decision.

Consumer Rule #9—Everybody works for somebody.

You know a person knows his rights as a consumer when you hear him say, "Let me talk to your immediate superior."

Suppose you are dining in a restaurant and are extraordinarily unhappy with the quality of the meal. You address the problem with the waiter, who will not (or perhaps cannot) give you satisfaction. Naturally, you ask to speak to his superior. If the manager is unable to mollify you, ask to speak with the owner.

When dealing with school systems, parents often forget this fundamental concept. I recall a mother once saying to me, "Sabrina needs extra help in reading, but I asked her third-grade teacher about it and she said that extra help is not possible or available. So, I guess Sabrina will have to struggle on."

Not so, Mom. Remember rule number nine! The teacher works for someone, and the person whom she works for works for someone, and on and on. Talk to the teacher's supervisor, then the vice principal, then the principal, then the superintendent, and so forth. At each level, inform the person that it is your desire to settle the issue at *his* level, and inform him of your plans when you have decided to go to the next level. Don't threaten or intimidate. Merely inform him that you are aware of your rights and options.

It is inappropriate (and largely ineffective) to skip levels (e.g., taking a conflict with a classroom teacher directly to the school board). Follow the chain of command.

As you attempt to advocate and intervene on behalf of your child, it is important that you establish and maintain positive relationships with the teachers and other school professionals. Minnesota's renowned PACER Center offers the following guidelines for effective parent-professional interactions:

- Disagree without being disagreeable. Continually emphasize the importance of the home-school partnerships.
- Be willing to apologize when and if it is appropriate.

- Accept responsibility for your part of the issue or solution.
- Pick your battles. Some battles are not worth fighting.
- Assume good faith on the part of those with whom you disagree. Reasonable, caring people *can* disagree on some issues.
- Try to focus the discussion on facts and data, not on opinions and emotions.
- Two effective methods for breaking a stalemate are to compromise and to use a trial period to see if the compromise works. ("We will meet again to discuss it on the twenty-eighth.")
- Often, the parent may have more knowledge about a child's disability (ADHD, nonverbal learning disabilities, auditory processing disorder) than the teacher does. This is understandable because the parent has made focused efforts to learn about the child's unique problem. Share this knowledge graciously. Do not use your superior knowledge as a way to embarrass or humiliate others.

SUCCESSFUL PARTNERSHIPS REQUIRE EXPECTATIONS

Over the years, numerous studies and surveys have been conducted to determine the expectations that teachers have for parents as well as the expectations that parents have for teachers. Invariably, these studies render nearly identical results. It is important that the adults in a child's life hold reasonable expectations for the other adults involved in this educational partnership. Further, it is crucial that all parties understand the expectations that are held for them by their partners.

Ten Things Parents Wish Teachers Would Do

- Enhance the child's self-esteem
- Set high but reasonable expectations for the child
- Provide the child with the support and the structure that will enable the child to reach those goals
- Ensure the child's safety in class; protect him from physical harm, humiliation, and rejection

- Deal with behavior in a fair and consistent manner
- Communicate honestly and openly with parents
- Assign effective and appropriate homework
- Use a variety of teaching methods to meet individual learning styles
- Genuinely care about the students
- Be aware of the child's needs, strengths, and weaknesses

Ten Things Teachers Wish Parents Would Do

- Be involved in the child's educational journey
- Set a positive example for the child
- Be supportive of school rules, policies, procedures, and goals—avoid unnecessary absences
- Act preventively—contact the teacher while problems are small and manageable, not only when a crisis occurs
- Inform the school of any home situations that may impact upon the child's performance in the classroom
- Provide the child with the material he requires to complete school assignments
- Assist the child with his homework by providing him with a time and place to study
- Treat school personnel with respect and dignity
- Give the child praise, encouragement, and support
- Become an active and supportive member of the school community

PARENTAL PRACTICES THAT SABOTAGE STUDENT MOTIVATION

In order to assist a child in establishing and maintaining school motivation, parents must understand the nature of motivation. Basically, a motivated and successful student does five things consistently:

- Motivates and "drives" himself (self-motivation)
- Accepts and handles responsibility

- Takes pride and satisfaction in his work
- Establishes and works toward goals
- Asks questions and requests help when necessary

Parents should focus their efforts on enhancing and reinforcing these traits and behaviors. It is the parent's role to establish a consistent *work ethic* within the child. By instilling this ethic, the parent will help the child develop habits and behaviors he will benefit from for the rest of his life. Every successful person, whatever his station or occupation, possesses a firm and effective work ethic.

It is important not to confuse "work ethic" with "puritan ethic." ("No play until the work is done.") Rather, a person with an effective work ethic is capable of initiating a task, staying with the task, bringing closure to the activity, and taking pride in the process and the finished product.

There are several mistakes that parents commonly make in their well-intentioned attempts to inspire and motivate their children. Among these are:

Tangible Rewards for Good Grades

Before we discuss this practice, we must first clarify the difference between *incentives* and *bribes*. I was once meeting with a dad, and I was encouraging him to provide his daughter with incentives and reinforcers when she made observable progress on challenging tasks. "No way," he responded. "I'm not going to bribe my own kid to do what she ought to be doing anyway."

This gentleman had a common misunderstanding of the difference between *bribes* and *incentives*. A bribe is offered to a person *in order to persuade him to do something wrong* (e.g., bribing an elected official to illegally use his influence to benefit the person who provides the bribe). Conversely, an *incentive* is offered to a person for *doing something right* (e.g., a bonus given to a professional ballplayer for making the All-Star team). We need to remember the difference between these concepts. Providing a child with a reward or reinforcement for a job well done is not a bribe but an incentive.

That being said, the common practice of giving a child a monetary reward for good school performance is a highly questionable one. ("Pedro, I will give you ten dollars for every A that you get on your next report card.") Parents who do this may believe that they are merely replicating the pay-for-play concept of the adult world where people are reimbursed for completion of assigned tasks. However, this practice is often counterproductive for children. Ideally, the child should be working in school out of a sense of interest, ambition, and pride. By promising the child a specific reward for good performance, his motivation focuses on the tangible reward rather than on the satisfaction of a job well done.

Several years ago, a large fast-food restaurant initiated a laudable corporate mission: to encourage children to love reading and become lifelong readers. In order to accomplish this, they instituted a program where children could go to their local franchised restaurant and receive a book, and a book report form to complete after reading it. When the child returned the report form to the store manager, she would be given a substantial restaurant gift certificate.

This well-intentioned program was minimally successful. The children's desire to read was not lasting or permanent. When the incentive program ended, the great majority of children ceased their independent reading and chose not to accept the free books that the restaurant continued to offer. The children were not motivated to be better, lifelong readers. Rather, they were motivated to get the gift certificates.

Rewards will entice a person to do something that he would not ordinarily do—as long as the reward is provided. When the reward is withdrawn, the behavior generally deteriorates or ceases altogether. In addition, behavior that is motivated by extrinsic rewards is generally noncreative when compared to behavior that is motivated by internal factors (pride, eagerness to please).

By providing the child with rewards for positive performance, you also run the risk of dampening or eliminating any intrinsic motivation that may exist. For example, a child might have a desire to learn how to play the piano. Her delighted parents promise to give her five dollars for every lesson that she takes. The girl begins to save for some new ski equipment. Eventually, her motivation becomes focused on the ski equipment and the piano becomes secondary, merely a means to the end. This is particularly true if the reward is tangible, desirable, and granted despite the *quality* of the performance.

In summary, *external* rewards are only effective if accompanied by internal (intrinsic) motivation. If you love your job and find it fulfilling and meaningful, your external reward (salary) serves to be a motivator. If you dislike your job and find it unfulfilling, your salary is not particularly motivating and you will continually search for another job. So it is with students.

Using Punishment to Improve Children's Performance or Motivation

Parents will often punish children at home for poor performance or misbehavior at school. This common practice can have a negative effect upon the child's attitude and motivation, and generally results in resentment and resistance from the child.

I recall consulting with an elementary school that was having difficulty managing the behavior of a third-grade girl. The teachers and the parents had devised a program wherein the child would be punished at home (early bedtime, no TV) for misbehavior at school. Conversely, she would also be punished at school (lost recess, extra homework) for failing to follow rules and regulations at home (e.g., refusing to get out of bed). I was asked my opinion regarding this strategy.

I reminded the teachers and parents that, as adults, we have two distinct aspects of our daily life: our work life and our home life. Imagine if your supervisor, disappointed in the quality of a report you submitted, informed you that you would not be allowed to play golf that weekend. Surely, you would not tolerate or accept this response.

Aren't children also entitled to have two distinct sides to their lives?

Requiring a child to go to bed early because of misbehavior in a math class would be as inappropriate as disallowing his involvement in recess because he failed to mow the lawn at home!

Punishment is, generally, ineffective in making long-term changes in a child's behavior. Further, punishment seldom impacts positively on a child's motivation.

There are several reasons why punishment simply does not work for most kids, most of the time.

- *Kids can become immune to the effects of punishment.* Children who struggle in school are punished often and severely. Eventually, the child becomes desensitized to this strategy and punishment has no impact upon the child's behavior or performance.
- *Punishment does not eliminate behavior; it merely represses it.* If you punish Jason for throwing rocks in the front yard in view of the kitchen, he will begin to throw rocks in the *back*yard, where he cannot be seen.
- *Punishment is not instructional; it does not model desired behavior.* By punishing your son for bullying his sister, you have merely informed him of what you *don't want him to do*. You have not provided him with any information related to the *appropriate* way to treat his sibling.
- *Punishment models aggression.* I recall watching a young father as he walked along a mall concourse with his two sons, who were perhaps seven and five years old. The older boy was continually pushing and teasing his younger brother. Suddenly, the dad turned to his son and slapped him firmly across the side of his head. "That'll teach you to hit your little brother," the dad said.

  He was absolutely correct. That *will* teach him to hit his little brother.

  The father showed his son that might makes right and that power can be used to intimidate and control.

- *Punishment does not generalize to other settings.* Punishment merely *stops* behavior; it does not make meaningful or lasting *changes* in behavior. If you punish your child for trampling through your garden, she will likely cease this behavior. But this punishment will not prevent her from romping through Grandma's garden when on a weekend visit to her grandparents'.

  If a child is punished for failing to complete his math homework, this will not improve his homework performance in science class.
- *Punishment is effective only as long as the threat of punishment exists.* We all make certain that we adhere to the speed limit when we see a police cruiser parked by the side of the highway. We all sit a little straighter and busy ourselves when the boss passes our desk. But when the cruiser is no longer visible in our rearview mirror and when the boss returns to his own office, our behavior reverts back to normal.

  This is evidence that punishment ceases to be effective when the *threat of punishment* is eliminated. If a dad punishes a child severely for failing to clean his room, the boy will maintain a clean room while his father is at home. However, when dad goes on an extended business trip, the condition of the child's room will deteriorate rapidly. The sole reason for the child's effort to keep his room clean was to avoid punishment. When the threat of punishment is removed, the motivation to maintain a clean room is eliminated.

  Quite simply, punishing the unmotivated child does not teach. Punishment serves only to enhance the child's feelings of inferiority, anxiety, and resentment.

One particularly troubling punishment often used by parents is the practice of barring the child from participating in his very favorite activity in response to misbehavior or poor school performance. This practice, unfortunately, is widely touted and recommended by child care experts. They recommend, "Find the one thing that the child likes best—his bike, his computer, his skateboard, his participation in soccer—and take it away from him when he is bad."

This strategy runs contrary to good, effective human relations. The technique is cruel, insensitive, and—most important—ineffective.

As an example, consider that the overwhelming majority of marriages that end in divorce generally are dissolved over the issues of sex or money. Basically, the spouse who controls the sex or the money attempts to use it as a reward or punishment. Sex or money is figuratively dangled over the head of the partner, with the promise of its delivery if the partner "behaves" . . . and with the threat of its withdrawal if the partner fails to please the controlling spouse. Eventually, the noncontrolling spouse tires of this game and dissolves the marriage.

This strategy sends a troubling and harsh message: "I am going to select an activity or a possession that I know you want—something that you love and need. Now I am going to take it away from you whenever you displease me, and I will allow you to enjoy it only when you meet my expectations."

Quite simply, this is an inappropriate way to treat another person.

Lecturing to Show the Connection Between Effort and Progress

Children generally respond poorly to lengthy, judgmental lectures and diatribes. Although parents may think these lectures will help the child to better understand the connection between his efforts and his progress in the classroom, youngsters hold a very different view. If a child knows that he will be on the receiving end of a lengthy sermon whenever he asks a question or seeks advice, it is highly unlikely that he will seek you out for counsel. Kids become easily bored by these lectures and often respond to them with inattention, yawns, and rolling eyes. This behavior, of course, angers Mom and Dad. Soon, resentment reigns.

Another reason that lectures are generally ineffective is that they are judgmental in nature. These homilies are often filled with advice as to what the child "should do" (e.g., "Work harder on your homework . . .") or "should feel" (e.g., "You should be grateful that . . ."). Although adults tend to be relatively cavalier about telling children they are not trying hard enough or that they must try harder, it is important to remember that it is exceedingly difficult for any person to accurately judge the motivation of another. The degree of effort that one applies to a task does not necessarily translate directly to one's performance on that task. It is possible for a child to fail at a task when applying significant effort; conversely, a child can succeed at a task with minimal effort. You simply cannot judge a person's effort solely by evaluating his performance. These lectures stifle positive and constructive communication between parents and their children.

Nagging Instead of Helping

Again, children view this behavior differently than parents do. Mom and Dad view these constant reminders as helpful for the child with a memory problem. Conversely, children view this strategy as "hassling." The intent of this strategy may be laudable, but it generally results in resentment and frustration.

Dr. Robert Brooks, author of *The Self-Esteem Teacher,* relates a story about a child who was greatly perturbed by the nagging of his concerned mom—and the simple, yet effective, solution that eliminated the problem.

The twelve-year-old boy and his mother had daily confrontations about his medication. He would often forget to take the breakfast dose of his prescribed psychotropic drug. His mother would remind him about the meds several times during the morning as he prepared to depart for school. This caused great frustration for the child and great friction between him and his mom. The boy generally boarded the school bus angry and upset after this troubling daily routine.

Dr. Brooks interviewed the boy and his mom and soon realized that they both had very different views of the situation. Mom viewed her "reminders" as a strategy to assist her son and felt that he was being very irresponsible about taking his medications, considering the significant improvements that the drugs made in his daily performance. She said that she tried to make her reminders gently and in a supportive way.

The boy viewed the situation quite differently. He considered the mom's reminders to be "nagging" and felt that her constant prompts reflected her lack of faith in him. Further, he said that it was the tone of her voice that bothered him the most.

The boy and Dr. Brooks developed a unique and quite effective solution. They taped a note card with "meds?" written on it to the end of a pencil. They asked the mom merely to hold the sign up whenever she wished to ask if the boy had taken his medications that morning. The mother readily agreed with the plan. Problem solved.

HELPING YOUR CHILD DEVELOP A WORK ETHIC

A recent survey of child psychologists and educators produced some interesting results. The professionals were asked to identify the trait that is the most important ingredient in adult success. Of course, a wide variety of answers were proposed. The most common response was "the ability and willingness to work." This trait will help the child succeed in any occupational area he chooses.

Parents can do much to promote a sound work ethic in their children. Every family creates its own unique culture. This culture is developed and supported by the family's rituals, traditions, and day-to-day behavior. By promoting a family culture that celebrates and fosters a solid work ethic, your child is more likely to develop lifelong habits of motivation, perseverance, and productivity. It is important that the parent avoid promoting the so-called puritan ethic ("No play until the work is done"). Rather, we should promote a family culture that values and celebrates a balanced lifestyle of productive work and enjoyable recreation and play.

If you wish your child to develop an effective work ethic, it is important to provide him with a positive role model regarding work and productivity. Chronic complaining about your job and responsibility will do little to build a solid work ethic in the child.

I was doing paperwork one evening in our kitchen. Our daughter walked through the room and asked, "Dad, why do you work so hard and so much?"

"Well, someone has to pay for your clothes and food," I replied.

As soon as I made the statement, I regretted it. I missed a great opportunity to teach Meghan about work ethic. I love my work. I take my responsibilities seriously and feel that my work is important and valuable. I should have explained that to her in that teachable moment. I could have (and should have) told her of the joy and sense of accomplishment that accompanies my work. Certainly, *every* job has its moments of tedium, but for most of us, our motivation to go to work every day goes well beyond the weekly paychecks. Great self-esteem, satisfaction, and fulfillment accompany a job well done. Work is not merely an obligation or a burden.

There are a number of traits and behaviors that characterize families that promote a good work ethic with their children. Among them are:

PROMOTING WORK ETHIC IN THE HOME

Acceptance: Each family member has unique needs, strengths, affinities, and interests. As a result, each member should play a special role in the family. By using and celebrating the individual strengths of each adult and child, everyone gets an opportunity to shine. Every member of the family is allowed and encouraged to contribute to the common good, and in turn, each person is recognized and reinforced for his efforts and accomplishments. In Boston, the Conigliaro family is noted for the baseball talents of the brothers, notably former Red Sox superstar Tony. The patriarch of the clan, Sal, once missed a crucial Red Sox–Yankee game during the pennant drive. When asked why he was not in attendance, he responded that Tony's kid bother had a Little League All-Star game that evening and, as Dad said, "That's important, too!" Nice.

Families that emphasize acceptance also minimize expressions of disappointment when dealing with one another. I have long felt that disappointment is the most damaging and hurtful emotion that one human being can convey to another.

Think for a moment of an influential and important person in your life. This is a person whose opinion you respect and revere, someone you trust and whose opinion is very meaningful to you. It may be a parent, a sibling, a spouse, a friend, or a colleague. Now, would you prefer to have that person *angry* with you or *disappointed* in you?

Most of us would choose *angry.* When someone says he is disappointed in you, he sends the devastating and discouraging message that you have let him down and not fulfilled his expectations of you. Imagine how you would feel and respond if that important person were to call you tonight and tell you he was *disappointed* in you. Doubtless, you would be hurt and distressed.

Remember this when expressing disappointment in your child. Although children *will* disappoint parents, be very wary of expressing this emotion to them. In his early writings, Mel Levine referred to the youngster with learning disorders as "the disappointing child." Through no fault or choice of their own, they are a constant source of disappointment to siblings, peers, teammates, teachers, and coaches. As parents, we must be sources of encouragement, support, and hopefulness. Expressions of disappointment are the exact opposite of what these children need.

Gregory Hemingway, son of renowned author Ernest, made an insightful comment in his memoir. When he received the news of his beloved father's unexpected death, his first thought was that he would never again have to see the look of disappointment in his dad's eyes.

Affection: Physical warmth and affection should be a critical ingredient in the parent-child relationship. Parents sometimes feel that they are clearly communicating their love for their child by feeding him, clothing him, and attending his school events. A father once told me, "Actions speak louder than words. I don't need to tell my son how I feel about him. He knows how much I love him because I take an active interest in him."

Sorry, Dad. You need to accompany your attentiveness with affection. Hugs and other expressions of affection can greatly strengthen and deepen the bond between a parent and a child. Children with special needs are often unable to understand or appreciate subtle expressions of love. Your demonstrations of affection must be overt and observable. Smiles, pats, affectionate eye contact, thumbs-up signs, and hugs are necessary ingredients in a parent-child relationship.

During the teen years, a child may become somewhat resistant to physical affection from his parents. Certainly, you will want to respect his feelings and his physical boundaries, but you should continue to demonstrate your affection in observable ways. Parents should not hesitate to be demonstrably affectionate with one another in the presence of their children. By doing so, the parents demonstrate appropriate ways to express affection and also provide children with ongoing assurance that their parents' relationship is strong and stable.

A parent's love and affection for the child should be unconditional and constant. Therefore, it is inappropriate and harmful to withhold parental affection in response to misbehavior or poor school performance.

Another effective and meaningful strategy that communicates affection, support, acceptance, and stability is the establishing and maintaining of family rituals and traditions. These are particularly valuable for the child who struggles in school, because they provide her with a home life that is comforting and predictable. This serves as a welcome counterpoint to the chaos and inconsistency that characterizes the child's school day. These traditions should not be restricted to holidays, but should be a regular part of every day. These activities should not be negotiated. If Dad creates a ritual of reading a story to Nancy every bedtime, this activity should occur regularly and should not be dependent upon behavior. ("Nancy, if you don't finish your dinner, there will be no story tonight.")

These rituals enhance the sense of connectedness between generations, emphasize shared values, and demonstrate a family's strength. Even during difficult and challenging times, these rituals endure.

Parents should look for opportunities to express their affection for their children. These activities may include:

- Call your child when you are traveling.
- Write an affectionate note and hide it in her lunch box or book bag.
- Cook a child's favorite meal or prepare his favorite dessert.
- Follow an old New England custom: Purchase a unique dinner plate that is a different color and design from the family's dishware. When a child has a personal accomplishment (makes the track team, improves on a math test, or takes his first swimming lesson), serve him his supper on the special plate as the family congratulates him.
- Brag about your child—when the child is within earshot.
- Cook a meal or dessert together.
- Turn off the radio and converse with your child as you chauffeur her about.
- Take a long walk with the child—at *his* pace.
- Have weekly rituals that the child enjoys (reading the Sunday comics together, walking to church, making pancakes every Saturday, having an in-home movie night with popcorn every Wednesday).
- Send her a card in the mail. Every child enjoys receiving mail.
- Play board games.
- Listen to *her* music and let her explain it to you. Let *her* be the expert.
- Give him a framed family picture for his room.
- Tell him made-up, original bedtime stories in which he and his friends are the heroes.
- Say "Please," Thank you," and "I'm sorry" to him—a lot.
- Tell her stories about your childhood—and hers.
- Be welcoming and kind to his friends.
- Tell him that you love him. Loudly and often.

The child must know that his parents' affection and love is unconditional and lasting. He must not fear that misbehavior or poor performance will eliminate or diminish his parents' affection for him.

You can even communicate your love when scolding or reprimanding your child if you use an affectionate nickname. ("Your room is a mess, honey. Please go upstairs and clean it.") This statement clearly shows that you are unhappy with the child's *behavior*, not with the child. In this way, you are simultaneously communicating *love* and *limits*.

By being affectionate with the child, the parents confirm and communicate that they are the youngster's allies. A good ally is always on your side, looks out for your interests, and can be depended on for assistance and support. Of course, allies need not be in complete agreement on every issue and may disapprove of one another's behavior and decisions. In fact, candid input is the responsibility of an effective ally.

Communication: In order to effectively foster motivation, a family must have ongoing and effective communication between and among the family members.

All communication is a two-way street: talking and listening. When talking to a child, the parent should be certain to encourage a two-way dialogue as opposed to a monologue in which the parent does all the talking. Children have a natural aversion to judgmental lectures or scolding. They seldom listen to or comprehend such communication.

The most effective parent-child communication is truthful, candid, and supportive. Nagging, yelling, constant criticizing, and rudeness are counterproductive. Although a parent need not tell the child every detail of every situation, you should never knowingly lie to the child. It is important that children see in you a positive role model for honesty. This also enhances the child's trust in you. Avoid lying or exaggerating in front of the child. It is confusing for the child to hear his parents lie to others.

Parents must learn to communicate criticism effectively and sensitively. Criticism is meaningful only if it is specific. "You need to make your bed before you go to the movies" is far better than "Your room is always such a disaster. I am tired of your room being such a disgrace. You don't care what I think or say." Avoid using the words "always" ("You always forget to do your chores") or "never" ("You never clean the sink after you use it").

Of course, it is occasionally necessary and appropriate for a parent to criticize a child. The adult must understand that the child will invariably become defensive when presented with criticism. This makes it difficult to communicate in a meaningful way. Try to make the criticism brief, supportive, and specific. Emphasize the concept that you are criticizing the child's behavior, not the child.

Many professionals recommend the use of I messages when communicating with kids. You messages ("You never help around the house," "You always misbehave when Grandma comes over") are accusatory and confrontational. I messages, on the other hand, communicate your own opinions and feelings ("I really need your help cleaning the house" or "I get embarrassed when you are rude to me in front of Grandma").

These I messages communicate that you are willing to listen to the child's opinion, and they tend to discourage escalation of the situation.

The second part of the two-way street of effective family communication is *listening.* Parents must learn and use effective listening skills if they expect the child to communicate with them about school and social issues. It is unlikely that a child will discuss these issues with the parent who automatically responds with scolding and lectures. By listening attentively and respectfully to your child, you will be able to gather the information that you need in order to foster his motivation, enhance the parent-child relationship, and solve mutual problems. In addition, the parent who listens well to his child is more likely to be *listened to* when he speaks to his child.

When listening to a child, remember that she may not expect (or want) an immediate, sage solution to her dilemma. Sometimes a child just needs to talk it out, and needs someone to listen attentively.

When a child wishes to engage a parent in conversation or ask a question, the adult would be well advised to use the tenets of active listening. This communication strategy clearly demonstrates that you are ready, willing, and able to listen to the child's input.

Among the steps of active listening are:

Focus: Communicate with your body language and behavior that the speaker's message is important to you. Put down the sewing, hammer, or dust cloth. Clear your mind of distractions and truly focus on the child's words, opinions, and emotions.

Imagine that your supervisor entered your office and told you that he wished to speak to you. You would, doubtless, put down your pen, turn in his direction, and make extended eye contact with him. These body language signals would clearly indicate that you were prepared and eager to receive his message. Often we fail to extend these simple courtesies to our children.

Repeat (Rephrase) the child's thoughts and feelings: This technique shows the child that you are truly listening. It also ensures that you understand what he is saying. ("You say that you are very frustrated about your history test grade because you studied very hard but the teacher included test items from a chapter that you hadn't read.")

In this step of the process, allow and encourage the child to correct any misconceptions or misunderstandings. ("No, I read all the chapters, but she told us that the test would cover only chapters 33 and 34. She asked questions about chapter 35, and although I *read* that chapter, I didn't really study it.")

Communicate nonverbally: The parent should occasionally nod or smile while he is listening to the child. This body language demonstrates that you are, indeed, listening to the child's input. Supplement this body language occasionally by saying "I see" or "I understand."

Reflect: During the conversation, identify and label the child's emotions. ("You are feeling pretty sad about this, aren't you?" "It sounds like you were surprised and disappointed by your grade on that paper.")

Self-disclose: Children will often complain when Dad or Mom begins to reflect on their own childhood memories, but youngsters take great comfort in hearing that their parents faced dilemmas and challenges when they were younger that are similar to those the child is currently confronting. This technique also demonstrates the parent's humanness and authenticity. ("Josh, when I was in high school, I had a math teacher who simply didn't like me. I tried everything to get him to change his mind but nothing worked. I found out that he collected model boats and I brought him a stack of my uncle's old model magazines. From then on, he was very friendly and helpful.")

Summarize: Conversations between parents and youngsters can be wide-ranging and can cover a variety of topics. For this reason, it is helpful for the parent to summarize the conversation at its conclusion. It is particularly important to be certain that both parties understand their responsibilities. ("Okay, John. I think we both understand that you are overwhelmed in your literature class and you cannot keep up with the required readings. You are particularly concerned about next week's midterm. I agree that you can stay home Sunday when the family goes to visit Grandma so you can study. You are also going to talk to Mr. Middleton about the exam and ask for extra help. You will also join the study group. Now, if Mr. Middleton can't or won't give you extra help, I will call him. Are we agreed?")

Parents may wish to discuss a child's academic struggles with him in order to better understand his problem and foster his motivation.

TIPS FOR PARENTS TO USE IN MOTIVATING A CHILD

- Success is the greatest motivator. Recognize, reinforce, and celebrate the child's successes and progress—even the small victories.
- Compliment children for good decisions.
- Reinforce the child for small gains in a difficult subject area. Reward direction, not perfection.
- When reviewing a test or report card with a child, always comment *first* on the positive aspects.
- Take an active (but not intrusive) interest in the child's hobbies and activities.
- Enjoy family activities in which all family members work cooperatively toward a common goal (e.g., gardening, family game nights, community service).
- Help children set realistic goals for their academic, social, and athletic performances. Use these goals to monitor and assess their progress.
- Speak positively and supportively about the child's school and teachers. If the child senses a parent's hostility toward the school, it is unlikely that the child will be motivated to succeed there.
- Be aware of the child's symptoms of anxiety (changes in eating habits, sleeplessness, nightmares, compulsive behaviors, shyness, defiance, physical symptoms, cruelty toward pets or younger siblings). Anxiety can have a significant impact on motivation by compromising the child's ability to make decisions, use sound judgment, memorize, and learn. Severe stress has been shown to impact judgment, decision making, memory, and learning.
- Monitor the child's health and secure medical intervention for any physical problem that may be interfering with her ability to attend and fully participate in school.
- Provide regular, nutritious, well-balanced meals. A child who is hungry or not receiving adequate vitamins and minerals is unlikely to be motivated in school.

- Be certain that the child gets sufficient rest and sleep. Tired children simply cannot learn. Research indicates that even a one-hour difference in the amount of sleep a child gets will impact upon the child's school performance the next day. Sleep allows children to process the previous day's events, and to consolidate learned and memorized information. In order for a child to reach a deep, restful sleep he must go to bed feeling safe, secure, and loved. Avoid parent-child conflicts at bedtime.
- Communicate to the child the esteem that the family holds for education. Celebrate and reinforce learning. Remind the child that education is a top family priority.
- Do not tell a child that a task "will be easy" in order to enhance her motivation. ("Come on, Beverly, let's get started on that map work. It should be a cinch!") This well-intentioned strategy often backfires. If the child does well on the task, she is not particularly delighted because the assignment was labeled "easy." Conversely, if she he has difficulty with the assignment, she has failed at a "simple task." Either way, the child's pride and self-esteem are not enhanced. A more effective approach is to say, "This task is a challenge, but I know that you can do it."
- Celebrate risk-taking behavior on the part of children. The willingness to take risks is fundamental to school success and motivation.
- Work with your child in an effort to improve his organizational, time management, and scheduling skills.
- Be willing and able to explain to your child's teachers and coaches that his lack of motivation may be the *effect* of his school failure, not the *cause*.
- Avoid comparing the child to her siblings. This practice merely builds resentment and anger, not motivation.
- Remember the importance of family traditions and rituals. Children feel comfortable and accepted in a home environment that features consistent and ritualistic events.
- Make an effort to take care of yourself. Maintain your physical health by eating right and exercising. Have a strong support

system and allow yourself the "luxury" of participating in activities that replenish your energy and boost your spirits. Recognize your own response to anxiety and give yourself permission to take a break occasionally. You will be less effective as an advocate and coach for your child if you are exhausted and drained yourself. There is a reason why airlines advise you to don the oxygen mask *first* . . . then offer assistance to others.

- Consistently demonstrate how much you value learning by supporting the policies and practices of your child's school. Avoid criticizing the child's teachers. Speak positively about your own school experiences and promote the idea that learning is a lifelong process.
- Show faith in your child and in her ability to learn. Although the child's academic performance may occasionally cause you concern, disappointment, and distress, avoid communicating this to the child.

In summary, families that *foster* student motivation are:

warm	supportive	cooperative
loving	encouraging	concerned
consistent	accepting	respectful

Families that *discourage* motivation may be:

tense	critical	aloof
chaotic	controlling	fearful
hostile	rejecting	unpredictable

12

The Parent's Involvement in Academic Issues

> "Parents need to fill a child's bucket of self-esteem so high that the rest of the world can't poke enough holes to drain it."
>
> —ALVIN PRICE

PARENTS AND READING

Parents can and should play an important role in the child's mastery of the reading process. The ability to read and comprehend the written word is fundamental to a child's success in school. Although the parents should not assume the responsibility of actually teaching the child to read, they can do much to monitor and improve the child's reading skills by doing the following:

Read aloud to your child. Make reading aloud a ritual that occurs several times each week. These readings need not be only at bedtime, and the content need not be a typical children's story. Reading to a child from the sports page prior to a game that you are about to watch together sends a clear message about the value and enjoyment of reading. There are several benefits to reading aloud to children. This practice can:

- Create a stronger bond between parent and child
- Enhance listening comprehension and vocabulary
- Lengthen the child's attention span
- Broaden his fund of information and experience
- Stimulate her imagination
- Foster development of values, self-esteem, and confidence
- Promote critical thinking skills

Be a reading role model. Let the child see you reading books, newspapers, and magazines. Let him know that you enjoy reading and find it interesting, informative, and entertaining.

Make reading materials available. Have books, periodicals, and newspapers around the house and available for the child. I often give magazine subscriptions to children as gifts. The magazines focus on their specific interests (e.g., baseball, video games, animals, airplanes) and they "receive" the gift twelve times a year!

Encourage the child to tell you stories. There is an undeniable link between and among the four language arts: reading, writing, speaking, and listening. By reinforcing one area, you make improvements in the others.

Make regular family visits to libraries and bookstores. Teach the children where and how to get books. Also teach them how to care for and respect books.

Read the same book. This strategy is particularly effective in the summer. Purchase two copies of the same book and read it as your child reads it. As the story progresses, discuss it; predict what will happen next; talk about the characters and the plot.

Encourage the child to read to her younger siblings. This can be an enjoyable bonding experience that, simultaneously, gives the older child practice in reading and the younger child practice in listening. Make a tape of her reading and send it to Grandma.

Remember—children learn by repetition. For younger children, most stories contain a great deal of repetition. Beyond this, your child may want you to read the same story or poem over and over . . . and over. Be patient! He learns with every repetition. Don't hesitate to assume different voices when reading character dialogue. Be animated.

Conduct informal, nonthreatening comprehension activities before, during, and after each reading selection.

- Before reading a story to the child, discuss the title and ask him to guess what the story will be about.
- Stop midpassage and ask the child to predict what may happen next.
- Ask basic memory questions—"Do you remember what the horse's name is?" "How many boys were in the boat?"
- At the end of the story, ask the child to devise an alternative ending.
- Discuss new words, the main idea, and so on.
- Have her draw pictures to illustrate the story.

Take the role of listener as a child reads aloud, and remember the following:

- Don't jump in and make corrections when he makes a reading error.
- Don't pressure or embarrass the child when he reads.
- Don't be surprised if she is unable to read a passage that she was able to read the day before; performance inconsistency is common among kids who struggle in school.

When selecting books to read, use themes and collections. Select books that relate to the child's interests or hobbies (baseball, fishing), and ask the child what types of books he prefers. Many publishers offer series of books that feature a group of characters who become involved in various adventures. Relate the current adventure to exploits from previous books. This technique can improve the child's comprehension and memory.

Parents should conduct reading activities that are enjoyable and fun for the child *and* the parent. In this way, the child associates reading with pleasant experiences. Sit close. Laugh. Use funny voices. Stop reading at crucial, exciting passages. Ask the child what *he* would do if he were in the character's place.

By reading to and with the child, you can do much to improve vocabulary, background knowledge, comprehension, and language usage. More important, it provides you with an opportunity to discuss your family's values, beliefs, and history.

ENHANCING CHILDREN'S BACKGROUND INFORMATION

Parents can play an important role in increasing the child's fund of background information. This knowledge will enable the child to better understand social conversations and classroom discussions. If she has an extensive fund of facts and information in a wide variety of subjects and topics, she will be more motivated to participate in these important classroom activities.

Adults have literally millions of pieces of "social information" in their brains. For example, suppose I check into a hotel and the receptionist tells me that I will be staying in Room 503. There is no need to ask him which floor the room is on. An item in my fund of social information is that the first digit in the number of a hotel room dictates the floor on which the room is located. When I leave the elevator and walk down the hallway, I see that Room 544 is on my left. I immediately know that Room 503 will be on my right because odd-numbered rooms are always located on one side of a hallway and all even-numbered rooms are located on the other side. Imagine the response of the desk clerk if I asked him what floor I should go to in order to find Room 503. He would be quite surprised that this concept was not included in my fund of social knowledge.

Consider how many pieces of social information you store in your mind. You know:

- that mayonnaise will go bad if left in the sunlight
- that P.M. means afternoon and A.M. means morning
- that stores place butter and milk in the same section
- that if Christmas falls on a Wednesday, New Year's Day will also be on a Wednesday
- that parking meters generally accept quarters only
- that fine jewelry is different from costume jewelry
- that felt-tip markers dry out if you leave the caps off
- that the initials FYI mean "for your information"
- that stamps should be placed in the upper right-hand corner of an envelope

Although you know all of the above facts, you doubtless cannot recall when or where you learned them or from whom. You simply *know* them. You learned them by osmosis . . . and added the facts to your fund of general knowledge. Unfortunately, children with learning difficulties do not master social information in that manner. They do not "soak up" facts. Rather, they must be directly *taught* the information that others may master through informal exposure.

Parents and caregivers should use every opportunity to increase a child's social information, particularly when out in the community. Encourage him to ask questions about things that he might find puzzling, and answer these queries patiently and thoroughly. Explain the limitless pieces of information that exist in his daily social environment. Again, his social success and status are largely determined by his ability to master these facts. Children with limited background knowledge are often viewed as unintelligent by adults and as "thick" by their peers.

A lack of background information can also hamper a child's academic progress because she often fails to understand comparisons and analogies that are made in literature, textbooks, or classroom discussion. For example, if a teacher says, "The father ran his family in the same way that Hitler ran Germany," the comment is meaningless if the child has no knowledge of Hitler and his reputation as a ruthless, cruel leader. Because of the child's lack of background information, she may often be unable to understand analogies, comparisons, and references that she hears or reads during the day.

HOMEWORK ISSUES

Many home-school disagreements occur over the issue of homework. Today's teachers have greatly increased their homework expectations in terms of both quality and quantity. This is occurring at a time when American families are under increased economic and social pressure. Single-parent families, blended families, and dual income families find that their hours are full to overflowing, and homework adds a significant burden to their lives. Inappropriate or excessive homework can contribute greatly to the child's (and the parents') negative view of school. It can also become a flash point for parent-child conflicts.

However, well-planned, appropriate homework can have significant motivational and academic benefits. It enables the child to use outside resources such as the Internet and the library and provides reinforcement and review of the day's lesson, which can be invaluable for a child with memory deficits or processing problems. Homework also helps the child develop his study, organizational, and time management skills. Homework becomes more important and valuable as the child proceeds through the grades. Although research demonstrates that consistent homework has limited positive impact upon the academic development of elementary school students, it has a significant effect on the academic progress and performance of students in middle school and high school.

The Teacher's Role in Homework

In 1998, the U.S. Department of Education published some basic guidelines for the amount of time that students should spend nightly on homework. They found that children in the early elementary grades should devote less than twenty minutes per day to home study; older elementary students should be assigned twenty to forty minutes of homework; middle schoolers should have ninety minutes of work nightly; high school students should have ninety minutes to two hours daily.

If students are to be motivated to complete their homework accurately and fully, the teacher must collect, correct, and return the assignments on a regular basis. If a child's homework is left uncorrected or he seldom receives feedback on his homework performance, his motivation will naturally wane. The teacher should develop and distribute policies and procedures related to homework that outline the expectations and responsibilities of the student, the teacher, and the parent. These policies should be maintained consistently throughout the school year.

Teachers should keep in mind the settings in which the students will be completing their homework assignments. They will be working in their kitchens or bedrooms and competing with a wide array of interruptions, disruptions, and distractions. These settings are drastically different from the structured, orderly environment of the classroom. As a result, the students will be able to complete far less work at home than in school. I generally recommend planning for a 3 to 1 ratio (a thirty-minute in-class assignment will take the child ninety minutes to complete at home).

Directions and instructions for homework assignments should be clear and readily understandable. Be certain that the students fully understand the directions before leaving class for the day. Some teachers allow students to complete the initial portion of the assignment in class to ensure that they understand the requirements.

When asking parents to assist the child with homework, the teacher should keep in mind the parents' schedules and skills. Many parents simply do not have the time to help a child with homework. This does not reflect parents' lack of interest in the child. Rather, it reflects the pressures parents face daily from siblings, work responsibilities, and household chores. Also, be cautious not to offend or embarrass parents by asking that they complete tasks that are beyond their academic level. Requesting that a non-English-speaking parent "check Hector's spelling list nightly" can cause resentment or humiliation for the parent.

Encourage parents to establish a set time and place for the child to complete her homework. Ask that the child be provided with a homework kit containing basic school supplies that she can keep in her study area. This eliminates the need for her to continually leave her study desk to search for a stapler or a role of tape. Encourage parents to oversee—but not control—the child's at-home study.

Homework should serve as a positive link between home and school and can provide the teacher with valuable diagnostic information about the student's knowledge and understanding of the targeted material.

Children are more likely to enjoy and complete homework if the teacher provides a degree of novelty and variety. Use a variety of formats in your homework assignments in order to maintain students' motivation.

The Parents' Role in Homework

Parents can play an effective and valuable role in the child's homework experience. Many teachers are troubled by parents' unwillingness to assist the child in this area, while other teachers bemoan parents' overinvolvement in the process. Ask the teacher to design and distribute policies regarding the role of parents in the completion of homework.

Good, effective homework assignments should be a review and reinforcement of the material covered that day in class. If the child requires intensive parental assistance to complete the homework, you may want to ask the teacher to reexamine and modify the home study assignments. Homework should be designed at a level that allows the child to complete it independently. If a parent finds it necessary to work nightly with the child on his homework for several hours, the assignments are probably inappropriate. Homework is designed to *reinforce,* not teach.

Your child is likely to have a negative view of homework. If the parent reinforces those feelings by speaking negatively and disparagingly about homework, the child's resentment and opposition will likely increase. Try to reflect a positive attitude toward homework and try to promote the idea that homework is an important and valuable part of the education process.

It is beneficial to have the child complete her homework at the same time and in the same place every night. Her homework area should have a shoe-box-size homework kit that contains all of the supplies that she will need to complete her assignments (i.e., pencils, paper, scissors, glue, stapler, etc.). Be sure that the kit is restocked and replenished on a regular basis. The kit will eliminate the need for the child to leave the area to search for the office supply product that she absolutely *needs* to have.

Conventional wisdom holds that the child should complete his homework in an area that is quiet and free of distractions. However, this is often not possible, particularly for children with significant attentional problems. For many years, children have wailed to parents, "I can study better with the radio on!" Perhaps the child was right! The highly distractible child is at the mercy of every visual, auditory, and tactile stimulus in his environment. By allowing him to have music in the background as he does homework, he has but *one* distraction—the music. His productivity often greatly increases. Instrumental music generally works best because it eliminates the distraction of the lyrics and singing along. Children often know which study environment is most effective for them. Discuss this with your child in order to develop a homework environment that is tailored to his needs, temperament, and learning style.

Parents need to determine how much assistance they should be offering to the child as he completes his nightly homework. Mom and Dad often unwittingly provide the child with more help than he needs. A child was once heard to tell a friend, "I can't play baseball with you after dinner. I have to help my dad with my homework." A

New York City school had so much difficulty with parental overinvolvement that they established and distributed a guideline for their families that "parents' pencils should never touch a child's homework paper." Reportedly, this approach did much to decrease the problem.

I met with a parent who was extremely upset with her child's teacher regarding homework issues. Each night, Mom struggled through her son's assignments with him, and most evenings ended in tears (hers and his) after three hours of effort to complete the homework that seemed to be well above the child's skills and capabilities. The mother was very concerned about the teacher's lack of sensitivity to the child's problems and needs.

I asked her if she had spoken to the boy's teacher about this issue, and she said that she had not. I then asked her to view the situation from the teacher's vantage point: She assigns the child homework that is consistently submitted punctually and neatly with all answers prepared accurately and completely. The teacher is, quite naturally, going to continue to assign the same quantity and complexity of assignments because all of the signals she is receiving indicate that the assignments are well within the child's capabilities. She has no idea that the assignments submitted to her are the result of three hours of blood, sweat, and tears from the student and his mom. All of her evidence seems to indicate that all is well. I advised the mother to write to the teacher and explain the nightly angst and frustration that the family was experiencing as a result of the homework. The teacher responded immediately and positively by stating that it was never her intention to cause such upset to the family. She modified the assignments significantly and asked Mom to monitor the homework and provide the teacher with a weekly informal assessment about the amount of time the child was spending and the amount of frustration that he was experiencing doing his homework.

Many families have established a quiet "study time" in their homes. This consists of a structured hour after supper when *all* the children are involved in quiet, reflective activities. Even if the child has no specific homework assignments that evening, he can spend that time reading, writing letters, or working on long-term assignments. Some children benefit from a parental "check" of homework when it is completed. Use this check to praise, encourage, and reinforce the child and his efforts.

If a child seems to be overwhelmed by the volume of homework, take the assignments away and give them to her one at a time. When she completes one assignment, hand her the next. This serves to make what seems to be a mountain of tasks more manageable. This technique is also effective for children who consistently save the worst for last by waiting until the end of the homework session to tackle the most difficult and dreaded assignment. Of course, this is counterproductive because the child works on the most complex assignment when he is fatigued and exhausted. He should attempt to do the most challenging assignment at the *beginning* of the session, when he is more fresh and alert.

The child's homework performance can be greatly enhanced by maintaining a wall calendar in his room that lists all of his long-term assignments, deadlines, and activities. This will enable the child to budget and plan his time more effectively. The calendar should list not only the final due dates, but also the dates of the various steps in the process of the specific assignment (e.g., "November 10—note cards should be completed for Lincoln essay").

In her brilliant book *The Organized Student,* Donna Goldberg also recommends that the *parents'* evening schedule be posted on the calendar. In this way, Michael knows that he cannot count on Dad's help on the science fair project on Tuesday evening because Dad will be attending an out-of-town seminar.

Many children with learning problems have marked difficulty with temporal concepts. This means that they have trouble with concepts and activities that involve time. As a result, they have great difficulty determining how long an activity or task will take. They are often exceedingly late (or early!) for events and have great difficulty planning their activities and their day.

Parents can strengthen a child's sense of time by asking the child how long she believes each assignment will take her to finish. Write her projected times on the assignments. Ask her to note the specific times when she begins and completes the task. Discuss how close her projections were. If a child is unable to make reasonably close estimates regarding how long such tasks will take, she will have significant difficulty with the long-term assignments that she will be given in the upper grades.

Many children benefit from "hurdle help," where the adult helps her to get started on an assignment and then the child completes it independently. In this way, the adult is able to be certain that the child understands the instructions and that the task is within the student's abilities.

It is useful to work regular breaks into the homework session. It is best to arrange these before the child begins his homework session. ("After you complete your math and your journal entry, you can go have a Popsicle and play with the kittens for five minutes. Then you can get started on your history questions.") Some parents use a kitchen timer to structure homework breaks. However, it is best to schedule breaks after completion of a given number of tasks, not a given amount of time. The latter strategy may result in unproductive clock-watching or daydreaming.

On occasion, I recommend the use of a "cognitive behavior modification" for a child with significant attentional problems. This is a simple, but effective, technique that can greatly increase the child's attention during independent tasks such as homework. Follow these basic steps:

1. Put a blank cassette tape into a recorder (sixty- to ninety-minute tape).
2. Fast-forward the tape for a few seconds. Stop the tape and record a beep (piano note, bell, finger snap).
3. Repeat this process one hundred times. The result will be a tape that contains one hundred beeps at totally random intervals (three minutes, one minute, two minutes, forty-five seconds, five minutes, seven minutes, two minutes, etc.).
4. Post a piece of paper on the child's desk. Instruct him to do his homework. Whenever a beep occurs on the tape, he should make

a mark on the paper. If he was working and paying attention when the beep sounded, he should mark an *X*; if he was daydreaming or inattentive when the beep sounded, he should mark an O.

5. At the end of the session discuss his attending behavior with him.

When I first heard of this strategy I was quite skeptical. I felt that the beeps would be distracting and that the child would become focused on *anticipating the beeps*, not on his homework. Despite my initial misgivings, I have found this approach to be extraordinarily effective with many highly distractible children. A great sense of accomplishment occurs as the child sees the increase in *X*'s and the simultaneous decrease in O's as time goes on.

Long-term assignments can cause significant difficulty and challenges for students with attentional and learning problems because the children are often unable to divide the massive mission into manageable chunks. As a result, they find themselves in a state of panic the evening before the assignment is due. It is important to understand that this inability to plan and prioritize is not the result of a lack of motivation or interest on the part of the child. Rather, it is a significant aspect of ADD and involves trouble with executive processing.

We all use executive processing several times a day, and a person with deficient skills in this area is at a great disadvantage. An example of common executive processing is as follows:

I decide that I need to do some yard work on a hot autumn Saturday morning. I grab bottled water, put it in my jacket pocket, and go into the garage to gather the necessary tools. I take a rake to collect the leaves; several hours of raking will surely require a pair of work gloves; and a tarp will be necessary to lift the piles of leaves that I will produce. The wheelbarrow will be required to transport the heavy leaf-filled tarp to the far corner of the yard. I put the rake, gloves, and tarp into the barrow and go to the yard to begin the cleanup. This type of executive processing is a fundamental part of everyone's daily routine.

The child who has poor executive processing skills is likely to approach the task in a far less efficient manner. He retrieves the rake and begins to gather the leaves. After he begins to get blisters on his hands, he goes to the garage to get work gloves. While in the garage, he decides that he needs a drink of water. He goes to the refrigerator, and he sees his favorite cartoon on the kitchen TV set. He sits down to enjoy it. Ten minutes later, Dad rages into the kitchen to inquire why the yard is not raked and why the rake is lying in the driveway. Sound familiar?

If it does, your child doubtless has executive processing difficulties and he will need help and guidance for any multistep tasks that require planning and prioritizing.

When the child is given a long-term assignment, discuss the process that he will need to follow in order to complete the task. Mark the final due date on the calendar, then count backward by posting the various steps that he must follow in order to complete the project. This strategy creates several mini-deadlines that the child should adhere to, thereby preventing a collective last-minute panic on the evening before the assignment is due. The adapted schedule might look like this:

- April 10 and 11 (weekend)—research on New Zealand; find out about geography, foods, and government
- April 12—draw map of New Zealand
- April 13—prepare note cards
- April 14—interview Uncle Carl about his trip to NZ
- April 15—design outline for Part I
- April 16—design outline for Part II
- April 19—write a rough draft
- April 20—Dad reviews rough draft
- April 21—write final draft
- April 23—paper due to Mrs. Shipley

Some children with significant learning, memory, or attentional problems benefit greatly from a parental preview of an assignment before beginning the task. This strategy can actually be more effective and helpful than the "on call" technique where the parent tells the child to "come get me if you get confused or if you have trouble." The preview strategy is proactive and will often enable the child to complete the assignment independently, without parental intervention.

A preview session might sound like this:

"Okay, Alex, before you begin your social studies assignment, let's take a look at it. The questions on the work sheet all pertain to the chapter on Chile that you read last night, so if you get stuck, take another look at the chapter.

"The instructions say that you need to use complete sentences for all your answers on the second part of the work sheet. Remember, that means that each answer must have a subject and a verb.

"Read those true/false questions carefully. They can be tricky!

"Your colored pencils are in your homework kit. You will need them to do the map work on the work sheet. Go sharpen them in the kitchen and then you are ready to work."

Homework is a multistep process and, as a result, may present significant difficulty and challenges for the child with special needs. A simple checklist outlining the steps that she completes each evening as she does her homework can be very useful. It also provides her with a sense of accomplishment and satisfaction to be able to check off each task as she completes it.

- Did I write my assignments on my pad at school?
- Did I bring home all the materials that I need?
- What time did I begin my homework?
- How much help did I need from Mom or Dad? None—A little—A lot
- Did I work hard?
- Did I proofread my written work?
- Did I check my math work for accuracy?
- Do the finished assignments look neat?
- Did I put the work into the appropriate folders?
- Did I put the folders into my backpack?
- What time did I finish?

Review, compare, and contrast these nightly sheets on occasion to identify areas and skills that may be particularly problematic (e.g., proofreading, filing completed work). Work with the child to remediate these difficulties. You may also want to share these sheets with the teacher on occasion to assist her in analyzing and remediating the child's study skills and learning style.

Below are some additional tips and strategies that parents may wish to use in order to make homework a more effective and successful activity:

HOMEWORK TIPS

- Use trial and error to determine the best time and place for your child to do homework. Do not be surprised if each of your children has a different profile or pattern for homework success. For example, Taylor may be more willing to complete her homework as soon as she arrives home from school and she studies most effectively in her bedroom. Sean, however, may be at his best after supper and he prefers to work at the kitchen table. Of course, the schedule must be somewhat flexible in order to accommodate sports practices, outside activities, and appointments. However, once a pattern and a schedule are established, the parent should make every effort to see that the child consistently completes her homework at the same place and time each day.
- Parents whose children are close in age and who get along well find it effective to have all (or some) of the children complete their homework together at the kitchen table or in the den. Older siblings can assist younger ones, and homework sessions can become quite productive and even enjoyable in this setting. Peer tutoring will probably motivate the older child if he is inspired by prestige, power, or people.
- If you are preparing a homework kit to keep in the area where the child studies, you may wish to place the following supplies in that box:

glue	calculator	pens
tape	pencil sharpener	pencils

paper clips	scissors	markers
stapler	hole punch	erasers
ruler	index cards	paste
thesaurus	dictionary	composition paper
scratch paper	almanac with maps	

A shoe box or tackle box can be used for this purpose, as it can be moved from place to place as needed. It is less effective to keep these basic supplies in a desk drawer.

- Parents may have difficulty determining if the appearance of a child's homework is acceptable to the teacher. Ask the teacher to provide you with one of your child's completed assignments that is satisfactory in regard to neatness or legibility. Keep this sample and use it to assess the neatness of the child's nightly assignments. ("Bobby, if you compare your work sheet with the sample that Mrs. O'Brien provided me, you will see that tonight's work is just too messy. Please carefully erase the final two answers and rewrite them more carefully.")
- When you check your child's completed homework, you are generally assessing only its neatness and completeness. It is not necessary to evaluate every answer, although a spot check of a few responses may be helpful.
- A good way to gauge your child's successful completion of homework assignments is to ask to see some of his homework that has been corrected. Make a note of the teacher's comments regarding accuracy, appearance, and effort.
- In many families, television is the archenemy of homework. Children may wish to have the television on while doing homework or rush through their assignments in order to watch their favorite programs.

  One creative and effective solution to this problem is to budget the child's television viewing. For example, you might allow him eight hours of television viewing each week. On Sunday, you and he review the upcoming week's television listings and he decides how he will "spend" his viewing budget.

Because his favorite reality show has a two-hour extended program on Tuesday evening, he may elect to watch no TV on Monday. The Friday evening basketball game could well consume three hours of his budget, so he may want to plan to join the program "in progress" and watch only the second half. Of course, the system would be flexible enough to accommodate special circumstances (Olympics, miniseries, etc.), but this technique encourages the child to be a more discerning and selective television viewer.

- Some professionals recommend devising a formalized reward/reinforcement system in order to encourage successful homework performance. I believe that relatively few students require such a reward system. But occasional, intermittent rewards that recognize and acknowledge outstanding homework effort are always a good idea. ("Max, you worked so hard on that report. I made some cocoa for you—with marshmallows. It's in the kitchen when you are ready." "While you were working so hard on that math work, I washed the dog so that you won't have to do it this weekend.")
- Most children in the upper elementary grades, middle school, and high school will have *some* homework nightly. View the child's claim that he has "absolutely no homework tonight" very skeptically.
- Some children with learning problems develop a pattern of working on an assignment until it gets difficult and then putting it aside and beginning another assignment. Although she fully intends to return to the first task later in the session, her memory and organizational difficulties often cause her to forget. To her surprise, she arrives at school the next morning with four half-done assignments. Encourage the child to do each assignment to its completion and to seek assistance when she confronts difficulty.

HANDLING THE REPORT CARD

Did you ever follow a school bus as it dropped off students on the day that report cards were issued? It is a study in contrasts. Some students bound off the bus and run joyfully toward the front door, eager to share their good news and their hard-earned victories with Mom, Dad, and Grandma.

Other kids (often siblings of the aforementioned bearers of great tidings) slowly disembark and solemnly plod up their walkways, shoulders stumped, heads bowed. They enter their homes with the facial expression commonly seen in the waiting line at the guillotine during France's eighteenth-century revolution. By virtue of the fact that you are reading this book, you know, love, or teach a child like this.

Parents of children who struggle face the report card dilemma several times a year. The report card provides definitive, concrete, observable evidence of the child's academic challenges. The parent may feel that the child's grades are subtle evaluations of his own skills and abilities as a parent. Parents view the document as an assessment of the semester just past and as a harbinger for the future.

It is important that parents develop a realistic perception of the report card ritual. Remind yourself that, although you are reviewing this *single* report card, the teacher completes *thirty* of them! Much of the data on the card is subjective, arbitrary, or dated. Report cards seldom give a clear, lucid picture of the child's level of functioning and are often inaccurate predictors of future academic success. It is not a meticulously designed portrait. It's a snapshot.

Try to view the report card as a launch pad for discussion, not a chiseled-in-stone evaluation. Although the card contains valuable information, it seldom tells the whole story. Examine the document for patterns or other significant data. Is the child struggling in all of his classes that require significant amounts of independent reading? Is he doing well in all his hands-on classes? Does his performance deteriorate significantly at the end of the day? How do his grades compare to previous report cards?

When you discuss the report with your child, remain calm. Look for areas of improvement or consistency that are worthy of praise and encouragement. ("It's good to see that you maintained your B in science, Ben.") When you discuss a poor grade, ask the child if he has insights into the grade. Is the class work too difficult? Is the pace too fast? Does he feel lost during class discussions?

Use the report card to create, with the child, long-term and short-term goals for the next marking period. Record and post these goals in his room and refer to them often in a positive, supportive way. Discuss these goals with the teacher so she can assist the child as he tries to improve. Review and reinforce his progress toward the goals on a regular basis.

Appropriate report card improvement goals could include:

- John will maintain his B in science
- Zander will raise his C in math to a B
- Chelsea will finish her science fair project by April 12
- Ellie will be tardy for school only one day in March

If you find that you are shocked and blindsided by a poor report card, there exists a problem in the communication among you, your child, and the school. The teachers should have formally or informally notified you if the child was going to receive a very poor grade. The fact that you were surprised by the grades also reflects the fact that you had not been reviewing or monitoring the child's homework, test scores, or day-to-day school performance. Some parents find it useful to discuss the upcoming report card with the child a few weeks before the card is issued. Ask him to honestly predict what his grade will be in each subject. Record his prediction. If his projections are significantly different from the actual grade, try to determine why this occurred!

Remember that school evaluations can be quite subjective. Some teachers pride themselves on being "tough graders" who seldom grant A's or B's. Other teachers may take the report card process far less seriously. At nearly every level of education, teachers generally have free rein to develop their individual criteria for grading. It is not an exact science. Caroline's math teacher may count homework as 50 percent of Caroline's final grade, while her science teacher might assign 75 percent of the grade to class work and participation. Her fifth-grade language arts teacher emphasizes the mechanics of writing (punctuation, spelling, capitalization), while her sixth-grade instructor celebrates the student's creativity and free expression. These factors could account for the discrepancies that may appear on the child's report card. Do not assume that this disparity necessarily reflects the amount of effort that your child is investing. ("Well, *obviously* you are trying hard in your math class and you are not trying in science.")

With all due respect to my teaching colleagues, you should know that teachers seldom invest concentrated, focused effort on every single grade that they record on the card. Few elementary school teachers are going to ruminate for hours over whether to give Aksheen a "satisfactory" or a "needs work" in second-grade geography. If a child goes from an "outstanding" to a "very good" in his handwriting skills, it is not a cause for panic or alarm. It does not even signify a drop in performance. Perhaps it merely reflects that the child had difficulty in the specific area of the curriculum that was covered during the marking period. Again, grading is largely a subjective process in elementary and middle school.

Parents should also be aware of the trite phrases that are often placed in the "teacher comments" section of the card. These comments are rarely individualized. If you check around with your neighbors, you will find that 90 percent of Mrs. Brennan's third-grade students were "a pleasure to have in class," and an equal number "has difficulty settling down after recess." Not to worry, Mom. These comments seldom give valuable insights into the child's progress or performance.

If you are upset or angry or disappointed in your child's report card, it is important to remember that the child is likely experiencing the same emotions. She may need your support and encouragement *more* than she needs a lecture or a scolding. Perhaps she is embarrassed or frightened. Acknowledge her feelings (and yours!) and provide her with some comfort and consultation.

Remember—as the proverb goes, "Kids need love *most* when they deserve love *least*."

In the words of educator and speaker Dr. Roger Taylor, "*A grade is an inadequate report of an inaccurate judgment by a biased and variable judge of the extent to which a student has attained an undefined level of mastery of an unknown portion of an indefinite amount of material.*"

13

Explaining Learning Disabilities to Your Child

"Self-knowledge must precede self-advocacy."

—MEL LEVINE, MD

A PARENT ONCE CALLED my special education school to request an admissions visit for her and her son, who was struggling mightily in school. She asked a strange question in her initial phone call: "Does the school have any signs or posters displayed that identify the program as a school for kids with learning disabilities?"

I asked her why she wished to know this.

She replied, "My son doesn't know that he has a learning disability and we don't want him to know."

He *knows,* Mom. Believe me, he knows.

I have long been puzzled by a parent's reluctance to discuss a child's learning disability diagnosis with him. The knowledge that the child has an identifiable, common, measurable, and *treatable* condition often comes as great comfort to the youngster. Without this information, the child is likely to come to believe the taunts of his classmates and feel that he indeed *is* a "dummy." After all, if your child had asthma or diabetes, you would surely explain to her the nature of these maladies and the precautionary steps that she could take to minimize the impact of the condition. So should it be with a diagnosis of learning disorders. The truth will set them free!

If a child does not have a basic understanding of the nature of his learning challenges, it is highly unlikely that he will be able to sustain his motivation in the classroom. Because he is puzzled and confused about the difficulty that he is experiencing at school, he is unlikely to be able to commit himself to his studies. In effect, self-knowledge is a critical step in establishing and maintaining a child's motivation.

When discussing the child's learning problems with her, it is critical to explain what the disorder is—*and what it is not*. You may find that the child holds many misconceptions about her disorder ("It goes away at middle school"; "It means I'm stupid"; "I'll never be able to read"), and it is important that you clarify and correct this misinformation. Again, if you do not provide the child with accurate information, she is likely to believe the incorrect input that she hears or overhears in the school yard, on the bus, and in the media.

During these discussions, emphasize her strengths and affinities and do not simply focus on her weaknesses and difficulties. Attempt to strike a balance between what she *can* do and what is difficult for her. Express optimism about her development and her future.

Continually remind the child that she can, indeed, learn but that she learns in a unique way that requires her to work hard and participate in classes and activities that are different from her peers' and siblings'. Emphasize the fact that this situation exists through no fault or choice of the child's. Explain that learning is a particular challenge for her and that it may take her longer to master skills than it will take her classmates. Remind her that she will "finish the race," but it might take her longer and she may have to take a different route. Constantly let her know that the adults in her life are solidly on her side and that she can count on your support and understanding.

It may be helpful to discuss some learning struggles and challenges that *you* faced during your school years and outline the solutions and strategies that you used at those times. This information can be quite comforting for a child. Although many professionals may disagree with me, I do not find it useful to cite famous people with learning problems as a means of inspiring and motivating the child. The media is continually reminding us that many notable entertainers, sports figures, entrepreneurs, and politicians have struggled with and "overcome" their learning disabilities. Children with battered self-esteem are unlikely to be inspired by these stories because these youngsters are unable to imagine themselves as successful adults and certainly cannot relate or compare themselves to world-renowned celebrities.

A more realistic approach might be to cite people whom the child knows as inspirational examples: *"Did you know that Uncle John also had a lot of trouble in school and he had to repeat third grade? It used to take him forever to do his homework and he still has difficulty writing. But he has a terrific job at the hospital and he is raising a great family. He enjoys cooking—just like you do—and nobody makes a better chili!"*

One of the most valuable and important roles that a parent can play in the life of a child with special needs is that of demystifier. The parent should explain the disability to the child, thereby demystifying the child's daily struggles. The youngster often feels greatly relieved once he realizes that his difficulties actually have a name and—most important—that others also have similar problems and challenges.

However, it is important that these explanations be made in a sensitive and age-appropriate way. This important information should not be communicated in one intense "let's discuss your learning disability" session. Rather, you should discuss the child's learning problems with him in a gradual, informal, and sequential way. Many of these discussions will be unplanned and will occur spontaneously in response to incidents that may occur at home or at school. These opportunities for discussion can be an invaluable tool in educating the child about his problems and enhancing his self-esteem. For instance, if the child is having difficulty setting the dinner table and becomes frustrated, you might use that opportunity to explain his sequencing and directionality problems.

"Carl, I know that this is difficult and frustrating for you and I really appreciate your willingness to stick with it. It's tough for you to remember the order you should follow when setting the table, but it will be easier if you refer to the checklist that we made last week. Remember? We keep it on the shelf near the dishes. After you have used the checklist for a while, we will begin phasing it out and I'll bet that you will be able to set the table by yourself within a few weeks. Remember that we followed that process when you learned to make your bed, and you do that chore really well now.

"Remember that the knife and spoon go on the side of the hand that you write with, and the fork goes on the other side.

"These problems that you have relate to something called sequencing and directionality. These skills will always be a little difficult for you, but you are doing much, much better. All of your hard work with Mrs. Carter in your OT class is really paying off. The extra lessons that Coach Simons is giving you in soccer should help your directionality, too."

Often, teachable moments may occur when a child asks a question related to his disability. Remember to answer his questions honestly and sensitively, and be wary of providing more information than the child can understand or handle. As an analogy, imagine that the child is an empty cup devoid of any information about the nature of his disabilities. You are represented by a pitcher, filled with data, reports, information, and knowledge about this disability. Slowly "pour" your knowledge into the cup until the vessel is full. Don't continue pouring until the cup overflows! Put the pitcher down and pour more knowledge into the cup later as it is requested or needed. During these discussions, carefully observe and listen to the child. You will recognize the signals that "his cup is full" and that the discussion should be concluded. Always end the conversation by encouraging him to ask questions, and assure him that you are eager and willing to have these discussions with him.

Of course, the adult should keep in mind the child's age and language skills when having these discussions. A parent-child conversation with a six-year-old is likely quite different from a disability-related conversation with a sixteen-year-old. You may refer to a six-year-old's hyperactivity as "feeling all wiggly"; the adolescent should understand the more clinical terms of "distractibility," "impulsivity," and "inattention." At times, you may want to compose a simple script before you begin a conversation that may be upsetting or troubling for the child (e.g., about medication, evaluation results, a change in program). Again, it is important that these discussions be open and supportive. They should be conducted in an upbeat, informational, and sensitive way. Always remember that the child's struggles are not his choice—or his fault.

During these conversations, continually remind him that he has a strong and intact support system consisting of adults who truly care about his well-being and his progress. Cite his teacher, grandparents, coaches, neighbors, and extended family. Often, the struggling child feels alone and abandoned. Remind him that he is neither.

When the child is in early elementary school, avoid using jargon or professional terms and use terminology that is readily understandable for her. As she gets older, begin to talk about accommodations and modifications that she may need. ("The teacher will give you more time to finish your test." "Mrs. Chapman has agreed to give you a little less homework than your classmates.") Encourage her to use teacher-pleasing behaviors in response to this extra help (saying please and thank you, making eye contact, being helpful). Reassure her that her negative, fearful feelings are natural and understandable. Emphasize that the child is different, not defective.

This demystification process is a crucial first step in the child's journey toward motivation, independence, and self-advocacy. As an adolescent and adult, she must know how to explain her difficulties and needs to teachers, coaches, supervisors, and employers *without* parental intervention.

DESIGNING A DOSSIER

A father of a special needs child once said to me, "You know, when you buy a new cell phone, computer, or lawn mower, you are given an instruction booklet to help you prevent and solve problems. It's too bad that kids don't come with instructions."

Well, maybe they should. If you are the parent of a child with learning problems, you realize that there are innumerable adults who pass through your child's life—babysitters, coaches, teachers, church personnel, bus drivers, school support staff, dentists, barbers, neighbors, and relatives. Most of these people are unfamiliar with learning disorders and, certainly, are not aware of your child's unique pattern of strengths, affinities, needs, and limitations. It is in the best interest of the child to provide those adults with some basic information that will help them better understand the child and his behavior. Further, this information can be used to generate techniques and strategies to monitor and improve the child's behavior and performance in a variety of settings. It also serves to shorten the amount of time that the adult will need to get to know your child.

President Ronald Reagan was governor of California for many years before entering the White House. As a result he had developed a number of very effective management strategies. He often cautioned his cabinet members and their subordinates: ***"Don't bring me problems . . . bring me solutions."***

Instead of entering the Oval Office and announcing, "Mr. President, we have a problem with House Bill number 96–182," they would simultaneously identify the problem and present several possible solutions that could be applied to the situation. "Mr. President, we have a problem with House Bill number 96–182. We could withdraw the bill from consideration, attach the substance of the bill to House Bill number 96–189, or assist the House leadership in amending the bill and resubmitting it. Which solution do you think we should try?"

As parents of children with learning problems, you would be well advised to apply Reagan's problem-solving strategy when dealing with the many adults who cross your child's path. Rather than bombarding them with information related solely to the child's weaknesses and needs, also provide them with strategies and approaches that have been shown to be effective for your child. Believe me, this input will be welcomed and much appreciated.

One of the most effective ways to provide this information is to develop and distribute a dossier. This is similar to the packet of information that a newly arriving diplomat presents to the leaders of the government of his host country. This brief (one to three pages) document provides data on the child's disorder but *also* offers suggestions that the adult can use to enhance the child's progress and performance. This document may even be helpful for the teachers who deal with your child every day, because it provides useful information that may not appear in the child's school records.

A well-designed dossier consists of seven sections:

- Introduction
- Diagnostic data
- Weaknesses
- Strengths
- Interests
- Supplemental personal information
- Suggested strategies

The introduction section should include some very basic data about your child and an expression of your appreciation and your willingness to assist the adult in any way. Include contact information and other basic data.

The diagnostic data should include a layman's overview of the child's diagnosis, with a brief explanation of the nature and needs of children with that particular problem. You will also want to address any common misconceptions that may exist regarding the disorder.

The section on weaknesses should list specific skills and activities that will present difficulty for the child. A brief explanation of the connection between the child's difficulty and her diagnosis may be helpful.

The section outlining strengths should emphasize the behavioral, social, and academic areas in which the child is successful. Be careful not to overstate her strengths, and remind the reader that these areas are "relative strengths" when compared and contrasted to her needs and areas of weakness.

In the section about the child's interests, outline the child's affinities and hobbies. This information enables the adult to view your child as multidimensional, and may enable him to use your child's interests in the activities that he conducts.

I refer to the supplemental personal information as the "You oughta know . . ." section. Every child has had positive or negative life experiences that may impact upon his day-to-day performance. In order for an adult to fully understand the child and her behavior, it is useful that he have this information that will enable him to view her behavior within a different context.

To help parents better understand the form and function of a dossier, I have designed one for a fictitious child.

The suggested strategies section should provide specific techniques that have been proven to be effective with the child in the past. The strategies should be explained in easy-to-understand language.

INTRODUCTION

Good day!

Drew is a ten-year-old student who has recently enrolled in your program. Although I am obviously biased, I feel that you will find him to be quite cooperative and eager to please. He is a diligent worker and is always willing to assist others whenever possible. His family and I greatly appreciate your working with him and are particularly grateful for your willingness to read this letter.

DIAGNOSTIC DATA

Drew has been diagnosed with nonverbal learning disabilities and auditory processing deficits. Although neither of these disorders affects his outward physical appearance, they will impact upon his ability to participate in your program, follow oral direction, and interact with others. In order to better understand and interpret Drew's behavior, it is important that you have some knowledge of these disorders.

A nonverbal learning disability can be a puzzling and complex disorder. The label is, as you will see when you meet Drew, a bit of a misnomer. Drew is highly verbal with a wide, expansive vocabulary. The disorder does not impact his ability to communicate verbally, but it will have a marked effect on his ability to function in your program. In fact, his ability to converse and discuss with adults often masks his confusion in social and academic settings. He has great difficulty with situations involving spatial skills, will often misjudge distances, and has a poor sense of direction.

The auditory processing disorder will also serve to complicate and compromise his involvement. It is important to recognize that Drew does not suffer from a hearing loss, per se. Rather, the message that enters his ears gets scrambled in some way, and as a result, there are subtle differences between what is said and what he actually hears. For example, he might hear the sentence "Matt and Drew went to town" as "Matt, Andrew went down." Of course, this makes it difficult for him to understand and follow verbal directions.

This disorder makes it difficult for Drew to process verbal language. In order to better explain Drew's difficulties, an analogy might be useful.

Have you ever gone into a restaurant or store where the waiter or clerk has a heavy foreign accent? As you attempt to converse with him, you frequently miss words that he says, and must interpret his meaning. You find this difficult, frustrating . . . and exhausting. This is very similar to the experience that Drew has with every conversation with his peers, family, and teachers.

WEAKNESSES

- Moderate difficulty with balance and coordination
- Difficulty understanding and following directions
- Difficulty reading facial expressions, body language, and moods of others
- Very naive; gullible; easily manipulated by peers
- Works slowly and deliberately
- Easily distracted by background noise
- May have high startle response to loud or unexpected noise

STRENGTHS

- Excellent reader (but may not comprehend all that he reads)
- Excellent rote memory (again, may have some difficulty understanding the material)
- Rich, expansive vocabulary and verbal skills
- Very kind and empathetic; generous
- Eager to please adults

INTERESTS

- Major League Baseball (Red Sox)
- Board games involving trivia and strategy
- Music (his uncle plays keyboards in a seventies nostalgia band, and Drew has a particular interest in music from that era)
- Collects sports memorabilia

SUPPLEMENTAL PERSONAL INFORMATION

- Drew was bullied and rejected at his previous school

and is easily intimidated by others. He becomes very quiet and withdrawn when he is fearful.

- His grandfather died suddenly last month. They were very close and Drew continues to have difficulty dealing with this. He may try to engage you in conversation about his grandfather.
- Drew recently began horseback riding lessons and he is very proud of his progress in this area.
- Drew is the youngest of three brothers. His siblings are very athletic and accomplished in sports. Drew feels very inferior in this area.

SUGGESTED STRATEGIES

Drew responds well to a signal or a gesture as a cue to modify or adjust his behavior. For example, when he needs to lower the volume of his voice, I get his attention and wink at him. This signal tells him to lower his voice but is not embarrassing for him in front of others. You may want to arrange some signals to use with him if he begins to behave inappropriately or manifest an annoying behavior.

Drew has difficulty making transitions from one location to another, or even from one activity to another. He handles these transitions far more effectively if he is provided with a warning or a heads-up a few minutes before the transition is to occur. ("Drew, you have about five minutes to work on your project and then we are all going outside for a demonstration.")

Because of past negative relationships with teachers, Drew is particularly sensitive to scolding or reprimanding and often shuts down when scolded in public. We find it helpful to emphasize that we are upset with his behavior—not upset with him. The behavior is bad—not Drew.

Drew has become quite adept at acting like he understands directions or instructions when, in actuality, he does not. He may make eye contact with you and nod knowingly. We find it useful to have Drew repeat the instruction back to us before he begins the task, in order to ensure that he truly understands.

Drew's verbal responses to others are often curt and can be interpreted as rude or dismissive. When he does this, please intervene and provide him with a more appropriate response.

Again, many thanks for your help. We greatly appreciate your assistance.

Best,

Drew's Dad

14

Household Chores and Work Ethic

"Work is nature's physician; it is essential to human health and happiness."

—GALEN

"God gives every bird his food, but he does not throw it into the nest."

—J. G. HOLLAND

A WORK ETHIC IS both a cause and a consequence of motivation; the two concepts are intricately connected to each other. A solid work ethic includes traits such as perseverance, initiative, and commitment. These traits are fundamental to student motivation. At the beginning of chapter 11, I cited the sage words of my mentor and friend, Mel Levine. He feels strongly that it is the responsibility of the parent to instill a work ethic in the youngster. The ability and willingness to accomplish assigned tasks are critical to adult success and prosperity. The child must learn to take initiative, use the proper tools, complete a job correctly, follow through on the task, and self-evaluate when the job is completed.

There is no more effective strategy for teaching these fundamental skills than household chores. Most families that function well assign defined jobs and responsibilities to each family member. When planned and assigned appropriately, the child does not view these tasks as tedious drudgery. Rather, they are seen as crucial in the family's ability to function effectively and efficiently.

Regular, consistent household chores provide the child with instruction and reinforcement in innumerable positive skills and traits. Chores foster a child's self-sufficiency, responsibility, confidence, self-esteem, fulfillment, and sense of belonging. A recent University of Minnesota study found that completion of regular household chores as a child is one of the most reliable predictors of successful adulthood. The well-intentioned parent who feels that she is doing her child a favor by not requiring the youngster to help around the house is, unfortunately, misguided. She is denying that child the opportunity to develop good work habits, self-esteem, and independence. There is a strong body of evidence that indicates that the work habits that are developed at home are carried over into the classroom and, eventually, into the workplace.

When the inherent value of household chores is recognized, parents can overcome and eliminate any guilt that they may feel about requiring the child to complete chores. A mom once told me that she did not believe in assigning chores to her children because "Kids should be allowed to be kids. Work is for adults. Play is for kids."

Although the mother's opinion was born of genuine affection for her child, it was ill advised. She was, unwittingly, depriving the child of a laboratory where he could learn skills and foster traits that will be fundamental to his future success. Chores also provide the child with a tangible and observable demonstration of the family's priorities and values.

Beyond this, regular household chores enable the child to master valuable life skills (e.g., cooking, cleaning, home maintenance) that he will need in order to function independently as a young adult. In previous generations, young people moved seamlessly from their parents' home to a home with their spouse. The current generation is marrying later in life, which requires the young person to be on his own for several years. His success in those years is largely dependent upon his ability to accomplish these important—albeit mundane—household tasks. Included in this chapter are some tips on the successful development of a chore system in your household.

Start 'em young! The aforementioned University of Minnesota research demonstrated the ineffectiveness of the oft-used "give the kid a free ride until his adolescence—*then* give him assigned chores" approach. Even the youngest child in the family can and should be expected to complete regular chores. Of course, the assigned tasks should be developmentally appropriate. Some suggested guidelines include:

- Two to four years old: pick up toys and clothes—ten minutes daily
- Five to seven years old: feed animals, retrieve mail or newspapers, basic cleaning, care of plants—ten to fifteen minutes daily
- Eight to twelve years old: vacuum, make own lunch, clear table, load dishwasher, sweep, take out recycling/garbage, simple food preparation—fifteen to twenty minutes daily
- Twelve-plus years old: prepare family meals, wash car, yard work, laundry, babysit for siblings, shopping errands, ironing—twenty to thirty minutes daily

One family that I worked with had a novel—and quite effective—strategy for establishing appropriate chores for their four children. On each child's birthday, Mom and Dad had a ritualized "birthday talk" with the child wherein they would discuss any new privileges that the child requested for the coming year (e.g., later bedtime, different weekend curfew). For each new privilege, the child was also given an additional chore or responsibility.

Children (particularly those with learning problems) need clear, understandable, detailed instructions related to chores. Merely telling the child to "go clean your room" is insufficient and will doubtless result in confusion, resistance, and conflict. Provide the child with a checklist that outlines the criteria for a clean room.

For example:

Your room is clean when:

- All dirty laundry is in the hamper
- All clean laundry is in the proper drawers
- Bed is properly made
- Books are reshelved
- Room is swept and vacuumed
- Toys are in toy box and athletic equipment is in garage bins
- Rubbish is emptied
- All food, cups, glasses have been brought to kitchen
- All clothes are in closet and dresser
- Desktop is clean

Provide the child with an estimate regarding how long each task should take to complete. Post a chore chart that lists each child's assigned jobs, which should be checked off or crossed out upon completion. These charts also serve as a reminder for the child and may eliminate the need for Mom and Dad to constantly nag him. In a sense, the chart—not the parent—becomes the "bad guy."

It is generally a good idea to teach one chore at a time. Once that chore is mastered, teach another task.

ASSIGN APPROPRIATE TASKS

In addition to the child's developmental stage, the parent should consider the child's skills and interests when assigning chores. If Joan enjoys being outside, she can rake leaves. If her sister enjoys cooking, she can prepare meals. Avoid assigning chores strictly along gender lines. Boys should learn basic cooking skills; girls should know how to operate the lawn mower.

Remember: One of the goals of household chores is for the child to learn skills that he will need in order to function independently in the future.

Allow and encourage children to switch tasks on occasion. This may break the tedium of the chores and provide the child with valuable experiences in alternative skills. Some families construct chore charts that rotate the assignments on a regular basis.

Not all assigned chores should be solitary. Occasionally, require kids to work together on a project. ("Meghan and Sean, I want you to clean the garage together on Saturday.") This strategy fosters cooperation among siblings because it is in both children's best interest to complete the task in a timely manner. Family chores ("Let's all work in the garden this afternoon") can promote family harmony and a sense of belonging.

Avoid "springing" chores on children. ("Jason, come in here now and clean your room.") This can build resentment toward the chore and toward the parent. Give the child the courtesy of a fair warning. ("Jason, sometime before supper, you need to clean your room. It should take you about thirty minutes and we're eating at seven o'clock. Okay?")

Earlier in the book, I wrote about the tendency to treat kids in a way that adults would *never* treat an adult. How often do you say to your child, "Matthew, go move your bike off the lawn and put it in the garage *right now*!" or "Turn off that TV *immediately* and feed the dog"?

Now reflect on how likely it would be that you would give such a command to your spouse. ("Nancy, come here *now* and help me figure out this electric bill." "Frank, the kitchen faucet is dripping. Fix it this instant!") Highly unlikely. Rather, we extend courtesies to adults that reflect our respect for them and their activities. ("Frank, the kitchen faucet is leaking again. Would you take a look at it when the ball game is over?" "Nancy, when you get a minute, can we figure out this electric bill?") We should extend the same respectful courtesy to our kids. ("Matthew, you need to put your bike in the garage. It is supposed to rain tonight. Please get it during the next commercial.")

PERSONAL AND *SOCIAL* RESPONSIBILITY

As adults we have a responsibility to care for ourselves (maintaining health, hygiene, etc.) and a responsibility to care for others in our community. You can reinforce this concept with your child by assigning chores that reflect the child's personal responsibility (e.g., bathing, room cleanliness, care of clothing, possessions) and social responsibility (e.g., care of common areas of the house, yard work, family laundry, cooking). The smallest unit of "community" is the family, and household chores reinforce the concept that the child has responsibilities beyond his own needs. He also has responsibilities for the common good.

As the child gets older, you may want to extend chores beyond the household. ("Melissa, as part of your weekly chores, I want you to help Mrs. Collins next door put away her groceries every Monday afternoon. She has difficulty with the heavier items and can no longer reach the top shelves in her pantry.")

Teaching a child to help a needy, infirm, or elderly neighbor provides an excellent lesson in social responsibility. You will also find that helping others is extraordinarily motivating for the child. One of the greatest human needs is the need to be needed. These activities provide the struggling child with a much-needed sense of contribution and accomplishment.

DEALING WITH CHORE-RELATED CONFLICT

Chores can become a flash point for parent-child conflict. Despite your best efforts, the child will occasionally view his chores as a negative intrusion.

When a child whines or complains about a chore ("Mom, I'm tired—I don't want to bring out the rubbish"), keep your cool. Don't give him a threat or command. ("You bring that rubbish out right now or you will be one sorry young man!") Rather, calmly provide him with a choice. ("I'll bet you are tired, Patrick. You've had a long day. The rubbish needs to go out before you go to bed. Would you rather do it after supper? Or I could ask your brother Scott to take the rubbish out now, but you will have to empty the dishwasher for him after dinner. It's your call!")

REWARDING THE CHILD FOR COMPLETING CHORES

Many parents provide their child with an allowance that is directly correlated to the successful completion of the child's chores. If the chores are done satisfactorily, the allowance is granted. If the child fails to complete, forgets, or neglects the chores, no allowance is given. Many professionals feel that this is a misguided and ineffective strategy.

Consider for a moment the reasons for assigning household chores:

To teach valuable life skills
To foster family values
To build confidence
To increase sense of belonging
To teach about the common good
To enhance self-esteem

Now consider the reasons why we give allowances to kids:

To foster independence
To teach wise spending habits
To teach wise saving habits

When these reasons are considered, it becomes clear that the allowance is not a reward—it is a learning tool. It is akin to a child's dictionary, encyclopedia, or computer. It is given to him in order to teach critical skills. Would you take away a child's dictionary if he failed to clean his room or feed the dog? Doubtful.

I believe that kids should be assigned chores regularly. I also feel that children should get consistent allowances. However, the chores and the allowances should not be connected.

The reward for the successful completion of chores should be the child's own sense of satisfaction, pride, and accomplishment, and affection, gratitude, and encouragement from others. If the child fails to or refuses to complete her chores, she should receive a natural consequence. For example, if your child leaves her toys in the front yard, those toys can be taken away for a few days. If she refuses to clean the den, she may be banned from the den for twenty-four hours. However, depriving a child of her allowance because of failure to complete chores defeats the objectives of both the chores and the allowance.

FAMILIES SHOULD ESTABLISH POLICIES AND PRACTICES RELATED TO ALLOWANCES

Some parents determine the amount of the allowance by basing it on a child's age (e.g., a nine-year-old receives nine dollars per week, a twelve-year-old receives twelve dollars per week). Try to avoid being overly judgmental or scolding when a child spends his allowance in a manner that you consider foolish. ("If you spend twelve dollars on that CD, you'll have no money until Friday.") Let the child learn about money management by experiencing the natural consequences of hasty or extravagant purchases. Besides, we all splurge on ourselves once in a while!

EXPRESS GRATITUDE AND APPRECIATION FOR COMPLETED CHORES

I was once giving a seminar on family dynamics and recommended to the audience that parents should always thank their children when chores are completed well. A dad raised his hand to vehemently disagree. "If you thank a kid for doing something as simple as feeding the dog, he'll expect you to thank him all the time—for everything!"

I had difficulty determining how a father could be averse to living in a home where people thanked one another consistently. Next time you go to a restaurant, take note of the number of times during the meal that you say "Thank you" to your waiter. You will doubtless express your gratitude a dozen times. Don't we owe our kids the same courtesy?

* * *

By requiring the child to complete assigned chores on a regular basis, the parent is creating and fostering a solid work ethic. The ability and willingness to work are traits that will be invaluable to the child as he enters adolescence and adulthood. By reinforcing his social responsibilities, you are preparing the youngster for a successful life in the community.

15

The Teacher's Role in Facilitating Parental Involvement

> "What the best and wisest parent wants for his child, the community must want for all its children."
>
> —JOHN DEWEY

TEACHERS OFTEN DECRY the lack of parental involvement in schools and cite low attendance at school open houses, lack of response to teacher phone calls, and parents' reluctance to participate in meetings regarding children's progress and performance. Interestingly, many *other* teachers bemoan the *over*involvement of parents, their intrusion into curriculum issues, and the constant parent-initiated communication—calls, notes, and e-mails. Needless to say, schools should endeavor to create a happy medium that facilitates home-school communication in a manner that allows parents to receive and respond to important information in an effective and efficient way.

The last decades saw significant time, energy, and money being invested in Effective Schools Research. Numerous universities and governmental agencies studied and analyzed schools that were effectively and efficiently educating students—in an effort to identify the traits and policies that made these schools effective. Although the various studies rendered different results, there was one universal truth among all the explorations: *Effective schools encourage and facilitate involvement by parents.* Further, this involvement generally translates to increased motivation among the student body.

Gone are the days when parents were willing to sit outside the school except for the occasional invites to a parent night or class play. We live in an age of consumerism wherein the customer wants to see, monitor, and evaluate the quality of the product. In many communities, parents take a consumerist view of school and wish to have input into the education of their children. This is a positive trend and can benefit children in a meaningful way. The key is to harness this parental energy to interact with school personnel in a productive and effective way. A survey by the National Parent Teacher Association confirmed these findings and reported that parental involvement in low income communities is particularly effective and valuable.

Teachers should not feel threatened by this parental involvement. Teachers should remember that parents have valuable, insightful, and comprehensive knowledge regarding their own children. You may be the expert in curricula or subject content, but Mom and Dad are the experts in *the child*. They have known him longer, have loved him more, and will be in his life longer than any professional. We can gain much from parental insights and information. Again, the child's motivation can be greatly enhanced by effective home-school communication.

INVOLVING PARENTS IN SCHOOL LIFE

One key to fostering parental involvement is to create an appealing and welcoming environment in the school. Welcome signs should be posted and maps of the facility should be clearly displayed. Some schools have created visitor's lounges where parents can enjoy coffee or cold drinks while waiting for their child or for an appointment. This room could also contain a lending library of parent resources or pamphlets of interest to families. A bulletin board could announce community or school events. Other schools have parents serve as "greeters" (à la Wal-Mart) for parents at the beginning and end of the school day. A school website could keep parents abreast of school events and activities.

Special events can also help create a positive, trusting relationship between home and school. Biweekly family nights where staff members and school families meet at the school for a potluck supper, a movie, or some other form of entertainment can break the ice. Some creative schools have sponsored school-wide murals, community gardens, family litter patrols, and other group projects that give parents, students, and faculty an opportunity to work together.

An effective vehicle to keep parents informed of the class events and activities is a simple weekly class newsletter. The time spent writing and distributing this newsletter is a true investment in enhancing your relationships with your parents. The newsletter will, eventually, *save* you time because it will prevent you from receiving fourteen phone calls about the departure time for Tuesday's field trip to the science museum. The newsletter could also be sent out in an e-mail, if appropriate. However, you should remember the "digital divide" that exists in many communities. Some of the parents may not have access to the Internet or e-mail.

An effective weekly class newsletter could include:

- Announcements of upcoming events
- Objectives and goals for field trips
- Reminders
- Study/homework tips
- Featured Student of the Week
- Acknowledgments and thank-yous for parents or students who have been helpful
- Suggestions to supplement curriculum content at home
- Reprints of timely articles
- Samples of students' writing or artwork
- Outline of plans for the upcoming week
- Classroom news
- Profile of featured Family of the Week

These formal communication vehicles should feature regular, weekly sections in a consistent format. A one- or two-page document would be appropriate, and it should be written in a somewhat informal and whimsical manner. The newsletter should convey the fact that the classroom is a joyful, caring, responsive, and productive environment.

Avoid use of educational jargon or a writing style that is overly formal. The newsletter should be distributed on the same day each week so parents come to expect and anticipate its arrival.

The newsletter should not, however, replace the occasional personal note sent from the teacher to a parent for a particular purpose. Parents generally appreciate receiving a handwritten note from a teacher regarding a child's progress or performance. Of course, these notes are particularly effective and meaningful if they carry *good news* about the child.

When I served as director of a residential school for students with special needs, I encountered a situation where a student showed unusual warmth and empathy. Aaron was nine years old and he actively fostered his reputation as a tough guy. He seldom showed his classmates or his teachers his sensitivity, lest they think that he was soft.

One day, he was missing from lunch, and I began searching the classrooms in an effort to locate him. I entered his science class and found him huddled on the floor holding the class guinea pig gently in his arms. The animal had been sick for several days and the students were quite concerned about her. Aaron was stroking the guinea pig's fur and softly singing an Irish lullaby to her. When I entered the room, he looked up at me sheepishly. A bit embarrassed at this display of sensitivity, he whispered, "This is what my grandma does for me when *I'm* sick."

I was so impressed and touched by this, and I knew that his mom would have truly enjoyed seeing what I had been privileged to see, so I immediately wrote her a note. It began "You missed a Kodak moment today . . ." and I then went on to describe the incident.

Aaron's mother called me the day my note arrived. She had faxed it to her husband, who was on an Asian business trip, and sent copies to all of Aaron's grandparents, aunts, and uncles, and displayed the note on the refrigerator, where it would be featured indefinitely. She was extraordinarily grateful. The simple gesture of a twenty-five-word note contributed greatly to Mom's feelings about Aaron's school. It also served to strengthen the relationship that I had with her.

Once I realized how effective and meaningful this strategy was, I decided to formalize it as part of the school's culture. I printed up sheets of special stationery containing the headline "You missed a Kodak moment today . . ." and placed them in the faculty lounge. I told the teachers to complete one and send it along to a parent whenever they witnessed a similar scene. That was over ten years ago. Parents have told me that they have saved those notes for a decade.

Parents of children who struggle in school tend to dread notes from teachers because these missives generally carry complaints, accusations, or problems. What a pleasant and unique experience for such a parent to receive a positive, upbeat message from a teacher reflecting that teacher's support and affection for the child. The teacher gains significant credibility with the parent.

MANAGING PARENT-TEACHER MEETINGS

Some teachers find it helpful to send a form to parents prior to a meeting, asking what concerns or questions the parent may have. This form can be used to establish an agenda for the session. ("Welcome, Mrs. Bacon. Today we should discuss Brad's plans for the science fair, his homework difficulties, and his spelling progress.") By setting an agenda, the meeting is more likely to be productive and focused. Always make an effort to begin and end the meeting on a positive note.

Another strategy to ensure that the meeting will be productive is to set a goal for each meeting and do your best to see that the goal is met by the end of the session. ("Mrs. Handel will agree to have Jack's glasses prescription reevaluated." "Mr. Brace will agree to have the language therapist do an evaluation.")

I advise teachers to begin the meeting with a positive comment that reflects your personal, individual knowledge of the child. ("*Max is so excited about going to the Red Sox game this weekend.*" "*Sherry tells me that you folks have a new dog. We just bought a dalmatian last week.*") This upbeat beginning is particularly important if you anticipate that the meeting may be difficult.

Design the setting of the meeting to be as comfortable as possible. Soft background music, simple refreshments, and adult-size furniture can lend an air of professionalism to the conference. Have paper and pens available in case the parent wishes to take notes. Have some basic art supplies handy to entertain the student's younger siblings, who often accompany the parent.

Be sure to place a CONFERENCE IN PROGRESS—PLEASE DO NOT DISTURB sign on your door. This not only prevents interruptions, but also communicates to the parent that this meeting is a priority for you and you take it seriously.

The teacher should focus the discussion on behaviors and performances that can be changed. For example, complaining to the parent about the child's learning problem is unproductive. In my first year as a teacher, I had a conference with the father of a child with a severe diagnosed attention deficit disorder. For the first ten minutes of the discussion, I outlined in detail the child's hyperactivity, inability to stay in his seat, and his disruptive behavior. After sitting patiently for a while, the understanding dad said, "Rick, I sent you an ADD kid and you are complaining that he moves around too much. That would be like if I sent you a kid with a broken foot and you complained that he limped." Point taken. Note to self: ***Don't complain about things that can't be changed.***

Parent-teacher meetings, by definition, involve complex and sensitive issues. As a result, even a well-planned meeting can become contentious and difficult. This is particularly true when the teacher is delivering bad or troubling news.

One way to prevent a difficult meeting is to avoid surprising or blindsiding the parent. If you feel that a child may fail a course, be recommended for grade retention, or require extensive testing, you should avoid dropping that bomb suddenly at a meeting. Frankly, if a parent is shocked by the news, the teacher did not do an adequate job of preparing the parent. The issue should have been mentioned as a possibility in previous discussions so that the topic would not come as a surprise.

If you have reason to believe that an upcoming conference may be difficult, solicit advice from the school's counselors or administration. You may wish to role-play and rehearse the meeting with a colleague or request that a supervisor join the meeting, or perhaps request that the supervisor stand by in the event that intervention or assistance is needed.

Approach the meeting positively and try not to appear anxious. Bring written notes if it would make you more comfortable and do not hesitate to take careful notes throughout the discussion. In the past, I have even offered to give the parent a copy of my notes to ensure that we both fully understood the proceedings and outcome of the meeting.

Be wary of sound bites. Avoid using highly charged, emotional words ("cheating," "lying," "stealing," "lazy," "rude") because these words will be long remembered and separated from the context in which they originally appeared. Measure your words carefully.

When our son Dan was in the fourth grade, his teacher began our parent-teacher conference by saying that Dan was "very belligerent." Dan was (and is) a very sweet and respectful person and we were greatly surprised by this comment.

Fortunately, I pursued the comment further and asked the teacher precisely what he meant by "belligerent."

"You know," he responded, "he squirms in his seat lot."

"But that's not what 'belligerent' means," I explained. "'Belligerent' means rude, disrespectful, and discourteous."

"Oh, no!" the teacher replied. "Danny is very polite and respectful. I guess that I have been using the wrong word."

I guess so. I wondered how many of his students' parents had punished their kids over the years because of this teacher's vocabulary weaknesses.

A reliable technique used in retail sales when dealing with an irate customer is to ask the person, *"What can I do to satisfy you?"* Interestingly, this empathic and solution-oriented approach often serves to calm the angry person and can significantly improve the dynamic and tone of the meeting. Try the technique with a frustrated or upset parent.

After completing a difficult or contentious parent meeting, contact all parties soon to arrange for a follow-up meeting to ensure that the agreed-upon steps are being taken. Call or write to the parents and thank them for participating in the meeting, and comment positively upon a specific suggestion or recommendation that they may have made. Look for opportunities to communicate positive news to them.

The teacher-parent conference can be an integral part of the relationship between home and school. This positive relationship, in turn, can serve to enhance the child's motivation and desire to succeed.

Below are some more suggestions that may enable the teacher to improve the quality and effectiveness of teacher-parent conferences.

- Avoid talking down to the parents. Remember that you are talking to competent adults, not to children. Make and maintain eye contact.
- Be diplomatic and sensitive, but always be honest and truthful. Remember that you speak for the school. Avoid making promises that you don't have the authority to keep.
- There are some situations in which it is appropriate to have the child included in the meeting. Discuss this with the parent prior to the meeting. If the child does not participate in the meeting, discuss the session with him the day after the conference.
- Bring samples of the child's work to the conference. You may also wish to bring some checklists, articles, or information sheets to give to the parents.
- Leave ample time at the end of the session for questions. At the conclusion of the meeting, summarize the various agreements that were reached and be certain that all parties understand the various assigned duties.

Effective home-school communication is particularly important at the beginning of the school year. As the adage goes, *"You never have a second chance to make a first impression."* If a teacher's first communication with a parent consists of a detailed list of classroom rules, a catalogue of school supplies that the child will need, and an outline of the consequences that will be meted out if the child fails to secure the required supplies, the teacher is off to a rocky start with her parent body.

Your first verbal and written communication should be positive and welcoming. Let the parents know a bit about yourself and your plans for the year. As you design the required supply list, be mindful of the socioeconomic status of your students and remember that many parents are purchasing supplies for several children in the family. Some teachers collect notebooks in June from students who were planning to discard them, and make them available to other students.

SOME STRAIGHT TALK FOR TEACHERS

> "Great, sincere appreciation of other people's children is one of the rarer virtues."
>
> —HARLAN MILLER

Unfortunately, most teachers have received minimal training in communicating with parents. I currently hold three degrees in special education and have never taken a course or a seminar about dealing with people in crisis. My twenty-year-old nephew is in training to be an emergency medical technician. Conversely, he has taken several courses in handling crises. The people who train EMTs recognize that trainees will spend their careers moving from crisis to crisis. After all, when a family summons an ambulance, there is a crisis occurring.

As a special educator, you must come to recognize that you, too, are in the crisis business. Nearly every time your telephone rings, the person on the other end is in crisis. Their child is not functioning at school. This invariably sends a family into crisis. It is quite unfortunate that preservice and in-service educational programs do not offer training to educational professionals in the various techniques used to effectively deal with a person in crisis.

One of the first concepts taught in a crisis-training curriculum is to not take the "victim's" behavior *personally*. People who are embroiled in a crisis often act in strange and inappropriate ways. It is not uncommon for people in crisis to actually strike out against their rescuers. It is very difficult to predict how a person will react and respond in crisis.

Teachers should remember this. Many teachers take the behavior of parents *personally.* (*"Mr. Barker raised his voice to me in the last meeting. I refuse to meet with him again."*) No one enjoys being treated disrespectfully, but the professional teacher must come to recognize that when a child is struggling in school, his family may well be going through a crisis in response to the child's failure. Take the parent's behavior *seriously,* but don't take it *personally.*

It is important to understand that parents—like all of us—have many "roles" that they play in their daily lives. Harriet Richards is a student in your fourth-period math class. As a result, you view Mrs. Richards as Harriet's mom. However, Mrs. Richards plays many other roles as well. She is mom to Harriet's siblings, a wife to Harriet's dad, a daughter, a sister, a cousin, a friend, a neighbor, a daughter-in-law, and an employee. These various roles create a complex and challenging life for Mrs. Richards.

Harriet has failed to complete her math homework for three days. The teacher telephones Mrs. Richards to discuss the matter and asks that she return the call by the end of the school day. The return call doesn't come. The teacher assumes that the parent's lack of response reflects the family's lack of interest in Harriet and her academic progress.

Perhaps the teacher's perception is incorrect. It is more likely that another of Mrs. Richards's "roles" has interfered with her ability to respond to Harriet's math difficulty. Maybe her father is hospitalized, her sister needs comforting after a divorce, a major presentation is due at work, or Mom is involved in a health crisis herself. We should not automatically interpret a lack of response as a lack of interest. It is difficult to establish an effective rapport with another person if you assume a highly judgmental attitude.

Most teachers give lip service to the idea of parental involvement in schools, but most research in this area indicates strongly that teacher attitudes are the greatest obstacle to parent participation. Teachers strongly resist parental involvement or influence in such critical areas as curriculum planning, student evaluation, staff evaluation, or policy development. Teachers greatly prefer that parental involvement be limited to fund-raising, school fairs, occasional parent nights, and chaperoning field trips. As a result, parents often feel ignored or patronized by schools.

John Dewey, America's consummate educator, reminds us that "education is a social enterprise." Therefore, a child's education should involve the focused efforts of the child, his teachers, and his parents.

The quality of a child's education is impacted by four relationships: his relationship with his classmates, his relationship with his teacher, his relationship with his parents, and his parents' relationship with his teacher. If any of these relationships is dysfunctional or ineffective, the child will be unable to reach his full potential. Parents are shareholders in the educational process and should be treated as such. Studies in this area also indicate that all parties benefit from parental involvement in the schools:

Students show marked improvement in attitude, behavior, attendance, involvement, and long-term academic achievement.

Parents gain greater understanding of the educational process, are better able to communicate with the child regarding school issues, can be of greater assistance with homework, and develop better and more positive attitudes toward the school.

Teachers gain a better understanding of the culture and mores of the community and establish more positive and supportive relationships with parents.

Everybody wins!

Of course, there are significant barriers to increasing parent involvement in the schools. Conflicting schedules can present challenges and obstacles, but these barriers can be overcome with some creativity and innovative programming.

Quite simply, most children view home and school as separate, unrelated planets whose orbits seldom intersect. This is unfortunate and it is the responsibility of the school to promote and enhance the teacher-parent relationship. Even in schools where school-home programs do exist, I find that most teachers merely tolerate these connections. Seldom do they embrace this concept or view it as an important ingredient in the student's success.

Beyond merely *tolerating* parents in our schools, teachers should do the following:

> *Inform*—Establish policies and procedures that keep parents informed about the class activities and the progress of their children. After all, if *you* don't tell them what is going on, they will accept the information given to them by the child, other parents, and the rumor mill.
>
> *Involve*—Seek counsel, advice, and opinions from parents. Use their skills and talents in your classroom.
>
> *Invite*—Let parents know and feel that they are welcome in your classroom. Extend formal and informal invitations.
>
> *Initiate*—Don't wait for the parents to come to you; initiate contact with them in a positive, supportive, collegial way.

Parents and teachers share a common goal: the education and development of the children. All parties can and should play a role in the educational process.

16

What Does Madison Avenue Know . . . That Maple Street Elementary School Doesn't?

"The key to successful selling is not in the ability to talk. It is in the ability to listen. Don't sell products . . . sell solutions."

—KLAUS LEISINGER

ALTHOUGH I MAKE MY LIVING as an educator, I have also had the opportunity to work with outstanding marketers through my involvement with SchwabLearning, PBS Video, and Simon & Schuster.

I have attended countless meetings in which the marketing staff discussed the research that has been done by Madison Avenue advertisers in an effort to determine what, why, and when children make purchases. I began to reflect on how valuable these marketing data would be for classroom teachers and I began studying the history and impact of children's advertising.

When America's soldiers returned from World War II, a baby boom of unparalleled proportions followed. By 1950, the child population in the United States had doubled the same population in 1935. This unprecedented population increase caused significant changes in every aspect of American life.

The impact (and financial potential) of the baby boom was not missed by America's manufacturers and retailers. A huge new market was created, and advertisers began developing strategies and techniques designed to attract and influence children to purchase their cereals, toys, clothes, and soft drinks. Retailers, who previously viewed the "kid market" as a child with five pennies and his nose pressed up against the candy counter, now realized that children have the potential to purchase billions of dollars of products annually. They also have significant influence over many of the purchases made by their parents. Thus, the "Kid Market" was born.

Marketing to children became increasingly widespread, creative, and (in some cases) inappropriate. In 1978, the Federal Trade Commission considered banning television advertisements aimed at children because of the ads' aggressive and manipulative nature. Childhood advertising is everywhere and it has proven itself to be wildly successful in motivating children to purchase specific products in specific stores. It is estimated that the average three-year-old can identify over one hundred brands by their logos or theme songs.

The Kid Market has increased and expanded significantly in recent years in response to several sociological phenomena that have occurred in our society. These cultural changes have resulted in a younger generation with significant monies to spend. It is estimated that the average ten-year-old has approximately fourteen dollars per week in allowance that he can spend independently. This marks a 75 percent increase over 1991. When this amount is coupled with gifts and earnings for chores/jobs, the Kid Market spends twenty billion dollars a year.

The twenty-first-century American child has far more purchasing power than did children of past generations. Not only do these children have significant monies to spend, they have marked influence on their family's purchases relating to food items, clothes, computers, electronics, cars, restaurants, and vacations—to the tune of $130 billion a year. Why else would *Sports Illustrated for Kids* carry ads for the Ford Explorer?

Mindful of these stunning data, marketers have invested millions of dollars in studying the Kid Market in order to design strategies that will inspire children to buy their products and services. Advertisers are in the motivation business. And they are very, very good at it.

Advertisers have been harshly and rightfully criticized for their unethical practices in marketing directly to children. Marketers have insinuated themselves into classrooms, educational media, textbooks, children's movies, and the Internet. Some of this advertising is inaccurate, misleading, and manipulative. Most children cannot distinguish between entertainment and commercials until age eight, so they may not even be aware that they are being sold something when watching an entertaining commercial. I do not defend these practices and I support attempts to regulate and control these strategies.

But I recall a history professor once telling me: "In order to understand a past generation, you should study the most influential and creative artisans of that era. If you wish to understand the ancient Romans, study their politicians. To understand the Greeks, study their philosophers. Study the great Elizabethan authors to understand Britain, and the moviemakers to gain insights into the twentieth century. When future generations wish to explore our culture, they will study *the advertising industry*."

The advertising industry is nearly incomprehensible in its scope and influence. Now that Madison Avenue has discovered the actual and potential power of the Kid Market, it has invested millions of dollars in discovering the likes, dislikes, fears, joys, and interests of children. This market research leads to a thorough understanding of the strategies and methods needed to motivate children to buy products and services. It seems both logical and appropriate that educators should familiarize themselves with these findings. After all, our goal as teachers and parents is to motivate children to buy *our* product—education! It makes great sense that we should attempt to gain insights and information from the extensive (and expensive!) research conducted by the advertising industry.

ARE WE HAVING FUN YET?

The most important tenet of the child marketing industry is the deceptively simple slogan **Kids Want to Have Fun.**

Initially, this statement may seem simplistic and obvious, but it is actually quite profound. Marketers define "fun" as "having your emotional needs met and satisfied." For a gregarious child, fun is being with his posse. For an autonomous child, fun means working alone on a project. Fun is working for an award in the mind of a child driven by achievement. There are many kinds of fun, and the definition of "fun" is different for each child. Basically, if a child's emotional needs are being met, he is having fun. If his basic needs are thwarted, he is not having fun. It is as simple, and as complex, as that. You must jettison the traditional definition of "fun" as joyful, pointless frolicking.

Included in this chapter are some basic findings of this research and some classroom implications for these findings.

There are marked and significant differences between the approaches that motivate boys and the strategies that motivate girls.

Market researchers invest significant time and money into studying and analyzing *centrics.* These are defined as the "core drives" that motivate people to purchase an item. Once a marketer can understand the centrics of a group, he is better able to design and market products that will appeal to that specific group.

These studies have shown that there are significant differences between the centrics of school-aged boys and the centrics of school-aged girls. Many people in our society continually strive to create a gender-neutral culture. This may be an admirable goal, but there are currently marked distinctions between the male and female of our species.

Of course, boys and girls do share many common needs and interests. Most children have strong needs to belong, to have power, to have freedom, and to have fun. Children want to feel intelligent, creative, and talented. They want to be accepted, popular, and independent. Further, they have common needs to have friends, to rebel, and to explore. But these needs appear to manifest in differing ways for boys and girls. For example, a boy's need for mastery generally involves physical skills, whereas a girl's need for mastery generally involves gaining a wide variety of skills and competencies.

What's Fun for Boys?

Boys are intensely interested in skill development and competence. They wish to get really good at something and will often obsessively practice a skill (video games, skateboarding) until mastery is achieved. This mastery provides much-needed power and independence. Boys generally gravitate toward being viewed and identified as "specialists" by their peers.

Competency, skill development, and victory are very important for boys, and teachers can enhance a boy's motivation by emphasizing these in the classroom. However, boys are not motivated by successes that are too easy to achieve, and, conversely, they can easily feel disillusioned and defeated if the victory appears to be out of their reach. The teacher must design activities that are challenging but achievable if she wishes to capitalize on the boys' need for competency.

Boys tend to take a simplistic view of conflict and view fictional or real-life conflicts as battles of good versus evil. Hence the popularity of movies and television shows wherein the delineation of good and evil is clear and observable (*A Nightmare on Elm Street, Star Wars*). Boys often have difficulty seeing or appreciating nuances and "shades of gray." They will tend to dislike or reject stories in which characters are multifaceted and ambiguous.

Boys are on a constant search for icons and heroes. They come to love and respect figures that are larger than life. This is reflected in their adoration of sports figures, mythical gods, and rock stars. Teachers can capitalize on this by selecting reading material that focuses on heroic figures.

"Grossness" is appealing to boys, particularly of middle-school age. Their delight in all things repulsive is rooted and reinforced by the aversive reaction that they observe in girls and adults when such topics are introduced. They may have a fascination with bodily functions, as represented in such boy-oriented products as *Ren and Stimpy* or Garbage Pail Kids. Advertisers know, *"If it's gross, it sells."* Rob Breakell, the finest and most effective science teacher that I have ever seen, would hold his male middle-school students spellbound for an entire semester as he explored the scientific human processes of elimination, urination, and perspiration. Students who had never taken an interest in science before were captivated by these discussions and demonstrations. Give the customers what they want!

Boys often have rather unsophisticated senses of humor. They can be quite silly and are greatly amused by pratfalls, pranks, and stunts. Sophisticated, subtle satire is generally lost on them. The teacher who delights in irony or pun-making will generally find his young male students unresponsive to and puzzled by his attempts at humor. A pie in the face? Now, *that's* funny.

Bravery is a greatly admired trait among boys. Every playground will find clusters of boys daring a classmate to attempt some risky act of courage. These rituals are fundamental to the boys' senses of self-esteem. Teachers should select stories that feature a courageous hero battling omnipresent evil.

There are many common "boy behaviors" that reflect this fascination with bravery. Our son would wear a bandage over his long-healed injury because, in the world of boyhood, a bandage is a badge of honor, courage, and daring. Boys take great pride in their injuries, and any boy fortunate enough to have a *scar* is greatly admired by his friends. Conversely, our daughter would seek out clear or flesh-colored Band-Aids because an injury was a source of embarrassment for her. Interesting.

Boys enjoy taking risks to demonstrate their boldness and valor. One brand of sour candy greatly increased their sales by adding a label that stated, *"Warning, this candy may be too intense for some members of the general public. The first fifty seconds are* extreme. *We double dog dare you to place two in your mouth at the same time."* Sales skyrocketed.

However, do not be fooled by this bravado and assertiveness. Boys are also interested in and capable of great affection. They may not be as demonstrative in their affection as their female counterparts, but a boy's simple act of saving the final Popsicle for Mom or smiling at the sister's new hairstyle is reflective of his affection.

Boys are often intrepid explorers who greatly enjoy new and risky challenges. They tend to be very inventive in their play and can easily imagine that the blanket over a coffee table is the interior of a submarine and the stick from the backyard is a magical, enchanted sword.

Boys also tend to do better than girls in visual-spatial tasks, physical strength, and gross motor activities.

Lest the reader think that the author—and the advertising industry—is sexist, note that neurologists and brain researchers *also* believe that there are observable and quantifiable differences between boys and girls. Current scientific evidence indicates that boys' brains develop and function in a manner that is quite different from the brains of their female classmates.

At the 2007 Learning and the Brain Conference sponsored by Harvard University, research was presented that clearly demonstrated the gender differences in brain development and function. Among the findings were:

- Girls tend to think more verbally than boys do; boys' brains tend to devote more cortical space to spatial-mechanical functions, whereas girls use more space for verbal-emotive functions.
- Frontal lobe development occurs earlier in the girls' brains and that enables them to read and make decisions sooner than their male classmates. Girls also tend to be calmer and better able to focus and attend to task.
- Boys' brains seem to need "rest" more often than girls' brains do. As a result they may "zone out" or become distracted more often than girls. Boys may also develop a repertoire of behaviors to keep

the brain stimulated (e.g., fidgeting, drumming fingers). Boys are, quite simply, more easily bored.
- Girls' brains seem to be able to "cross talk" between hemispheres more effectively. As a result, girls are better able to multitask and make transitions easier than boys.

Schools can operationalize this research by designing "boy-friendly" classrooms. Among the characteristics of these classrooms are:

- Ongoing opportunities for movement and activity by using experiential and kinesthetic teaching approaches.
- Increased emphasis on spatial-visual activities (e.g., manipulatives, boardwork).
- Allowing male students to use academic materials that are directly related to their areas of interest (e.g., video games, sports) and encouraging the boys to choose the materials they wish to use.
- Decrease in the volume and expectations related to homework and providing parents with specific advice and guidelines for home study.
- Increase of single-gender learning activities where the boys and girls work separately.
- Increased emphasis on the practical, pragmatic uses for the material learned in class.
- Exposure to male role models via classroom guests and male characters in books and stories.

What's Fun for Girls?

Girls' interests and motivators are significantly different from boys'. It is not sexist to say that there are significant differences between boys and girls, just as there are distinctions between men and women. One need only observe an elementary school playground to see these differences. While the boys engage in large-group rough-and-tumble and somewhat mindless physical games, the girls gather in small groups to talk, commiserate, and share.

Girls develop an early interest in beauty, as reflected in an intense interest in art and the early fascination with candy necklaces and kiddie cosmetics. This fascination is reflective of the girls' need to feel grown up. They often take great care in selecting their clothing and fixing their hair. They are very interested in making a positive physical impression on others. This is a vehicle through which girls express themselves and reflect their self-esteem. In fact, a significant warning sign for depression among school-aged girls is a lack of concern for hygiene and appearance.

Because girls tend to develop emotionally more rapidly than boys do, they become intensely interested in the lives of others. This is reflected in their fascination with the personal lives of celebrities as well as their intense discussions about the lives and experiences of their friends and classmates. Where boys tend to be very secretive about their home lives and have little interest in learning about the private issues in their friends' lives, girls are very willing to disclose the details of their home lives and are fascinated by the domestic adventures of others.

Teachers will find it very effective to use biographies and autobiographies in order to motivate girls and to teach history using a "personality approach" that explores the personal lives and backgrounds of historical figures.

Many—and perhaps *most*—young girls have strong maternal instincts and a need to "mother" and nurture others. This accounts for the popularity of dolls and small pets in the world of girlhood. The loving and lovable Cabbage Patch dolls with their adorable faces and outstretched arms have engendered sales of nearly one billion dollars since their arrival in the 1980s. The marketing of these dolls encouraged girls to "adopt" the Cabbage Patchers, not to "buy" them. Some adoption advocates felt that this marketing approach trivialized the adoption process, and this is probably true. But the strategy was pure genius on the part of the marketers because it satisfied girls' natural desire to rescue and nurture.

The theme of nearly every Disney movie that is popular with girls is "nurturing" (*Beauty and the Beast, Finding Nemo, 101 Dalma-*

tians). The most popular reading series for girls is the Baby-sitters Club, which features girls who are responsible for nurturing young children—and one another.

Girls can also be silly and may enjoy games and rituals that seem mindless to adults. The telephone ritual of "you hang up first—no, you—no, you" is a classic example. But girls can also be capable of sophisticated and subtle humor and of appreciating irony and puns.

Like boys, girls are also interested in competence and mastery. However, girls are often more broad-based in their interests and are not as focused on becoming an "expert" in a specific area or skill. They are more interested in acquiring significant skills in a variety of activities or endeavors.

A significant sociological shift has occurred among girls in the past few decades. In the 1950s and 1960s girls were taught to avoid competition and were cautioned to be ladylike and demure. With the onset of the long-overdue Women's Rights Movement and the resultant legislation and changes in societal expectations, girls are now far more willing and eager to participate in competitive pursuits in the classroom, in the community, and on the playing field. Again, this is widely viewed as a very positive and constructive change in our society. Girls now have outlets for their needs for mastery and accomplishment that are very similar to the outlets boys have.

From a physical viewpoint, girls tend to be more sensitive to sound, pain, and touch and often have superior fine motor skills and dexterity. The quality and clarity of their speech is often more advanced than boys' of their age, as is their short-term memory. They can also process verbal language faster and more accurately than their male classmates.

Although there *are* distinctive and measurable differences between motivators for boys and motivators for girls, below are some motivational forces that exist for all children, despite their gender.

Belonging
Popularity
Friendships

Power
Mastery
Intelligence

Assimilation	Superiority
Association	Control
Affiliation	Excellence
Freedom	***Fun***
Individuality	Imagination
Uniqueness	Simplicity
Independence	Sensation
Exploration	Creativity
	Amusement

The wise teacher will plan her classes to include as many of the above-listed motivational forces as possible.

It is important to remember that each of the forces has manifestations that are positive and negative. For example, a child's wish to be "popular" is undoubtedly a positive drive; however, if he attempts to become popular by bullying others or being disrespectful toward the teacher, the force becomes a negative.

WHAT MAKES A TV COMMERCIAL WORK– OR NOT WORK?

Commercial television time is extraordinarily expensive, and advertisers are reluctant to continue showing a promo if it is not effective in selling the product. When evaluating the effectiveness of a commercial, seven aspects are addressed:

- **Attention:** Does the commercial capture and hold the viewer's attention?
- **Comprehension:** Does the viewer fully and readily understand the message of the commercial?
- **Involvement/Engagement:** Is the viewer fully involved in the commercial—does she sing along with the jingle? Does he know the tagline slogan?
- **Yield:** Does the viewer have a positive opinion about the commercial?

- **Action:** Does the commercial propel the viewer to action? Does he purchase or use the product?
- **Reaction:** Does he enjoy the product and does he feel that the commercial fairly and accurately explains and describes the product?
- **Communication:** Will the viewer tell others about the commercial and/or the product? Did it make a sufficient impact on him to the extent that he will participate in word-of-mouth marketing?

This formula has been extraordinarily effective in evaluating commercials and products and it has become an industry standard.

Perhaps we teachers can modify this formula in order to evaluate the effectiveness of *our* "marketing" and motivational approaches.

- **Attention:** Do my introductions and the initial minutes of my class capture the student's attention? Is each child sufficiently challenged and involved throughout the lesson to sustain his continued attention and focus? Are my materials attractive and appealing? Is my curriculum material of sufficient interest and relevance to my students?
- **Comprehension:** Are my instructions and directions stated clearly and thoroughly? Do students understand our long-term and short-term objective? Are students frequently "lost" or confused? Do I continually evaluate students' comprehension during a lesson? Do students feel comfortable asking questions or requesting clarification? Is the curriculum on an appropriate and realistic level?
- **Involvement/Engagement:** Do I use strategies that ensure that all students are actively engaged in curriculum-related tasks? Do I adequately monitor group work and independent activities? Are all students allowed and encouraged to volunteer and participate? Do I use methods that encourage this participation? Are student responses accepted positively by the teacher and the class members? Is there accountability for student participation? Is active participation reinforced and recognized?
- **Yield:** Do my students enjoy my class? Do they enjoy my

company? Do they smile and laugh during class? Are they eager to please me? Do they feel safe and comfortable in my class? Do my students get along with one another?

- **Action:** Does my curriculum inspire students to learn more about my subject area? Do students do their homework regularly? Do they volunteer actively in class? Do they spontaneously bring in material or newspaper clippings related to the subject area that I am discussing?
- **Reaction and Communication:** Occasionally, poll or survey your students to secure information about their opinions on the format and progress of the class. These surveys can be done formally or informally and can be conducted via written forms, individual conferences, or brainstorming sessions. Many teachers report that through these activities students provide invaluable and insightful information that can be used to improve the content and tone of the classroom.

Marketing research has indicated that there are characteristics that ensure the success of a product or advertisement. There are also characteristics that will doom the product or advertisement to failure.

> **Positive Attributes:** Children are attracted to approaches and products that make them feel smart, powerful, popular, skilled, connected, in control, grown up.
>
> **Negative Attributes:** Children are repelled by products or approaches that make them feel dumb, controlled, rejected, incompetent, inferior, patronized, isolated.

Teachers and parents should review their daily policies and procedures to determine whether their approaches provide the children with the characteristics necessary to ignite and maintain their motivation.

The Importance of Updating

Products and approaches must be continually updated and modernized in order to be viewed as current and meaningful to students.

The most popular and widely distributed toy in American history is Barbie. This doll has been continually updated and modified over her fifty-year life. A glaring example is the metamorphosis of Nurse Barbie of the 1950s to Doctor Barbie of the 1980s. Barbie continues to make significant changes in her wardrobe and accessories to reflect these societal changes.

Teachers are well advised to make continual and ongoing adjustments in their curricula and approaches. Lessons should reflect the latest research and findings in the field of education.

WHAT MARKETERS HAVE LEARNED ABOUT PARENTS

The advertising industry can also provide us with information that will help teachers better understand parents.

Extensive marketing research and surveys have rendered interesting data about America's parents and their hopes and desires for their children. Teachers should be aware of this research, as it can help us better understand and relate to the parents who cross our paths daily.

Parents hold three basic goals for their children:

1. They want them to be *happy.* Parents want contentment and joy for their children. They recognize that a positive outlook on life will be fundamental to their development and they wish to protect their children from undue worry and anxiety. They feel that happiness is the best antidote for depression and discouragement.
2. They want them to be *healthy.* Today's parents understand the correlation between a happy mind and a healthy body. Many parents are very proactive regarding the health of their children, as reflected in their interests in nutritious foods and healthy lifestyles. Car seats, bicycle helmets, and infant swim lessons are clear indicators of parents' concern for the safety of their children.

3. They want them to be *prepared for the future.* Many sociologists feel that this generation of American parent is far more future-oriented than previous generations. Parents of elementary school children want their youngsters to be prepared for middle school; middle-school parents want assurance that their children will be prepared for high school; and the parents of high schoolers are often obsessed with ensuring that their sons and daughters prepare for college life.

As teachers, we should recognize and respond to these parental needs whenever we interact with the parents of our students. If you wish to motivate these parents to cooperate with and assist you, let them know that you share their concern for their child's happiness, health, safety, and future success. This will go far in convincing the parent that their child is in capable, caring, and competent hands.

WHAT MARKETERS KNOW ABOUT CHILDREN'S FEARS

Marketers have also invested significant effort in analyzing the common fears among children.

Advertisers recognize that it is in their best interest not to produce and market products that would frighten children. Webster's dictionary defines fear as *"a distressing emotion aroused by impending or imagined pain, danger, or evil."* As teachers and parents, we should be aware of the situations or factors that create fear for children. As a child's world expands, his fears and worries expand as well. The huge stuffed animal industry owes its success to children's need to feel safe and comforted at night.

Interestingly, many children have a desire to experience fear in manageable, controlled doses. This is evidenced by children's fascination with amusement park rides, horror movies, and ghost stories. Child marketing expert Gene Del Vecchio refers to this phenomenon as the child's desire to "tickle" fear. Children wish to experience fright but under controlled, protected conditions and in small doses.

These activities allow the child to demonstrate bravery and independence while maintaining his safety.

Numerous studies have found that children's fears are fairly predictable and that these fears change as the child matures. Younger children may have irrational fears of noises, monsters, or separation from parents. The elementary school student may fear new situations, parental divorce, personal danger, or injury. The middle schooler may develop fears of kidnapping or being alone. The adolescent may fear social rejection, terrorism, drugs, or sexual relations.

Adults should avoid exposing children to these fears or exploiting the fears in any way. (*"If you keep acting this way, Daddy is going to leave us." "Your behavior had better change or you won't have any friends at all."*) Children have basic, primal reactions to fearful situations and will generally choose flight or fight as a response. Both of these reactions can create disruptions in the classroom or crises in the home.

Adults should be aware of the child's fears and assist the youngster in overcoming them. A fearful child is unlikely to be motivated.

AGE-APPROPRIATE APPROACHES TO MOTIVATION

An advertising executive, not a psychologist, coined the term "age appropriate." Market researchers have learned much about the ways that a child's needs and drives change as she matures. A product or a marketing approach that is successful and effective for a seven-year-old is unlikely to excite or inspire a seventeen-year-old.

Below are some of the basic research findings that outline the age-related variations in the needs and drives that motivate children at various stages of their development. Of course, whenever we examine or analyze large groups of children in order to make generalizations regarding behaviors or interests, we develop stereotypes. That is the point and the goal of this type of research—to determine the characteristics of the *typical child* at a given age. As a parent or teacher, you might think, *"My kid doesn't fit that pattern!"* You are probably right.

Ages eight through twelve

Characteristics

Children at this stage are quite impressionable and tend to admire and imitate adult role models. They are intrigued by fantasy and often have a strong need to collect (toys, cards, dolls). They are more interested in quantity than quality at this stage.

As children progress through this stage, they want adults to recognize and praise their burgeoning development. They are very sensitive about being linked with younger children. They are also developing a more sophisticated sense of right and wrong. They begin to recognize moral subtleties and no longer view the world as good or bad, angelic or evil.

This stage of development features minimal rebellion. Children want to be accepted by everyone and are unlikely to challenge authority in a significant way. The opinions of their caregivers are very important to them. Most preteens are relatively compliant and rarely put forth independent thought. Conformism is the key. He wants to fit in and to have approval of the adults and children in his life.

Interests and Needs

Sports: Most eight- to twelve-year-olds are interested in participating in sports activities. They are less interested in following professional sports teams.

Collecting: At this stage, more is better. They are interested in carving a niche for themselves in the classroom and in the family. Becoming the resident expert in a selected area or accumulating a collection of cards, bottle caps, stamps, coins, or ball caps often satisfies this need.

Acceptance: Children at this stage have a strong need to be accepted by others. They openly seek the approval of parents, teachers, and peers. They continually compare themselves to their classmates in order to determine their own level of attractiveness, intelligence, athleticism, and talent. They often develop self-images that are contrary to reality (e.g., a physically attractive child feeling that she is ugly).

Success: Children at this age have a strong need for success and achievement. It is for this reason that boys may seek out and develop an area or skill wherein they can enjoy success and recognition (e.g., skateboarding, computer games).

Collaboration: Children at this age enjoy working in pairs and groups, whereas preschool children prefer solitary play. You will note that television advertising that targets children seldom features a child being or playing alone. Marketing research shows that children will be more motivated to buy a product if the advertising features groups of children sharing good times together.

"Billboard effect": Marketer Dan Acuff coined this term to illustrate the preteen's need for acceptance and conformity. The ten-year-old may still enjoy playing simple board games (Chutes and Ladders) and taking his Winnie-the-Pooh to bed. But he would never admit this to his friends or teachers. Children view themselves as "on a billboard" and they develop a public persona that may be quite different from their private persona.

Humor: The preteen's sense of humor is often irreverent and dark. Much of the appeal of this humor lies in the fact that older children, parents, and teachers find it to be distasteful. What little boy does not enjoy the look of repulsion on his mom's face as he shows her his gooey green candy that is dispensed from the nostrils of a plastic nose?

At this age, a child's sense of humor is fairly unsophisticated and he doesn't "get" the subtle humor that adults enjoy (word play, puns, etc.).

Ages thirteen through fifteen

Characteristics

Early adolescence is a period of significant and often puzzling changes for the child. Her body undergoes significant developments and her mind becomes more open to abstract thought and reasoning. She begins to understand and enjoy some of the subtle and sophisticated language and concepts that had previously been incomprehensible to her.

It is at this stage that the child begins his inevitable push away from the adults in his life. He no longer views his parents and teachers as perfect and is not as eager to gain their approval. He may be confused by these feelings and manifest this confusion by long periods of sullen, noncommunicative behavior. Mood swings and other unpredictable behaviors are also common. Marketers capitalize on these emotions by portraying parents and teachers in commercials as incompetent or insensitive.

As the child enters adolescence, he seeks to establish his identity. He does this by affiliating himself with a subgroup of peers who provide him with the acceptance, camaraderie, success, and approval that he craves.

The key to understanding children at this stage of their development is to recognize that they are *managed by the moment*. In effect, these children have no recallable past and no foreseeable future. Whatever incident or event is occurring in her life at that given moment is the most important occurrence in the history of humankind. When the early adolescent wails, *"Becky didn't invite me to her pool party. My life is over!"* she means it.

Once early adolescence is viewed from that perspective, many of the puzzling behaviors that we see from these children become more understandable. Their fixation on the present can cause significant anxiety, fear, and even depression.

Interests and Needs

Identity: Because the early adolescent is struggling to establish his identity, he may attempt to do so by creating a patchwork that consists of the values and beliefs of his parents combined with the values and beliefs of his peers. Adults often view this process as a rejection of them, and the adult-child relationship begins to deteriorate. However, the separation from the attitudes and interests of parents is a necessary step in the child's development.

Sexuality: This stage finds the child both confused and thrilled about his emerging sexuality. He begins to explore the various moral and ethical views related to sexuality, and his sexual needs begin to occupy much of his time and thoughts.

Morality: The early adolescent no longer views the world as good or evil. She recognizes subtleties in morality and this can be confusing for her. She no longer feels it's necessary to follow every adult rule and mandate, and gravitates toward the less structured and less demanding morals of her peer group.

Humor: Slapstick, pie-in-the-face humor becomes less appealing for the early adolescent. Her sense of humor becomes more edgy and subtle. She enjoys sarcasm and innuendo.

Ages sixteen through eighteen

Characteristics

The human being has two periods of extraordinary change and metamorphosis. These periods occur in the first two years of life and between the ages of sixteen and eighteen.

During late adolescence, significant neurological development occurs and the brain becomes capable of increasingly sophisticated and subtle thought. The young person becomes more adept at planning, problem solving, and philosophizing.

The adolescent focuses much of his time and energy on establishing and developing relationships. Because he can now drive a car, these relationships are no longer restricted to his neighborhood or his community, and he greatly enjoys this newfound freedom and independence.

Teenagers begin trying on various roles as they search for and solidify their identities. They dabble in Goth, rocker, and jock personas. They hold a series of part-time jobs in their search for an identity that fits. Adolescence was once described as: *"I am not what I was; I am not what I am; I am not what I will be."*

Marketers often find that young people in late adolescence respond to advertising in the identical manner that adults do because they are more adultlike than childlike. This is an important concept for teachers and parents to understand and embrace.

Needs and Interests

Love/affection: Even though the adolescent may make a concerted effort to reject the affection of her parents and seems unwilling to invest significant time or energy into these relationships, she *does* have strong needs to be loved and accepted. However, these needs are generally met within her peer group.

Autonomy: The late adolescent recognizes that he must learn to function independently. He often rejects offers of assistance and advice from elders and wants to make decisions on his own.

Success: Teenagers want and need an area or skill where they can enjoy success and recognition. Unfortunately, some teens meet this need for recognition through socially unacceptable or even illegal activities.

FAVORITES THAT MOTIVATE

Youth Marketing Systems, Inc., conducted extensive research and surveys to determine the interests, favorite activities, favorite characters, and favorite settings for boys and girls ages eight through eighteen.

The implication of this research for marketers is obvious. But teachers, parents, and coaches could also use these data when planning activities, curricula, incentives, and programs. (Items do not necessarily appear in rank order.)

FAVORITE ACTIVITIES

Boys 8 to 12	***Girls 8 to 12***
Video games	Group play
Bowling	Movies
Comics	Video games

Jigsaw puzzles
Collecting
Bike riding
Pets
Skateboarding
Making maps
Internet
TV viewing

Shopping
Internet
Pets
Arts/crafts
TV viewing
Writing stories
Music
Puzzles

Boys 13 to 15

Video games
Martial arts
Movies
Collections
Sports
Concerts
Skateboarding
Camping
Amusement parks
Internet

Girls 13 to 15

Movies
Dancing
Pets
Beach
Concerts
Swimming
Horseback riding
Gymnastics
Internet

Boys 16 to 18

Electronic games
Martial arts
Movies
Amusement parks
Magazines
Sports
Playing cards
Concerts
Drawing
Tools, woodworking
Internet
Science fiction

Girls 16 to 18

Movies
Pets
Concerts
Playing cards
Gymnastics
Swimming
Nature
Music
Design, art
Fitness
Internet
Television

CHARACTER IDENTIFICATION

Boys 8 to 12	***Girls 8 to 12***
Action heroes	Singers, movie stars
Pro sports stars (male)	Pro sports stars (male and female)
Political figures (male)	Models
Soldiers	Dancers
Adolescents	Teachers/parents
Cartoon characters	Gymnasts

Boys 13 to 15	***Girls 13 to 15***
Sports celebrities	Movie stars
Comedians	Strong female leaders
Coaches/teachers	Music celebrities
Music celebrities	TV celebrities
Movie stars	Models
Political figures	Teachers/parents
Religious/spiritual leaders	"Hunks"
Race car drivers	Comedians

Boys 16 to 18	***Girls 16 to 18***
Sports stars (male)	Sports stars (male and female)
Movie stars	Movie stars
Political figures	Music celebrities
Race car drivers	TV celebrities
Coaches	Models
"Edgy" cartoon characters	Strong female leaders

FAVORITE SETTINGS

Boys 8 to 12	***Girls 8 to 12***
Amusement parks	School
Caves	Stage
Castles	Skating rink
Circus	Wedding

Rollerblade track
Outer space
Ocean/underwater
Foreign lands
Prehistoric
Water park
Mall

Beach
Islands
Jungles
Zoos
Mall
Theater
Party

Boys 13 to 15
Sporting events
Video arcade
Beach
Amusement park
Concert
Convenience store
Music store
Basketball court
Racetrack
Mall

Girls 13 to 15
Beach
Video arcade
Sporting events
Mall
Movie
Convenience store
Ocean/underwater
School
Concert
Park

Boys 16 to 18
Sporting events
College
Urban areas
Beach
Parties
Amusement parks
Concert
Mall
Movie theater
Travel destinations

Girls 16 to 18
College
Concert
Beach
Movies
Mall
Park
Music store
Home
School

SALES TECHNIQUES IN THE CLASSROOM

Another area of the business world that has invested tremendous resources into the study of human motivation is the field of sales and salesmanship. Companies and corporations spend millions of dollars training their sales staffs how to motivate customers to purchase their products and services.

As teachers, we often serve as salespeople. Our customers are our students and our products are mathematics, language arts, history, and science. We can improve our teaching and motivational skills by examining the policies, procedures, and practices commonly used by salespeople.

You may be familiar with the manipulative sleight-of-hand sales strategies used by door-to-door salesman of the past. They would use guilt ("If you *truly* loved your child, you would be willing to buy this twenty-four-volume encyclopedia"), embarrassment ("Do you want to be the only house in the neighborhood without a new mailbox?"), or fear ("Eight of ten families are robbed at some point in their lives, but you can prevent becoming a statistic by purchasing this new alarm system"). These techniques were very effective and these skilled salespeople made sales quickly and often. However, these salesmen were only interested in making one solitary sale per customer. Once the purchase was made, the relationship between the seller and the buyer concluded.

The strategies that salespeople currently use are far different from the sales techniques of the past. Now salesmen are trained in practices that are designed to build mutually beneficial and long-term relationships between the retailer and the customer. The key concepts are customer service and the creation of return customers who will recommend the company's goods and services to others. Again, the objectives of a salesperson are very similar to the goals of a teacher.

The current buzzword in salesmanship is "relationship selling." This approach is designed to create a long-term, mutually beneficial relationship between the salesperson and the customer. The relationship is based upon trust and is created by listening to and responding to the customer's needs. The salesperson also attempts to determine the *fears* of the customer and makes an effort to allay those fears. For example, if the owner of a shoe store confides to his distributor that he is concerned about his summer cash flow, the distributor may devise a deferred-payment program for the customer that allows him to pay for his summer orders with revenues from his back-to-school promotions.

Salespeople are trained to take a low-key, nonaggressive approach with their customers. Their role is to *support,* not merely to *sell.* They endeavor to become dependable, reliable, trustworthy allies of the customer—someone who recognizes and responds to the customer's needs.

The key to establishing and maintaining this relationship is ongoing, consistent personal contact. The salespeople keep in constant touch with customers using a variety of communication vehicles (phone calls, e-mails, mailings, meetings) and inform the customer that they are available on short notice for questions, concerns, crises, or emergencies. This brings great comfort and reassurance to the customer.

Among the other strategies and techniques used by "relationship salespeople" are:

> *Respond to the customer's emotional needs.* Show a genuine interest in the customer and "tune in" to his emotional state during meetings and phone calls. Provide him with reassurance, praise, empathy, or comfort as it is needed. By clearly demonstrating your concern and understanding, you show the customer that you view him as a person, not merely as a purchaser. The salesperson's loyalty and sensitivity will be remembered and appreciated.

> *Focus your attention and language on the customer.* Salespeople are trained to avoid using first-person language when meeting with prospects and customers ("*I think that . . .*" "*Let me show you . . .*"). Rather, they use third-person language ("*You should have . . .*" "*You will need . . .*"). This strategy focuses the attention on the customer and,

again, demonstrates the salesperson's responsiveness to the needs of the purchaser.

Know the customer. Salespeople are trained to learn as much as possible about the customer and his company before the initial sales call is made. This research is greatly appreciated by the customer, as it reflects the salesperson's concern, creativity, and responsiveness. This technique also enables the salesperson to be fully aware of the customer's needs, strengths, and weaknesses and to design a proposal that responds to these specific needs.

Focus on why the customer should buy—not their objections. The customer will naturally have concerns, questions, and anxieties. He will have numerous reasons why he should not make the purchase. It is the responsibility of the salesperson to focus the customer's attention and energies on the reasons why the customer will benefit from the purchase.

Reread the last few paragraphs and as you read, substitute the word "teacher" for "salesperson," "student" for "customer," and "lesson" for "product." Any teacher would be well advised to apply these sales techniques to her daily interactions with students in her classroom.

Madison Avenue's research into the needs and desires of children has resulted in tremendous information and insights into the ways that youngsters are motivated. This research can be viewed as a gift given to educators and parents who daily attempt to solve the paradox of childhood motivation.

This research clearly demonstrates that children have "keys" to their individual motivation. However, there are four basic needs that are fundamental to igniting motivation in children. Nearly every child needs:

Sentience—a need for sensory stimulation and experiences using the various senses

Association—a need for meaningful, significant relationships with others
Achievement—a need to overcome obstacles and enjoy success
Change—a need to do new and different things

However, the marketing world also understands the concept of fusion. That is, a *combination* of the above needs must be met in order for the child to be truly motivated and inspired. A child will not be motivated, for example, merely because the teacher introduces a new and novel activity (change). The change must be accompanied by a sense of belonging and achievement. The child will not be inspired by achievement unless he also has a sense of sentience and/or association.

The Pokémon cards are an outstanding example of this concept. Their unprecedented popularity is doubtless due to the fact that the Pokémon cards meet all four of the needs that spark children's motivation.

Sentience—The cards are extraordinarily attractive and intricate.
Association—Cards are designed to be traded with friends and are used to play games.
Achievement—Cards are collected and great celebrations are shared when a child secures a rare and difficult-to-find card. The fact that parents are generally clueless about the intricacies of the cards and the game also gives children a sense of power and achievement.
Change—The publishers are constantly issuing new and updated versions of the cards.

When faced with an "unmotivated" child, parents would do well to examine the above list and determine which of these needs are not being met for the child.

AFTERWORD

Human motivation is a complex and intricate process that has been studied and analyzed for decades. As teachers and parents we must have a pragmatic understanding of the factors that enhance or decrease the motivation of the children with whom we interact each day.

There are many ongoing controversies in the area of student motivation, but there are ten concepts that are widely accepted as "facts." Remember these when attempting to motivate the child who struggles at home or in the classroom:

1. *All human behavior is motivated.* Even the child who *appears* to be unmotivated is actually motivated. For example, a child's refusal to participate in class discussions may actually be *motivated* by his fear of embarrassment because of his limited vocabulary or lack of knowledge about the subject at hand. It is inaccurate to say, "The child is unmotivated"; a more accurate statement would be "The child is not motivated *to do that which I want him to do.*"
2. *Tangible rewards may create temporary behavioral changes, but rewards are unlikely to increase the child's motivation.* When a child is involved in a reward system, the *reward* often becomes the primary source of motivation. For example, if a parent offers to give a child twenty dollars for passing a history test on the War of 1812, the child is *not* motivated to learn history; she is motivated to receive the monetary gift. The knowledge of the War of 1812 is merely a means to an end and will soon be forgotten.

3. *Learning and attentional problems have a marked impact on student motivation.* Children with learning problems experience failure and frustration in school at an early age. They develop feelings of helplessness and are often rejected and isolated by their peers. They view failure as inevitable and, therefore, are unwilling and unable to invest themselves in academic pursuits. This lack of investment naturally causes increased failure—and a vicious cycle is created.
4. *Competition is an ineffective motivational approach for most children, most of the time.* The only person motivated by competition is the person who feels he has a chance of winning. Therefore, the child who struggles academically will not be inspired by spelling bees, contests, quizzes, and competitive games. Only the competent, capable student will find these activities motivating.
5. *Motivation is greatly impacted by primary physical needs.* If a child's physical needs (hunger, thirst, safety, air, etc.) are unmet, the child will not be motivated to learn. The physiological (mind/body) sensations caused by these unmet needs will overshadow and overpower her motivation to learn.
6. *Students have unique, individual patterns of motivation.* Just as each child has his own temperament, personality, and learning style, each child also has a unique motivational profile. Activities and approaches that are highly motivational for one child may be totally ineffective with another.
7. *Coaching techniques are often effective in motivating the child who struggles academically.* The responsive, individualized, structured techniques used in coaching often provide the child with the balance of support and challenge that he needs in order to learn. For this reason, many children respond more positively to coaching techniques than they do to traditional teaching strategies.
8. *Punishment, like reward, will result in temporary behavioral changes, but will do little to foster motivation.* The use of threats, intimidation, and punishment will not enhance a child's intrinsic

motivation. The use of punishment implies that the target behavior is within the child's capabilities and that the threat of retribution will force the child to perform to his potential. If the student has a genuine learning problem that prevents him from mastering the target material, the use of punishment is unfair, inappropriate, and ineffective.

9. *The only effective, long-term motivator of human behavior is success.* When a child experiences success in academic or social tasks, she becomes increasingly motivated to experience more and greater success. These successes serve to inspire the child to reach her greatest potential. But as special education pioneer James Chalafant reminds us, "Success breeds success only when the child feels that his initial success is genuine and earned."
10. *In order for a person to be motivated to invest herself in an activity, three factors must be present:*

    a. She must feel that the goal is attractive.
    b. She must feel that the amount of effort required to meet the goal is realistic.
    c. She must feel that it is likely that she can accomplish the goal.

    If *a, b,* and *c* are present, the child is motivated. If any one component of the formula is absent, the child will not be motivated. In order to illustrate this concept, let's examine three scenarios wherein a child is not motivated:

I. The geometry teacher introduces a new math unit that requires Garvin to master twenty-five complex formulas. She attempts to motivate him by telling him that she has confidence in his ability to master the formulas because he has accomplished similar tasks in the past. She assures him that—with a little extra study time—he can be successful in the unit.

   Despite her efforts, Garvin is not motivated to participate in the unit.

   The missing element is a. *Although Garvin knows that he*

probably can *accomplish the task (c) and that it will not require overwhelming time and effort (b), he sees no purpose in completing the task. The goal is simply not attractive enough to inspire him. In this case, the teacher needs to accomplish* a *by explaining to Garvin that these formulas will be very useful as he designs his science fair project and, further, that these formulas are used daily by architects—a profession that holds great interest for Garvin.*

II. The drama coach at Jessica's high school approaches her in the hallway. He tells her that he plans to have a production of *Romeo and Juliet* in the spring and he would like her to audition for the role of Juliet. He reminds her that nearly every student in the school attends the spring production and that the female lead in the play has subsequently been elected prom queen for the past five years. He also says that this activity will greatly enhance her college applications. The coach knows that she will be able to master the complex dialogue because of her stellar performance as Lady Macbeth during her sophomore year. He assures her that her English teacher, Miss Nichols, has agreed to help her master the lines. He shows her extraordinary sketches of the five costumes that Juliet will wear during the production.

Jessica politely declines.

The coach did a fine job of making the goal very attractive and appealing for Jessica (a). He also provided assurances that this task was within her capabilities (c). However, Jessica is a senior and is currently overwhelmed with college applications, SAT study groups, yearbook editing, varsity sports, and a very active social life. She feels that the addition of one more major activity will be unmanageable and that the amount of effort required (b) is a deal-breaker.

The coach should give her assurances that the task is manageable and provide her with guidance and assistance to enable her to juggle her various responsibilities. Remind her that yearbook, SAT study groups, and college applications will all be completed by spring, thereby giving her ample time for rehearsals and performances.

III. Doug's father wants him to try out for the cross-country team. Dad was a runner in high school and college and he recognizes Doug's natural potential. His endurance and long stride will make him a very successful long-distance runner.

Dad talks to Doug about the camaraderie of team sports and the importance of keeping in shape. He shares stories of his days on the track squad and reminds Doug that colleges often give scholarships to students who excel at fall sports. He assures Doug that practice and conditioning for cross-country runners is actually fun. He reminds him that Doug runs every day anyway, so he may as well run for a team!

Dad's best efforts and most convincing arguments fail to sway Doug. He does not try out for the team.

Dad was wonderfully effective at making the goal of joining the cross-country team very *appealing (a). He also convinced Doug that the task would not be particularly taxing or difficult (b).*

However, Doug has never tried out for a varsity sport before and he is concerned that he will not make the team. He fears the embarrassment of being cut from the squad, and despite Dad's assurances, he does not think that he can accomplish the goal.

Dad would be well advised to have Doug meet with the cross-country coach and get information about the coach's perception of Doug's talent and potential. Doug may also wish to consider joining the less competitive junior varsity program. If his talents are outstanding, he will soon be promoted to a varsity position.

Whenever a child is unmotivated to attempt or complete a task, it is likely because an ingredient in the ABC formula is missing. The challenge of the teacher or parent is to determine which factor is missing and provide the child with information that makes the formula complete.

In some cases, student motivation is as easy as ABC.

RECOMMENDED READING

A Bird's-Eye View of Life with ADD and ADHD: Advice from Young Survivors, Chris A. Zeigler Dendy and Alex Zeigler (Cherish the Child Publishing).

All Kinds of Minds: A Young Student's Book About Learning Abilities and Learning Disorders, Mel Levine, MD (Cambridge, MA: Educators Pub. Service, 1993).

Assertive Discipline: Positive Behavior Management for Today's Classroom, Lee and Marlene Canter (Los Angeles: Canter and Associates, 2002).

At Home in Our Schools: A Guide to Schoolwide Activities That Build Community, Child Development Project (Oakland, CA: Developmental Studies Center, 1994).

The Challenging Child: Understanding, Raising, and Enjoying the Five "Difficult" Types of Children, Stanley I. Greenspan, MD, and Jacqueline Salmon (Reading, MA: Addison-Wesley Publishing Company, 1995).

The Different Drum: Community Making and Peace, M. Scott Peck (New York: Touchstone, 1995).

Discover Your Child's Learning Style: Children Learn in Unique Ways—Here's the Key to Every Child's Learning Success, Mariaemma Willis and Victoria Kindle Hodson (Rocklin, CA: Prima Publishing, 1999).

Driven to Distraction, Edward M. Hallowell and John J. Ratey (New York: Pantheon Books, 1994).

Finding Help When Your Child Is Struggling in School, Lawrence J. Greene (New York: Golden Books, 1998).

Handbook of Resilience in Children, Sam Goldstein and Robert B. Brooks, editors (New York: Springer Science and Business Media, Inc., 2006).

The Kids Market: Myths and Realities, James U. McNeal (Ithaca, NY: Paramount Market Publishing, Inc., 1999).

Kids, Parents, and Power Struggles, Mary Sheedy Kurcinka (New York: HarperCollins, 2001).

Leadership for Students: A Practical Guide For Ages 8–18, Frances A. Karnes and Suzanne M. Bean (Waco, TX: Prufrock Press, 1995).

Learning to Listen: Positive Approaches and People with Difficult Behavior, Herbert Lovett (Baltimore: Paul H. Brookes Publishing Co., 1996).

Live It, Learn It: The Academic Club Methodology for Students with Learning Disabilities and ADHD, Sally L. Smith (Baltimore: Paul H. Brookes Publishing Co., 2005).

Looking in Classrooms, Thomas L. Good and Jere E. Braphy (New York: Harper & Row, 1987).

A Mind at a Time, Mel Levine, MD (New York: Simon & Schuster, 2002).

Mom's Guide to Raising a Good Student, Vicki Poretta and Marian Edelman Borden (New York: Wiley Publishing, 2002).

Motivating Hard to Reach Students, Barbara L. McCombs and James E. Pope (Washington, DC: American Psychological Association, 1994).

The Myth of Laziness, Mel Levine, MD (New York: Simon & Schuster, 2003).

No Such Thing As a Bad Kid: Understanding and Responding to the Challenging Behavior of Troubled Children and Youth, Charles D. Appelstein, (Weston, MA: The Gifford School, 1998).

On Playing a Poor Hand Well: Insights from the Lives of Those Who Have Overcome Childhood Risks and Adversities, Mark Katz (New York: W.W. Norton & Company, 1997).

The Optimistic Child, Martin E. P. Seligman, Karen Reivich, Lisa Jaycox, and Jane Gillham (Boston: Houghton Mifflin Co., 1995).

The Organized Student: Teaching Children the Skills for Success in School and Beyond, Donna Goldberg and Jennifer Zwiebel (New York: Simon & Schuster, Fireside, 2005).

Painful Passages: Working with Children with Learning Disabilities, Elizabeth Dane (Silver Spring, MD: NASW Press, 1990).

People Skills: How to Assert Yourself, Listen to Others, and Resolve Conflicts, Robert Bolton, PhD (New York: Simon & Schuster, 1986).

Punished by Rewards: The Trouble with Gold Stars, Incentive Plans, A's, Praise, and Other Bribes, Alfie Kohn (Boston: Houghton Mifflin Co., 1993).

The Road Less Traveled: A New Psychology of Love, Traditional Values and Spiritual Growth, M. Scott Peck (New York: Touchstone, 2003).

The Self-Esteem Teacher, Robert B. Brooks, PhD (Circle Pines, MN: American Guidance Service, 1991).

Teacher and Child: A Book for Parents and Teachers, Haim G. Ginott (New York: Macmillan, 1972).

The 10 Commitments: Parenting With Purpose, Chick Moorman and Thomas Haller (Merrill, MI: Personal Power Press, 2005).

20 Questions to Ask If Your Child Has ADHD, Mary Fowler (Franklin Lakes, NJ: Career Press, 2006).

Underachievement: Reversing the Process: A Parents Guide for Assisting Your Underachiever to Success, Carolyn Warnemuende and John H. Samson (Sunset Beach, CA: Family Life Publications, 1991).

The Unmotivated Child: Helping Your Underachiever Become a Successful Student, Natalie Rathvon, PhD (New York: Simon & Schuster, Fireside, 1996).

What Do You Do with a Child Like This? Inside the Lives of Troubled Children, L. Tobin (Duluth, MN: Whole Person Associates, 1991).

What Kids Buy and Why: The Psychology of Marketing to Kids, Dan S. Acuff and Robert H. Reiher (New York: Free Press, 1997).

What to Look for in a Classroom . . . and Other Essays, Alfie Kohn (San Francisco: Jossey-Bass, 1998).

When You Worry About the Child You Love: Emotional and Learning Problems in Children, Edward Hallowell, MD (New York: Simon & Schuster, Fireside, 1997).

10 07